THE
Strategic
Teacher

THE
Strategic
Teacher

Selecting the Right Research-Based Strategy for Every Lesson

Harvey F. Silver ▪ Richard W. Strong ▪ Matthew J. Perini

Merrill
is an imprint of

Upper Saddle River, New Jersey
Columbus, Ohio

Library of Congress Cataloging-in-Publication Data

Silver, Harvey F.

   The strategic teacher : selecting the right research-based strategy for every lesson / Harvey F. Silver, Richard W. Strong, Matthew J. Perini.

      p. cm.

   Includes bibliographical references and index.

   ISBN 978-1-4166-0609-3 (pbk. : alk. paper) 1. Effective teaching. 2. Learning, Psychology of. 3. Lesson planning. I. Strong, Richard W., 1946- II. Perini, Matthew J., 1973- III. Title.

LB1025.3.S548 2007

371.102–dc22

2007025820

Association for Supervision
and Curriculum
Development

1703 N. Beauregard St. • Alexandria, VA 22311-1714 USA
Phone: 800-933-2723 or 703-578-9600 • Fax: 703-575-5400
Web site: www.ascd.org • E-mail: member@ascd.org
Author guidelines: www.ascd.org/write

We acknowledge the use of nine strategies from *Classroom Instruction That Works*. Copyright 2001, McREL. Adapted by permission of McREL, 4601 DTC Blvd. Suite 500, Denver, CO 80237. Phone: 303-337-0990. Web: www.mcrel.org/topics/products/19/

ASCD publications present a variety of viewpoints. The views expressed or implied in this book should not be interpreted as official positions of the Association.

All Web links in this book are correct as of the publication date below but may have become inactive or otherwise modified since that time. If you notice a deactivated or changed link, please e-mail books@ascd.org with the words "Link Update" in the subject line. In your message, please specify the Web link, the book title, and the page number on which the link appears.

This special edition published by Merrill Education/Pearson by arrangement with the Association for Supervision and Curriculum Development.

Vice President and Executive Publisher: Jeffery W. Johnston
Publisher: Kevin M. Davis
Director of Marketing: Quinn Perkson
Marketing Manager: Erica M. DeLuca
Marketing Coordinator: Brian Mounts

This book was printed and bound by Edwards Brothers. The cover was printed by Phoenix Color Corp.

Published 2009 by Pearson Education, Inc., Upper Saddle River, New Jersey 07458.

Merrill
is an imprint of

10 9 8 7 6 5 4 3 2 1
ISBN-13: 978-0-13-503584-9
ISBN-10:   0-13-503584-8

To Abigail—

for making sure we got it right.

Contents

Acknowledgments

One of our favorite quotes comes from physicist Victor Weisskopf, who earned the title of "the ultimate civilized man" thanks to his accomplishments as a scientist, musician, leader, and teacher. The quote is "The only sin is if you hear a good idea and don't steal it." What we like about that line is that it reveals one of the deepest truths about individual success: It is, in large part, stolen from others. Through the prodigious talents of Victor Weisskopf, we alleviate some of the guilt we feel in presenting this book to teachers, who are its rightful authors.

Some of the teachers who've lent us their work appear by name in this book. We begin by giving them special thanks. Thank you to Barbara Heinzman, formerly of Geneva City Schools, Dr. Claudia Geocaris of Hinsdale South High School, Robin Cederblad of Downers Grove South High School, Toni Johnson of Penn Yan Academy, Michael Ledford of Dewitt Elementary School, Sherry Gibbon, formerly of Penn Yan Academy, and Carl Carrozza of Catskill Middle School. However, we know all too well that there are others—many others whose ideas have found their way into these pages. Though we have made every effort to reach all of the teachers whose work is found here, we fear that some have eluded us. We hope we have done their work justice, and we wish to thank them all.

A special thanks is also due to Jay McTighe, Grant Wiggins, Robert Marzano, and Giselle Martin-Kniep, whose tireless work in helping schools get better has deeply influenced us, our book, and the Strategic Dashboards you'll find throughout the book. An additional thanks is due to McREL for their help in making the dashboard concept a reality.

Next, we would also like to express our appreciation for many other people who contributed their talents, ideas, and time to this project. Among the many names we would like to mention are Abigail Silver, Robin Young, and Lori Barnett for the depth and quality of their feedback and revision notes; Allyson Palmer and Meredith Lee for their thoroughness as researchers; and all the people who stuck with us through our endless series of drafts: Peta Feiner, Alexis Canonico, Bethann Carbone, and especially Justin Gilbert, who somehow managed to make it all come together.

Last but not least, we would like to thank two of the most accommodating organizations we've ever had the pleasure of working with. To Barbara Schadlow, Allanna Wayne, and Joanna Siebert at Laureate Education and to Scott Willis, Darcie Russell, Nancy Modrak, and the wonderful staff at ASCD: We are thankful for your support—and humbled by your patience.

Foreword

Today, when we talk about educational research, we are generally talking about two different types of research. First, and most commonly, we are talking about meta-analysis, or the technique of combining existing research studies on a particular technique or strategy (say, a set of studies on the benefits of cooperative learning) in order to create a larger and more reliable field of data. Using this enlarged research pool, educational researchers are able to tease out patterns, make generalizations, and translate their findings into numerical data such as effect sizes, percentile gains, and the like.

A second type of educational research is known as *action research*. Action research seeks to set up controlled, scientifically valid experiments in classrooms. For example, an action research project might be set up with the intent of proving or disproving this thesis: *Teaching students how to form images while reading leads to significant improvement on reading test scores.* The teachers in Classrooms A, B, and C would then use an agreed-upon methodology for teaching image making to their students. Meanwhile, by deliberately *not* teaching image making in their classrooms, the teachers in Classrooms D, E, and F would serve as a control group. Test scores from the respective classrooms would then be compared, conclusions drawn, and there you have action research in a nutshell.

Over the last 10 to 15 years, education has seen an explosion in both meta-analytic studies and action research projects. Without question, this proliferation of research has made a difference in schools across the country and across the globe. In fact, I have spent the better part of the last two decades actively pursuing both of these lines of research and working to turn the abstractions, generalizations, and numerical data they create into practical techniques and strategies that schools and teachers could apply immediately and with confidence.

Yet, I have long sensed that a vital piece of the puzzle was missing. Researchers, for all the insights they provide, are bound to the tools and techniques of their discipline. What they were missing was the biggest and richest data field of all—the collected wisdom of our teachers who apply their craft daily in helping our children. In effect, we were getting better at the science of teaching: finding patterns, conducting experiments, making generalizations. What was missing was the art. That's where this book and its authors come in.

I have been paying close attention to the work of Harvey Silver and Richard Strong for 20 years now. Their model for integrating learning styles and teaching strategies to meet the full range of student diversity is, in my opinion, the best and most sensible approach to differentiation in education. I have also had the pleasure of working with them on a number of projects and professional development initiatives. What makes Harvey and Richard's work stand out is how collaborative it is. Under their Thoughtful Classroom professional development model, learning is a communal process. The consultant is never some sole authority lecturing to a room of note takers. Instead, teachers, administrators, and even students play an active role in shaping the learning experience so that it works for everyone. In addition, when it comes to the actual workshops, so much of their work takes place in the classroom. More than any other professional developers I know, Harvey and Richard look for every opportunity to work directly with teachers, not as researchers, consultants, or evaluators, but as fellow teachers committed to helping every student experience the wonder and the power of learning. In many ways, then, the work of Harvey Silver and Richard Strong is the mirror image of my own. I have always taken an approach that begins with the research and then worked to put that research into action. The authors of this book reverse the pattern. Their work originates in classrooms and schools and connects what happens there to the bigger picture provided by the research.

What connections they make. Through an innovation known as the Strategic Dashboard (see page 20 for an example), they show how each strategy in this book relates to nearly every idea that matters in instructional research: how the strategy serves as a unit design tool; how it can be used to differentiate instruction; what skills, facets of understanding, and types of knowledge it builds in students; how it is supported by current research. What's so attractive about this approach, other than its immediate usefulness to teachers, is how well it aligns with what I have found coming from the opposite direction as a researcher. Perhaps we should consider *The Strategic Teacher* a touchstone text, one of the very first documents in a new and exciting field where the science of teaching—the empirical reliability of meta-analysis and action research—is perfectly aligned with the art of teaching and the wisdom of the teachers who practice it every day.

—Robert J. Marzano, President
Marzano & Associates

PART ONE

Introduction

Welcome to Strategic Teaching: The What, the Why, and the How

The word *strategy* comes from two ancient Greek roots: *Stratos,* meaning "multitude" or "that which is spread out," and *again,* meaning "to lead" or, we might say, "to bring together." Thus, at its heart, the word *strategy* celebrates the difference between teaching and nearly all other professions: Most professionals see their clients one at a time, but teachers' clients come to them as groups of diverse individuals brought together by birth date, scheduling demands, and, occasionally, interest. The goal of teaching is to weave together a conversation that unites these disparate individuals around a common core of learning. Strategies are the different types or styles of plans teachers use to achieve this goal.

Although teachers have always used strategies (think of Socrates's dialogue, Jesus's parables, the medieval birth of the lecture), until recently most teachers had only a handful of generic techniques at their disposal: discussion, demonstration, lecture, practice, and test. Over the the last 50 years, however, teachers and researchers have created, revised, tweaked, and recast these five basic elements into hundreds of new forms.

In *The Strategic Teacher* we have collected 20 of the most reliable and flexible of these strategies (along with dozens of variations) and organized them into four distinct styles of instruction: a *Mastery* style that emphasizes the development of student memory; an *Understanding* style that seeks to expand students' capacities to reason and explain; a *Self-Expressive* style that stimulates and nourishes students' imaginations and creativity; and an *Interpersonal* style that helps students find meaning in the relationships they forge as partners and team members, united in the act of learning. The goal of *The Strategic Teacher* is therefore simple indeed: to provide teachers with a repertoire of strategies they can use to meet today's high standards and reach the different learners in their classrooms.

We have designed this book to be read, but also to be used. To this end, we address these questions:

- What does strategic teaching look like?
- How are teaching strategies the same but different?
- Why does every classroom teacher need a repertoire of teaching strategies?
- How do we select the right strategy for a particular teaching and learning situation?
- How can we get the most out of our use of teaching strategies?

What Does Strategic Teaching Look Like?

Let's begin by peering into four different, but equally thoughtful classrooms. Gabrielle, Martin, Stephen, and Rimi don't work harder than their colleagues do. Rather, they work more strategically. Strategies help them and their students by providing a plan that addresses three questions:

1. What kind of structure will help my students achieve our purpose?
2. What role will I play in achieving this purpose?
3. What role will my students play in achieving this purpose?

In this way, strategies work like a kind of open-ended script that helps both teachers and students move thoughtfully toward their goal. To see how, let's focus on Gabrielle D'Abo's Mystery lesson on dinosaur extinction (from Figure A).

Like any good lesson, Gabrielle's began with a clear *purpose*. Gabrielle wanted students to practice and develop their abilities to reason and weigh evidence while using the concepts they were learning during her unit on extinction. The Mystery strategy supplied Gabrielle with a *structure* that helped her formulate her mystery, develop a set of guiding questions, and design 20 clues related to dinosaur extinction. The Mystery strategy also made the *teacher's role* clear to Gabrielle: She posed the mystery to students, explained what students were to do during the lesson, listened in on and coached student groups as they were assembling clues, and served as devil's advocate to help students shore up gaps in their emerging explanations. *Students' roles* were made obvious as well—they became detectives charged with studying clues; weighing evidence; and forming, testing, and revising their explanations of how and why a planet's worth of large and exotic beasts vanished from Earth.

FIGURE A   Four Classrooms

Making Memories	The More We Are Together
On the upcoming final, students in Martin Finn's 11th grade civics class will be responsible for knowing and explaining 12 different principles of constitutional government. To help the class prepare, pairs of students are delivering brief lectures on each principle. Here's the twist: Each student lecture includes an opening discussion, a visual organizer, and a set of review questions that engage different forms of thinking. Students learned this format from Martin. They call it New American Lecture.	Rimi Meyer's 6th graders are studying biography as a writing genre. Today, the students are arranged in their regular Friday Community Circle groups. Today's topic: *Life Challenges: Where Do They Come From and How Do We Overcome Them?* Each group monitors and runs its own discussion as students explore the topic in their own lives and in the lives of the biographies they are reading together. A visitor to the classroom comments to Rimi, "I just can't believe how well these kids listen and how well they empathize with these historical figures and one another."
A Mystery Explained	**Mathematical Connections**
Gabrielle D'Abo's 4th graders are entering the third day of a three-week unit on extinction. For today's lesson, Gabrielle has designed a Mystery lesson. Working in groups of four, students examine and assemble a set of clues related to the extinction of dinosaurs. Each group's goal is to build chains of evidence that explain why the dinosaurs disappeared.	Looking back over last week's work on polynomials, Stephen Mulhall can see that his decision to use the Inductive Learning strategy has paid off. He began by asking students to create at least five different ways of categorizing polynomial expressions. The class then discussed the labels they gave each group, explained their reasons for grouping them the way they did, and worked to form generalizations about how each group might need to be treated mathematically. As they progressed through the unit, students revised both their categories and their generalizations. Now, with the unit nearly over, Stephen can see how much more flexibility and insight his class has when it comes to applying what they have learned in problem-solving situations.

Now, take a second look at the other teachers' strategic lessons shown in Figure A. Can you get a sense of the structure, teacher's role, and students' role from these descriptions?

How Are Teaching Strategies the Same but Different?

Words like "structure" and "role" make us think not merely in terms of plans but beyond that as a kind of drama. In this way, we can see teaching strategies as a new kind of script—a script designed to accommodate improvisation, student engagement, and response. All teaching strategies are similar in their universal commitment to structure, engagement, purpose, and response. What makes teaching strategies different is their *style:* differences in purposes, structures, roles, and means of motivating and engaging learners. We group our strategies into four broad instructional styles, plus one group of strategies that integrates all four styles. The styles and their strategies are listed and described in Figure B.

Take another look at the four classrooms described in Figure A. Can you see how each teacher's strategy lessons represent the Mastery, Understanding, Self-Expressive, and Interpersonal styles respectively?

Why Does Every Classroom Need a Repertoire of Teaching Strategies?

While teaching strategies are not new to most educators, many educators have not been given the training or support needed to develop a repertoire of effective strategies. Research and experience demonstrate that teaching strategies are critical to the overall health of the classroom and to the academic success of our students for at least six distinct reasons:

1. **Strategies are tools for designing thoughtful lessons and units.** As teachers, lesson and unit design questions exert a profound influence on classroom decision making. It should come as no surprise, then, that educational researchers have spent many years working to develop clear

FIGURE B   Style Strategies

Mastery Strategies	Interpersonal Strategies
focus sharply on increasing students' abilities to *remember* and summarize. They motivate by providing clear sequence, speedy feedback, and a strong sense of expanding competence and measurable success.	foster students' need to relate personally to the curriculum and to each other. They use teams, partnerships, and coaching to motivate students through their drive for membership and *relationships*.

Four-Style Strategies

engage all four styles simultaneously, thereby encouraging students to develop a balanced and dynamic approach to learning.

Understanding Strategies	Self-Expressive Strategies
seek to evoke and develop students' capacities to *reason* and use evidence and logic. They motivate by arousing *curiosity* through mysteries, problems, clues, and opportunities to analyze and debate.	highlight students' abilities to imagine and *create*. They use imagery, metaphor, pattern, and what if's to motivate students' drive toward individuality and *originality*.

and practical models for lesson and unit design—from Madeline Hunter's (1984) classic lesson design model, to Grant Wiggins and Jay McTighe's approach to *Understanding by Design* (2005), to Robert Marzano's work in classroom curriculum design (2003). From these models, we can extract five questions that every teacher needs to answer when developing a lesson or unit:

- How will the material be introduced?
- How will new information be presented?
- How will students practice and apply what they are learning?
- How will student learning and progress be assessed?
- How will students reflect on what they learn and their own learning process?

No single strategy can respond effectively to every question. Although New American Lecture is an ideal tool for presenting new information, it is notably weaker when it comes to promoting independent practice or assessing student progress. Only a repertoire of strategies guarantees that each and every element of effective design—introduction, new knowledge, practice, assessment, and reflection—gets its due in the lessons and units we teach.

2. **Strategies make the work of differentiating instruction manageable for teachers and motivating for students.** Let's begin our investigation into the relationship among strategies, motivation, and differentiation by listening to two students responding to the question: *Who was your favorite teacher?*

Kenny R.: My favorite teacher had to be Ms. Gibbon. Ms. Gibbon taught U.S. history in a way I'll never forget. She used to teach historical periods and movements as recipes. I still remember my ingredients list: yeast makes dough rise, warm water activates yeast, salt brings out natural flavors, sugar adds sweetness, and so on. So, for particular periods or movements in U.S. history like the Progressive Era and the Civil Rights Movement, we would have to analyze the historical forces at work and use the recipe metaphor to explain the effects and reactions of each of these historical factors as if they were food ingredients. Sometimes, we would even have bake-offs, where we would present our recipes for teachers and other students to judge.

Rosalynne F.: More than anyone else, Ms. Lacey got me ready for college because she was the first teacher who really taught me how to take notes. First of all, Ms. Lacey took the time to show us how she made notes. She'd put these difficult passages from textbooks or articles up on an overhead and she'd just sort of talk her way through them, stopping to summarize, asking questions, and making arrows and margin notes. Then we'd have these group practice and study sessions where we'd have to apply what she had taught us. Ms. Lacey was always there to give group members feedback on how we were doing and suggestions on how we could get better, so we always mastered new note-taking techniques pretty quickly.

Right away, we can see that Kenny and Rosalynne have very different ideas about learning. Kenny is drawn to the novel and imaginative aspects of learning, Rosalynne to practical skills, such as taking effective notes. Kenny favors teaching practices that allow him to explore surprising connections, such as the connection between history and cooking. For Rosalynne, good teaching looks an awful lot like good coaching, with an emphasis on modeling skills, practice sessions, and instant feedback. Finally, Kenny and Rosalynne evaluate their teacher's success in reaching them using different criteria. Ms. Gibbon gets high marks from Kenny because she was able to make history come alive in exciting and unforgettable ways. Rosalynne judges Ms. Lacey's success according to how well she prepared Rosalynne for the rigors of information management at the college level. The differences in how Kenny and Rosalynne approach, process, and relate their classroom experiences are the result of *learning styles.*

The long and prestigious history of learning styles begins with Carl Jung (1923), who discovered that the way we process and evaluate information develops into specific personality types. Later, Kathleen Briggs and Isabel Myers (1962/1998) expanded on Jung's foundation to create a comprehensive model of cognitive diversity made famous by their Myers-Briggs Type Indicator. Since then, new generations of educational researchers, including Bernice McCarthy (1982), Carolyn Mamchur (1996), Harvey Silver and J. Robert Hanson (1998), Edward Pajak (2003), and Gayle Gregory (2005) have studied, applied, and elaborated on learning styles and how to use them to improve teaching and learning. In synthesizing this expansive body of research with our 30 years of experience in helping schools and teachers motivate all students, we have identified four distinct learning styles. Figure C outlines these four styles.

Perhaps you're asking what all this has to do with research-based instructional strategies. The answer is *a lot.* As teachers, we have students like Kenny and Rosalynne in our classrooms, along with many other students with different learning style profiles. We can effectively differentiate instruction to motivate our Kennys, our Rosalynnes, and every student in our classroom by developing a repertoire of teaching strategies. Students are not the only entities in our classrooms with style preferences. Teaching strategies also have styles. Some strategies emphasize the successful application of content and skills and speak to Mastery learners; others engage Understanding learners by piquing curiosity and facilitating critical investigation; some strategies celebrate originality and address the imaginative side of Self-Expressive learners; still others motivate Interpersonal learners by focusing on the development of personal relationships and the classroom community.

Thus, the strategies in this book, which are organized by style, serve as a framework for differentiating instruction. By rotating strategies to incorporate all four styles into your instructional design, you will

FIGURE C   The Four Learning Styles

Mastery Learners	Interpersonal Learners
Want to learn practical information and procedures. **Like** drills, lectures, demonstrations, and practice. **May experience difficulty when** learning becomes too abstract or when faced with open-ended questions. **Learn best when** instruction is focused on modeling new skills, practicing, and feedback sessions.	**Want to** learn about things that affect people's lives. **Like** group experiences, discussions, cooperative learning activities, role playing, personal attention. **May experience difficulty when** instruction focuses on independent seatwork or when learning lacks real-world application. **Learn best when** their teacher pays attention to their successes and struggles.
Understanding Learners	**Self-Expressive Learners**
Want to use logic, debate, and inquiry to investigate ideas. **Like** reading, debates, research projects, independent study, making cases or arguments, asking "Why?" **May experience difficulty when** there is a focus on the social environment of the classroom (e.g., cooperative learning). **Learn best when** they are challenged to think and explain their ideas.	**Want to** use their imaginations to explore ideas. **Like** creative and artistic activities, open-ended and nonroutine problems, generating possibilities and alternatives, asking "What if?" **May experience difficulty when** instruction focuses on drill and practice and rote problem solving. **Learn best when** they are invited to express themselves in unique and original ways.

naturally motivate all learners by addressing their preferred styles, and you will help students grow by challenging them to work in styles they might otherwise avoid. In addition, unlike methods of differentiation that quickly become overwhelming for teachers (and isolating for students) by emphasizing all the possible differences among students, a style-based approach makes the work of differentiating instruction eminently manageable.

3. **Strategies provide the tools needed to bring thoughtful programs alive in the classroom.** Many effective and thoughtful teaching and learning programs, including Grant Wiggins and Jay McTighe's *Understanding by Design* (2005), provide schools and teachers with invaluable guidance in designing, evaluating, and adjusting units of study so that they lead to deeper learning. Nevertheless, teachers often need some-

thing beyond a plan—they need a set of tangible strategies to direct the implementation of these plans in the classroom.

When Grant Wiggins and Jay McTighe sat down to create *Understanding by Design,* they developed six facets of understanding as indicators for determining the depth and quality of student comprehension:

- *Explanation:* Summarizing and retelling big ideas and critical concepts
- *Interpretation:* Making sense of "interpretable" content, such as texts, data, art, and arguments
- *Application:* Using skills and knowledge in new and authentic contexts
- *Perspective:* Examining situations from an objective distance and recognizing the legitimacy of different viewpoints
- *Empathy:* Appreciating and identifying with others' ideas, situations, and motivations
- *Self-knowledge:* Developing the self-awareness needed to reflect on performance and grow as a learner

What teachers quickly discovered was that these facets could also play a critical role in defining the goals of instruction: What facets of understanding are essential to develop in relation to what I am teaching, and how will I help students build that understanding? A repertoire of teaching strategies does more than make possible the achievement of instructional goals that begin at the end—that is, with the end state of student understanding in mind. Strategies help teachers make the path to these goals clear and concrete.

4. **Strategies build the skills needed for success on state tests.** When state testing was relatively new but beginning to change the educational landscape in the United States, we initiated an investigation driven by a single question: What separates high achievers from low achievers on these new and increasingly prominent tests? For us, and for educators in general, this was a critical question because teachers and schools were being held accountable for students' success on standardized tests at exactly the same time that the very notion of standardized testing was changing radically. How were tests changing? Perhaps we can best represent this shift to the new generation of testing by looking at two test items (Figure D). One question typifies an older and more traditional standardized test item. The second represents the demands of the current generation of tests and test items.

What's the difference between these two items? In a word: skills. The traditional item, though it requires students to make the distinction between *endangered* and *extinct,* focuses squarely on finding a correct answer, on remembering a specific bit of information. The new item assesses students' deeper understanding of a key concept—*adaptation*—and asks them to demonstrate that understanding by applying multiple academic skills: interpreting visual information, conducting an analysis

FIGURE D   Traditional Versus New Test Item

Traditional Test Item	New Test Item
Which of the following animals is **not** endangered? A) African elephant B) American alligator C) Blue whale D) Dodo bird E) Florida manatee	Below is an imaginary animal called a *Woggle*. **Based on its characteristics**, what **scientific** inferences can you make about its niche and habitat? In other words, tell about where it might live, what it might eat, and what role it might serve in its community. **Explain your thinking.**  50 cm *Illustration courtesy of the Connecticut State Department of Education (2001).

using criteria, making inferences, and writing a coherent explanation. Clearly, standardized testing had evolved.

We assembled and categorized test items from every state and in every major content area, extracted the skill sets required by various items, even conducted informal test-taking and interview sessions with groups of students identified by their teachers as high, average, and low achievers. What we found surprised us: Regardless of the grade level or content area being tested, student success hinged on a relatively small set of core skills—12 in all. Then came a bigger surprise: We found that these skills were radically undertaught and rarely benchmarked. In some cases, skills that proved especially vital to students' performance—skills like taking good notes or developing plans to address complex questions—were never mentioned in state curriculum documents. Therefore, we decided to call these skills, so critical to student success but often overlooked by schools, the Hidden Skills of Academic Literacy (see Figure E, p. 10).

If we expect students to perform well on state tests, we must teach them how to apply these skills without cutting into content. A repertoire of strategies represents the single most effective way to achieve this double purpose of managing content while developing the Hidden Skills of Academic Literacy. In fact, the strategies selected for inclusion in this

FIGURE E   The Hidden Skills of Academic Literacy

Reading and Study Skills	Reflective Skills
• Collect and organize ideas through note making. • Make sense of abstract academic vocabulary. • Read and interpret visual displays of information.	• Construct plans to address questions and tasks. • Use criteria and guidelines to evaluate work in progress. • Control or alter mood and impulsivity.
Thinking Skills	**Communication Skills**
• Draw conclusions; make and test inferences, hypotheses, and conjectures. • Conduct comparisons using specific criteria. • Analyze the demands of a variety of higher-order thinking questions.	• Write clear, well-formed, coherent explanations in all content areas. • Write comfortably in the following nonfiction genres: problem/solution, decision making, argument, comparative. • Read and write about two or more documents.

book have all been chosen based on their capacity to develop at least two (and sometimes as many as six) of these Hidden Skills.

5. **Frequent use of strategies leads to consistent and significant gains in student achievement.** Perhaps no question in educational research has been answered more clearly over the last decade than this one: Do instructional strategies really make a difference in student achievement? The answer, a resounding *yes,* can be attributed to several meta-analytic research studies (studies that create a larger and more reliable pool of data by combining the findings from many other studies) conducted by researchers, including Kathleen Cotton (2000) and Arthur Ellis and Jeffrey Fouts (1997). Far and away the most important and influential of these meta-analytic studies came from the research team of Robert Marzano, Debra Pickering, and Jane Pollock (2001) under the title *Classroom Instruction That Works: Research-Based Strategies for Increasing Student Achievement.* Marzano and his team compared the effects of various teaching strategies on student performance and ranked the strategies according to the academic gains students made when exposed to each one. The findings are eye-opening, with strategies associated with *identifying similarities and differences* and with *summarizing and note taking,* for example, consistently yielding percentile gains of 30, even 40, points. From this research, nine distinct classroom practices are proven to make a positive difference in student performance. Marzano and his team refer to these classroom practices as "instructional categories." We prefer to think of them as "best bets" for raising student achievement.

Here are the nine categories or best bets for teachers and schools interested in helping their students reach higher levels of success:

1. Identifying similarities and differences
2. Summarizing and note taking
3. Reinforcing effort and providing recognition

4. Homework and practice

5. Nonlinguistic representation

6. Cooperative learning

7. Setting objectives and providing feedback

8. Generating and testing hypotheses

9. Cues, questions, and advance organizers (Marzano, Pickering, & Pollock, 2001)

All the strategies you'll find in this book have been selected with this important research in mind. Our goal in making this deep connection to *Classroom Instruction That Works* has been to make easier the difficult work of planning and delivering lessons and units in the age of accountability. Not only can teachers rest assured that each strategy is backed by a powerful and reliable research base, but they can also use the included Strategic Dashboards to document how they are incorporating current and widely respected research into their instructional plans. (More on these Strategic Dashboards later.)

6. **Strategies build different kinds of knowledge.** Imagine you were hired tomorrow to teach two lessons: (1) the causes of World War II, and (2) how to read a battle plan. Chances are you would not use the same strategy for both lessons. Teaching always includes finding a balance between *what* and *how,* between *content* and *skills,* between *declarative knowledge* and *procedural knowledge.* While it is true that good teaching strategies incorporate content and skills, it is also true that some strategies are better suited to helping students learn how to serve a tennis ball, write an essay, or construct a mathematical proof; meanwhile, other strategies slant toward the declarative side of content, enabling teachers and students to explore essential questions and delve into the riches of the various disciplines.

Of course, different students, situations, and instructional purposes make some of these reasons more important than others for different teachers. Which of these reasons for developing a repertoire of strategies is most important to you? Are there any other reasons?

Reasons are one thing. They offer us the *why,* the arguments for using strategies, but can they provide more? Can reasons go beyond the *why* to tell us *how* we can make good decisions about teaching? Can they give us clear guidelines for selecting the best strategy for particular situations? They can. In the next section we will introduce you to a practical tool for instructional decision making based on these six reasons. We call this tool the Strategic Dashboard.

How Do We Select the Right Strategy for a Particular Teaching and Learning Situation?

The Strategic Teacher supports teachers as they work to bring high-impact, research-based strategies into their classrooms. A quick survey of the contents reveals that the four learning styles provide the overarching structure for this book. Parts 2 through 5 contain a set of strategies in the Mastery, Understanding, Self-Expressive, and Interpersonal styles, respectively. Part 6 discusses Four-Style strategies, or strategies that challenge students to work and learn in all four learning styles. As such, the book offers teachers a simple, effective method for differentiating instruction.

Nevertheless, differentiation using learning styles is only one argument for the regular use of research-based strategies in every classroom. We have also witnessed how strategies improve unit design, develop different facets of understanding, build academic skills, raise achievement levels, and teach both declarative and procedural knowledge. What we have learned from the teachers we work with is that these six reasons for using strategies correlate strongly with the questions teachers ask themselves when deciding which strategy to use. Together, we turned this insight into a decision-making tool called the Strategic Dashboard. Much as a car's dashboard offers drivers the "vital statistics" of driving instantly and in a visually appealing format, each Strategic Dashboard provides teachers with a concise, visual profile of a particular teaching strategy. Figure F shows the Strategic Dashboard for the Self-Expressive strategy called Mind's Eye.

Notice how the dashboard is divided into six panels. The six panels correspond to the six reasons for developing a repertoire of strategies; each reason has been recast as a question related to selecting strategies for the classroom:

- How does the strategy fit into unit design?
- What learning styles does the strategy engage?
- What facets of understanding does the strategy develop?
- What hidden skills does the strategy build?
- How does the strategy incorporate the research on instructional effectiveness?
- What types of knowledge does the strategy teach?

Each panel on the dashboard visually answers a question so that teachers can see, at a glance, the vital statistics of any given strategy to determine how well it meets their instructional purposes. To understand better how the Strategic Dashboard works, let's take a tour of each of its six panels:

- **Panel 1: How does the strategy fit into unit design? (Blueprint for Learning)**—There are five kinds of lessons required for a unit to be successful: introduction, presentation of new information, practice and application, assessment, and reflection. This dashboard panel contains a "blueprint for learning" consisting of five squares—one for each type of lesson. The key appears on the right side of the panel and shows how

FIGURE F   Strategic Dashboard for Chapter 12—Mind's Eye

How does the strategy fit into unit design?
(Blueprint for Learning)

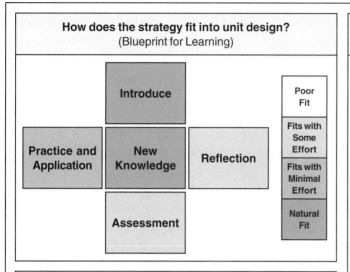

Introduce	Poor Fit
Practice and Application / New Knowledge / Reflection	Fits with Some Effort
	Fits with Minimal Effort
Assessment	Natural Fit

What skills does the strategy build?
(The Hidden Skills of Academic Literacy)

Read and Study
- ● Collect/organize ideas through note making
- ● Make sense of abstract academic vocabulary
- ● Read/interpret visuals

Reason and Analyze
- ● Draw conclusions; make/test inferences, hypotheses, conjectures
- ○ Conduct comparisons using criteria
- ○ Analyze demands of a variety of questions

Create and Communicate
- ● Write clear, coherent explanations
- ● Write comfortably in major nonfiction genres*
- ○ Read and write about two or more documents

Reflect and Relate
- ○ Construct plans to address questions and tasks
- ○ Use criteria and guidelines to evaluate work
- ● Control/alter mood and impulsivity

What learning styles does the strategy engage?
(Motivation/Differentiation)

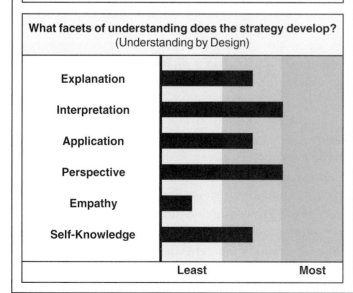

Mastery | Interpersonal
Success | Relationships
Curiosity | Originality
Understanding | Self-Expressive

How does the strategy incorporate the research on instructional effectiveness?
(Classroom Instruction That Works)

- ○ Identifying similarities and differences
- ● Summarizing and note taking
- ○ Reinforcing effort and providing recognition
- ○ Homework and practice
- ● Nonlinguistic representation
- ○ Cooperative learning
- ○ Setting objectives and feedback
- ● Generating and testing hypotheses
- ○ Cues, questions, and advance organizers

What facets of understanding does the strategy develop?
(Understanding by Design)

Explanation
Interpretation
Application
Perspective
Empathy
Self-Knowledge

Least — Most

What types of knowledge does the strategy teach?

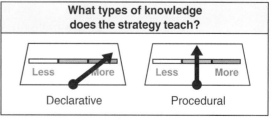

Less — More   Less — More
Declarative   Procedural

*Mind's Eye is especially useful for building students' descriptive powers as writers.

well each strategy fits each kind of lesson. The darker the shading, the better the fit.

  • **Panel 2: What learning styles does the strategy engage? (Motivation/Differentiation)**—Learning styles are the key to motivating students and to managing differentiated instruction. The learning styles panel indicates the learning styles that each strategy engages. It also includes a keyword reminder linking each style to its motivational principle:

  ◦ Mastery learners strive for *success.*
  ◦ Understanding learners are driven by *curiosity.*
  ◦ Self-Expressive learners see learning as an outlet for their *originality.*
  ◦ Interpersonal learners learn by building *relationships.*

This dashboard panel is best described as a radar screen depicting a "cloud cover" over the four learning styles. The more cloud cover in each quadrant, the more the strategy will appeal to students with that style.

  • **Panel 3: What facets of understanding does the strategy develop?** *(Understanding by Design)*—This dashboard panel represents each of the six facets of student understanding as presented by Grant Wiggins and Jay McTighe (2005). Each type of understanding—explanation, interpretation, application, perspective, empathy, and self-knowledge—is represented with a bar. The distance the bar travels from left to right signifies the degree to which a particular strategy corresponds to that particular facet of understanding.

  • **Panel 4: What skills does the strategy build?** (The Hidden Skills of Academic Literacy)—Each and every strategy evokes and models two or more of the Hidden Skills of Academic Literacy. There are 12 skills in all that are grouped into four categories. This dashboard panel is a simple checklist: dormant skills have empty circles and appear in gray, while applicable skills have filled-in circles and are presented in black.

  • **Panel 5: How does the strategy incorporate the research on instructional effectiveness?** *(Classroom Instruction That Works)*—This dashboard panel presents the research on instructional effectiveness underlying each strategy. For efficiency and ease, we have decided to follow the nine categories outlined in Marzano, Pickering, and Pollock's (2001) well-known *Classroom Instruction That Works.* This dashboard panel is a simple checklist: Dormant instructional categories have empty circles and appear in gray, while applicable instructional categories have filled-in circles and are presented in black.

  • **Panel 6: What types of knowledge does the strategy teach?**—This panel presents two meters, one for declarative knowledge and one for procedural knowledge. The meters indicate whether the strategy is more useful or less useful when teaching either type of knowledge.

Now that you have walked through one dashboard, for the sake of comparison, take a minute to examine a dashboard for a very different strategy, say Graduated Difficulty (p. 44) or Community Circle (p. 194). What differences are immediately noticeable?

In addition to the Strategic Dashboard that opens each of the 20 chapters, you'll also find that each chapter is organized into six sections:

1. *The Strategy Overview* provides a brief introduction to the strategy.

2. *The Strategy in Action* shows a teacher using the strategy in the classroom.

3. *Why the Strategy Works* explains the research base supporting the strategy and the benefit to the students.

4. *How to Use the Strategy* describes how to implement the strategy by following a list of clear steps.

5. *Planning a Lesson* leads the reader through the planning process, providing steps, examples, and suggestions for designing superior lessons.

6. *Variations and Extensions* provide teachers with additional tools, strategies, and resources for adapting and expanding their use of the strategy.

How Can We Get the Most Out of Strategic Teaching?

Before we launch the 20 strategies, here are four quick tips for becoming a more strategic teacher:

1. **Apply the 4-S approach to teaching:**
   ◦ Standards
   ◦ Students
   ◦ Situations
   ◦ Strategies

   Make *students* as important as *standards* by clarifying your learning *situation* and selecting the *strategy* that best fits your situation and motivates your students.

2. **Name that strategy.** Tell students what strategy you are using. Teach them the specific steps you will be moving through and the roles each of you will be playing. Research shows that classrooms where students are taught explicitly the steps and roles of the strategies teachers use become classrooms where students use strategies independently and thoughtfully (Brown, Pressley, Van Meter, & Schuder, 1996). Gabrielle D'Abo's classroom contains eight posters that describe the roles students play for each of her most frequently used strategies. Figure G (p. 16) shows her steps for the Reading for Meaning strategy.

3. **Practice strategic rotation.** Use all five types of strategies regularly and keep a record of what styles you use, along with how the students respond. Don't be afraid to experiment: If students are struggling, try using

FIGURE G   Reading for Meaning Strategy Poster

Reading for Meaning

READ the Reading for Meaning statements carefully before you read the text.

ESTABLISH a tentative hypothesis. (Decide if you agree or disagree with the statements.)

AS you read the text, collect evidence for both supporting and refuting the statements.

DECIDE if the evidence is sufficient to support or refute.

SHARE your ideas and evidence with your readers' group:
- Listen carefully to other members of your group.
- Try to come to a consensus.
- If the group cannot agree on a statement, revise it.
- Take time to write an explanation of your thoughts.

a different strategy. Concept Attainment (Understanding) or Metaphorical Expression (Self-Expressive), for example, will help students grasp concept-heavy content. You can build a more collegial learning environment among students and foster better classroom relationships with Interpersonal strategies such as Community Circle or Reciprocal Learning. Content acquisition and focused skill building are usually best accomplished with Mastery strategies. To help all students become more complete and balanced thinkers and learners, try a Four-Style strategy such as Do You Hear What I Hear? or Task Rotation. The possibilities are endless and exciting; however, remember that styles are never pigeonholes. High-quality learning demands all styles of thinking, and teaching students how to get the most out of their minds means rotating strategies across all styles.

4. **Keep moving forward by regularly looking backward.** Try not to use a strategy without sparing at least a few minutes to help your students reflect on the learning process. How did it affect their approach to learning? What obstacles did they confront? How did they overcome those obstacles? How can they improve their performance next time? Strategic teaching always involves helping students reflect on where they have been and assess the quality and depth of their current learning. Then—and only then—can we expect students to move forward as we work with them to enhance their ability to learn more in the future.

As authors, we try to keep our word, and as the title of this introduction suggested we should, we have spent the last 4,000 or so words discussing the *What* (what strategies look like and the differences among them), the *Why* (the reasons teachers need a repertoire of research-based strategies), and the *How* (guidelines for selecting strategies and implementing them in the classroom) of teaching strategies. All that is left are the strategies themselves.

PART TWO

Mastery Strategies

Mastery Strategies

Mastery strategies focus sharply on increasing students' abilities to remember and summarize. They motivate students by providing clear sequence, speedy feedback, and a strong sense of expanding competence and measurable success.

Strategy Chapters

1. New American Lecture is a strategy that makes lecturing interactive, memorable, and brain-compatible.

2. Direct Instruction employs a four-phase approach to skill mastery that leads to student independence.

3. Graduated Difficulty is a technique that allows teachers to differentiate instruction by ability or readiness level while helping students set and reach meaningful goals.

4. Teams-Games-Tournaments organizes students into cooperative study groups where they review critical content and help one another prepare to compete against students in other study groups.

How does the strategy fit into unit design?
(Blueprint for Learning)

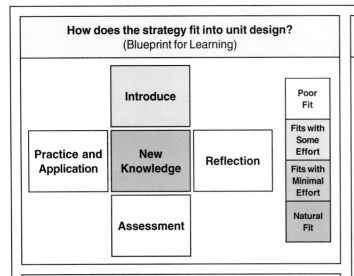

What learning styles does the strategy engage?
(Motivation/Differentiation)

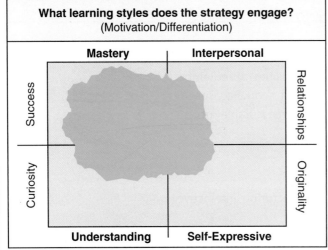

What facets of understanding does the strategy develop?
(Understanding by Design)

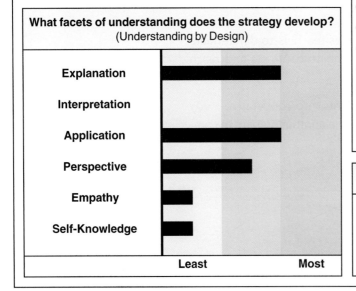

What skills does the strategy build?
(The Hidden Skills of Academic Literacy)

Read and Study
- ● Collect/organize ideas through note making
- ● Make sense of abstract academic vocabulary
- ● Read/interpret visuals

Reason and Analyze
- ○ Draw conclusions; make/test inferences, hypotheses, conjectures
- ○ Conduct comparisons using criteria
- ● Analyze demands of a variety of questions

Create and Communicate
- ○ Write clear, coherent explanations
- ○ Write comfortably in major nonfiction genres
- ○ Read and write about two or more documents

Reflect and Relate
- ○ Construct plans to address questions and tasks
- ○ Use criteria and guidelines to evaluate work
- ○ Control/alter mood and impulsivity

How does the strategy incorporate the research on instructional effectiveness?
(Classroom Instruction That Works)

- ○ Identifying similarities and differences
- ● Summarizing and note taking
- ○ Reinforcing effort and providing recognition
- ○ Homework and practice
- ○ Nonlinguistic representation
- ○ Cooperative learning
- ○ Setting objectives and feedback
- ○ Generating and testing hypotheses
- ● Cues, questions, and advance organizers

What types of knowledge does the strategy teach?

Declarative

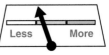

Procedural

1

New American Lecture

Strategy Overview

New American Lecture is a strategic way of lecturing. The strategy is designed to answer two questions: (1) What does direct instruction look like when applied to the teaching of declarative content rather than the development of procedures and skills? (2) How can incorporating what current brain research tells us about how to make information memorable improve the classic lecture format? In developing and implementing a New American Lecture, the teacher provides students with five kinds of support:

1. To connect the learner to past knowledge and to build new connections, the teacher designs an activity that hooks students into the content and a bridge that links students' initial ideas to the content to come.

2. To organize and teach students how to collect information, the teacher provides students with a visual organizer that lays out the structure of the lecture content.

3. To increase involvement and make content memorable, the teacher uses memory devices and active participation techniques.

4. To help students process and integrate the information, the teacher conducts periodic thinking reviews.

5. To help students apply and evaluate their learning, the teacher provides synthesis and reflection activities.

The Strategy in Action

High school history teacher Aja Tucker introduces her unit on sectionalism (the period in U.S. history beginning around 1820, when the northeastern, southern, and western states became increasingly divided) by setting the stage as follows:

> Between 1820 and 1840, the differences among the Northeast, the South, and the West became so pronounced that during the election of 1836, the Whig Party ran three separate presidential candidates: one in the North, one in the South, and one in the West. The idea was to divide up the electorate, prevent the Democrats from winning a majority, and throw the election to the House of Representatives. This strategy is amazing for two reasons. First, it almost worked. Second, if you think back to our last unit, you'll remember that the country was more united than ever after the War of 1812. How did our country go from the Era of Good Feelings to a sharply divided nation in only a few short years? What factors and issues led to this level of disunity so quickly? Today, we're going to find out using a strategy called New American Lecture.

After piquing students' curiosity, Aja refers students to the map in their textbooks showing the geographic features, natural resources, and primary modes of economic income across the eastern half of the United States. "What I would like everyone to do," says Aja, "is spend two minutes studying this map while thinking about these questions:

- What are the key geographic features of each region?
- What do you notice about the resources and economies of each of these regions?
- How might these differences have contributed to the rise of sectionalism?"

Students jot their ideas down in their notebooks before pairing up to share and compare their ideas with a fellow student.

After surveying and recording students' responses, Aja distributes a blank matrix organizer, which previews the content of her lecture and provides space for students to record key information as Aja presents it. (Figure 1.1, p. 24, shows the completed organizer.)

Aja then begins her lecture by describing the key geographic features of the northeast, south, and west while using the map as a visual aid. As she describes geographic features, she asks students to close their eyes so they can "see" the rivers, coasts, and plains in their minds. After five minutes of presenting, Aja stops and instructs students to see what they remember by covering their organizers and describing the geographic features of each region. She calls on three different students to describe each region before moving to the topic of immigration.

Once again, as Aja presents, she reminds students to try and make a deep sensory connection with the information by mentally putting themselves in the shoes of the Irish, German, and African people who came to the United States during this period. Again, Aja makes sure she presents for no more than five minutes before posing her next review question. Because she knows the importance of engaging students in different styles of thinking, she is careful to rotate the styles of the review questions she asks. This time, Aja wants students to explain rather than recall, so she asks, "Why did more German immigrants move west while more Irish immigrants settled in the Northeast?"

Aja completes the lecture in this way, stopping every five minutes and asking students to process and review the new content by asking questions that require different styles of thought. For example, after her presentation on the economic bases of these three regions, Aja has her students make inferential connections by asking, "What links and relationships can you find between the geography of each region and the economic base that developed there?" After the fourth and final segment of her presentation on key political issues, Aja engages students in a more personal form of thinking by posing this question: "If you were living in one of these three regions, which issue do you believe you would feel strongest about? Why?" By the end of the lecture, students' organizers look like Figure 1.1.

To synthesize the lesson and help students apply their learning to current events, Aja presents students with this task:

> Imagine you are a professional speechwriter. The year is 1840, and congressional campaigns are kicking into full gear. Pick one of the three regions we discussed in class, and imagine that a congressional candidate has hired you to write a brief speech that will have maximum appeal to voters in the selected region. Select at least three political issues from your organizer and be sure to work them into your speech. Remember to craft your speech to rally voters around your candidate.

Second grade teacher Callie Murtaugh also uses New American Lecture. Today, she is using the strategy to deliver a language arts lesson on how sentences are constructed. She begins by asking students to examine two sentences and decide which one is more interesting:

1. Girls skipped.
2. The girls skipped happily to the circus.

After students have collected, shared, and discussed their ideas on how and why the two sentences are different, Callie builds a bridge to the lesson, telling students that they will be planting "sentence gardens" by asking *Who? What? Where?* and *How?* to build and expand new sentences. Callie begins by writing the words "boys run" in the "Who?" and "Does what?" positions on the sentence garden organizer. Then, as Callie

FIGURE 1.1   Completed Lecture Organizer

Sectionalism
1820–1840

Definition	Northeast	South	West
Geography	• Narrow coast • Natural harbors • Little arable land between mountains and coast	• Wide coast • Few harbors • Wide, navigable rivers	• Plains • Lots of open, fertile land
Immigration	• Primary immigration from Northern Europe • Many Irish people came to work in factory jobs	• Primary immigration from Africa—slaves	• Central European immigrants • Many Germanic people became farmers
Economic base	• Commercial and industrial	• Slave economy • Agrarian emphasis on tobacco, then cotton	• Agrarian emphasis on grains
Political issues	• Favored national bank • Favored high tariffs • Favored increased immigration • Mixed on expansion • Favored road and canal development	• Opposed national bank • Opposed tariffs • Opposed new immigration • Favored expansion • Opposed road and canal development	• Opposed national bank • Mixed on tariffs • Favored increased immigration • Favored expansion • Favored road and canal development

continues to present, students fill out key information on their sentence garden organizers (see Figure 1.2).

As Callie and her students complete more sentence gardens during the lecture, Callie makes sure she stops every three to five minutes to allow students to process what they have learned. To facilitate processing, Callie asks students different styles of questions after each new sentence garden is complete. Callie's questions are as follows:

• What are the questions we use to expand our sentences? (Emphasizes recall)

• Can you expand the sentence "Butterflies fly"? (Emphasizes application)

• How is writing a sentence like planting a garden? (Emphasizes metaphorical thinking)

FIGURE 1.2   Sentence Garden Organizer

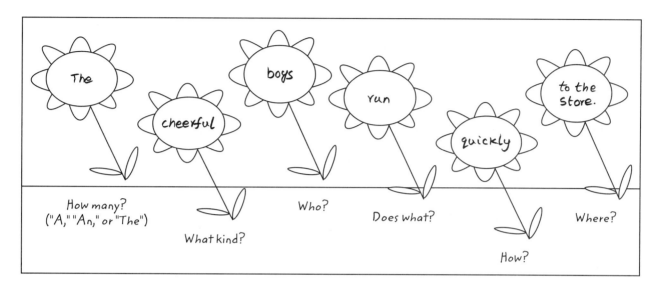

• Which part of our sentences do you like best? Can you tell why? (Emphasizes justifying personal preferences)

After completing the lecture, Callie allows students to talk in pairs and then with the whole class about what they learned and what they liked best about the lesson. As a way to help students practice and build inter-disciplinary connections, Callie asks students to use their sentence garden organizers to create five sentences about different people they would find in their communities.

Why the Strategy Works

In recent years the lecture has fallen on difficult times. Prominent researchers have questioned its value, claiming it relies too heavily on audi-tory input and makes students passive recipients as opposed to active learners. Yet, most of us have attended or delivered wonderful lectures that have provided new insights or opened our minds to new worlds and new possibilities. Without question, lectures can be potent instructional strate-gies, great for conveying a large amount of information in a short time.

New American Lecture (sometimes called Interactive Lecture) pro-vides teachers with a strategic format for designing and delivering lec-tures. The earliest manifestations of the strategy can be found in the work of David Ausubel (1963, 1968) whose theory of "meaningful verbal learning" sets the groundwork for upgrading the lecture through an antici-patory set or "hook" and a clear, visual organizational structure. Since

Ausubel's initial work, New American Lecture has evolved significantly, mostly in light of new and current research on human memory. Why this connection to memory? Because so much of the success of the lecture depends on students' abilities to get the content we deliver into their permanent memories. If students remember what we present, then the lecture proves to be a marvel of efficiency, allowing us to cover a lot of ground quickly; but if students lose the context within hours, then lecturing becomes a waste of precious classroom time. Viewed in this light, the question for educators is "How can we design and deliver lectures that will help students get key content into their permanent memories?"

Thanks to the work of cognitive scientists and psychologists, we now know a great deal about how to help students develop permanent memories. For example, we now know that there is only one type of memory but that memory serves different functions. We also know that three critical functions of memory are to (1) temporarily store the input we receive through the five senses (sensory memory); (2) permanently store and allow us to access all our accumulated knowledge (permanent memory); and (3) receive information from both permanent and sensory memory so that it can be processed at any particular moment (working memory) (Anderson, 1995). We know that processing information in multiple ways builds stronger memories (Paivio, 1990). Best of all, we know from the work of educational researchers such as Marilee Sprenger (2005), Eric Jensen (2005), and Robert Marzano (2004), how to incorporate these findings into our teaching to get students' attention through sensory memory, activate the processing capacities of working memory, and help students convert what they learn into permanent memories. In synthesizing this research, we have been able to extract four distinct principles of memory related to lecturing in the classroom:

1. Connection
2. Organization
3. Dual coding
4. Exercise and elaboration

The Principles of Memory

The Principle of Connection. The more that new information connects to a clear purpose and to students' prior knowledge, the easier it is to get students' attention and prime their memories. Here's how the New American Lecture incorporates this principle:

- The teacher uses a *hook* to capture the attention of the sensory memory and activate prior knowledge from the permanent memory.
- Students *kindle* their responses by jotting down ideas and pairing up to test them.
- The teacher builds a *bridge* between student responses and the content of the lecture.

The Principle of Organization. Organized information is easier to process and store in memory than information that lacks an organizational framework. Here's how the New American Lecture incorporates this principle:

- The lecture is designed around a visual organizer that helps students see the lecture's overall structure and "chunks."
- The teacher presents information one chunk at a time, allowing students to process information through the working memory before moving to the next chunk.

The Principle of Dual Coding. When the lecture incorporates visual, auditory, physical, and emotional experiences along with words, the information gets stored in multiple parts of the brain, thereby deepening the connection and facilitating recall. Here's how the New American Lecture incorporates this principle.

- The teacher ensures that processing using the working memory is strong and deep by
  - Using visuals
  - Inflecting his voice
  - Demonstrating ideas
  - Speaking with emphasis and emotion
- Students repeat, reinforce, and enrich their understanding of important ideas by
  - Defining them in their own words
  - Sketching them
  - Making physical representations
  - Exploring feelings associated with them

The Principle of Exercise and Elaboration. Giving students opportunities to elaborate on and practice using new information keeps the working memory active and its experiences varied, thereby facilitating the development of permanent memories. Here's how the New American Lecture incorporates this principle.

- The teacher stops every five minutes and poses a review question.
  - The teacher rotates questions to engage different styles of thinking:
    - Recalling and reviewing information (Mastery style)
    - Drawing conclusions and making inferences (Understanding style)
    - Imagining and asking *What if?* (Self-expressive style)
    - Exploring feelings and values (Interpersonal style)
- Students apply their new learning to a synthesis task or comprehension test.

How to Use the Strategy

1. Prepare students for the lecture by "hooking" their attention with a provocative question or activity, allowing them to jot down and compare ideas with a partner ("kindling"), and then building a "bridge" between student responses and the new content.

2. Distribute, or work with students to create, a visual organizer.

3. Present information using auditory, visual, kinesthetic, and/or emotive cues to make information vivid and memorable.

4. Stop presenting every five minutes or so. Allow students to review and process learning by posing questions that engage different styles of thinking.

5. Allow students to evaluate and reflect on the content and the process of the lesson.

6. Assess learning using a synthesis task or more traditional evaluation technique such as a comprehension test.

Planning a New American Lecture

Planning a New American Lecture involves five basic steps:

1. Identify your topic
2. Design the visual organizer
3. Develop review questions
4. Design the hook
5. Develop a synthesis task

Identify Your Topic

You need to collect and chunk the information. If you think back to the sample lessons, you will remember that the collecting phase is when the students collect information by taking notes on the visual organizer. In the planning stage, it is your job to collect the information you want your students to collect during the lesson. The best way to collect information is to jot down key words related to the content. Do not feel you need to be orderly about this; jot down whatever pops into your head. For example, a 1st grade teacher who was planning a lesson called "A Walk Through the Four Seasons" jotted down the following words for winter:

> cold, snow, no birds, Christmas, sledding, snowball fights, Hanukkah, jackets, gloves, mittens, snow days, skiing, hot chocolate, hibernation, bare trees, snowmen, short days, snow boots, sweaters, New Year's Day, Martin Luther King Jr. Day, inside

After you have generated your information, you need to understand how it all fits together. Look at all the key words you have identified and group them into categories. For example, even though the 1st grade teacher already had the natural categories of the seasons built into her content, she further broke up her lecture into these categories: clothing, holidays, activities, and nature/weather. Categories help you recognize the chunks in your lecture. As you group information, you may discover key words or concepts that need to be added.

Design the Visual Organizer

Visual organizers illustrate how information fits together to form a larger picture. Once you identify your content and explore how it all fits together, you can design a visual organizer that both you and your students will use during the lecture. Designing a good organizer depends on your ability to recognize different conceptual patterns information can take. Figure 1.3 (p. 30) shows a variety of organizers highlighting common conceptual patterns.

Develop Review Questions

As you make your plans to present information in roughly five-minute lecture sessions, decide on stopping points at which you will use questions to review material and engage all students. By rotating the styles of questions you pose to students during these review-and-process sessions, you give all students the opportunity to think about the content according to their preferred learning style. Moreover, by using an arsenal of questioning techniques, you create variety, arouse interest, and challenge students to move beyond their style preferences by thinking in all the styles. Figure 1.4 (p. 31) is a brief guide to the four styles of questions, along with examples from a variety of disciplines. (For more on the relationship between the four learning styles and classroom questioning, see Task Rotation, pp. 241–252).

Design the Hook

A *hook* is a provocative question or introductory activity that attracts student interest, focuses thinking, and opens memory banks closely associated with the new topic. In creating a hook, you should look over your organized information. What theme or concept unites your material? As with your review questions, you may want to use learning styles to differentiate the types of hooks you develop. Four teachers' style-based hooks are given on pages 31–32. Along with the way each teacher bridged students' responses to the lesson.

FIGURE 1.3 A Potpourri of New American Lecture Organizers

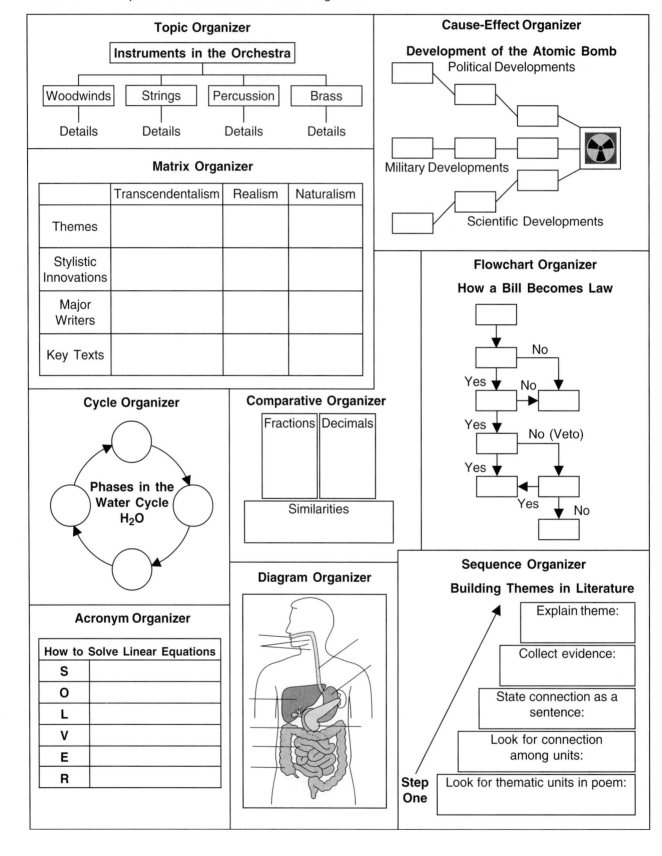

FIGURE 1.4   Questions in Style

Mastery questions emphasize recalling information:	Interpersonal questions emphasize feelings, values, and personal experiences:
• Summarize: In your own words, restate what we've said. • Prioritize: What were the two most important points? • Remember: Turn your paper over and see how much you can remember from this part of the lecture.	• Feelings: Which of these issues do you feel strongest about? Why? • Preferences: Which step in solving polynomial equations is hardest? Which is easiest? Why? • Role play or empathize: Suppose you are a student in Nazi Germany. How would you react if a friend had to wear a band declaring his religion?
Understanding questions emphasize analysis and use of evidence:	**Self-Expressive questions emphasize imagination:**
• Compare and contrast: What are the similarities and differences between U.S. attitudes toward the British in 1763 and in 1773? • Hypothesize: Identify some possible causes and effects for the information on the organizer. • Support with evidence: Find information in your organizer that proves or disproves this statement: *Long division is simply a complicated form of subtraction.*	• Metaphor: Create a metaphor for the commutative property. • Symbols: Design a flag that stands for what we know about Spanish explorers. • What if?: What would happen if Newton's third law were false? Suppose every reaction were double the force of the original action. Suppose it were half.

1. **Mastery**
   ○ **Hook:** Think for a minute about anything you know about scientific classification. What do you know about how scientists classify organisms?
   ○ **Bridge:** Good! You really know a lot about classification. Now let's build some new information on what you already know.
2. **Understanding**
   ○ **Hook:** Here are four long-division problems, two that involve remainders and two that don't. What differences do you notice? Why might there be these differences?
   ○ **Bridge:** Good! Now let me show you some more long-division problems, and we'll see which of your ideas are true.
3. **Self-Expressive**
   ○ **Hook:** Imagine that you came back to the United States 200 years from today, only to discover that it was no longer a superpower. What could have caused this change?
   ○ **Bridge:** Good! Now let's look into the fall of the Roman Empire and see if we can find any similarities.

4. **Interpersonal**
   ◦ **Hook:** Think back on a time when someone persuaded you to change your mind. Why did you change your mind?
   ◦ **Bridge:** Good! You've described the way people can be persuaded. Let's look at how a great speaker persuades her audience and see what else we can learn about persuasion.

Develop a Synthesis (or Comprehension) Task (or Comprehension Test)

You may choose to have students integrate and apply the knowledge they have gained in your lecture immediately, or you may choose to put assessment off until a later time. Because New American Lecture has the same instructional goals as a traditional lecture, you may choose to assess students' knowledge with a comprehension test. Alternatively, you may choose to have students complete a synthesis task in which they apply their learning to the creation of a meaningful product. For example, after a lecture on the four seasons, the 1st grade teacher we met earlier in this chapter challenged students to create a "Diary of a Tree" with pictures and entries for each of the four seasons.

Variations and Extensions

Student Presentations

Making presentations is an important academic and life skill. Students are introduced to the art of presenting as early as kindergarten when they are asked to give a book talk or present an item for show and tell. By the time they reach high school, students are asked to participate in debates and deliver engaging presentations. Furthermore, today's job market seeks workers who have the ability not only to collect, classify, and understand the constant flow of information, but also to present that information clearly and coherently so others can understand it.

Student presentations serve two purposes. First, you can use them to assess your students' comprehension of the content: Is all of the key information accounted for? Is it organized in a clear structure that shows the relationship between main ideas and details? Second, asking students to design and deliver a presentation allows you to assess their competence in key research, information management, and communication skills.

Of course, there is a wide variety of presentation methods students can use or be asked to use. Figure 1.5 outlines seven common types of presentations and links each to a purpose and to assessment criteria typically used to determine the quality of each type of presentation.

Once the parameters of each type of presentation have been made clear, you can develop tasks accordingly. The following narrative-based presentation task designed by a 5th grade English teacher demonstrates what we have discussed in Chapter 1.

> Over the next few weeks we're going to read several short stories. As we read, we will pay close attention to how the authors create characters (What are their feelings? How do they respond to events in the story? etc.), and how they develop a plot or story (What happens? Where does the story take place? What problems arise? How are the problems solved?). After we have completed our readings and you have gathered notes and information on how writers create characters, settings, conflicts, and resolutions, you will be asked to create a story of your own. Your story must have at least two characters, take place in an interesting setting, and pose some sort of problem or conflict to be solved. You will read your story to the class, and your story will be assessed according to these criteria:
> - Does it have a well-formed and creative narrative?
> - Does it show an understanding of narrative techniques that we learned in our unit?
> - Was your reading to the class passionate and engaging?

FIGURE 1.5   Seven Types of Presentations

Type	Purpose	Assessment Criteria
Recount	To tell what happened	Accurately describes sequence of events
Instruction	To present a lesson or demonstrate a skill	Clearly describes the content or how to perform or execute the skill
Narrative	To entertain, to inform, to share thoughts and reflections	Describes information in an entertaining way
Information Report	To describe what is known about a certain topic	Presents information in a clear and organized way
Explanation	To explain causes and/or effects	Provides logical reasons behind causes and effects; tells *why* rather than describes *what*
Argument	To lay out a position and support it	Lays out a clear position, cites evidence and reasons, considers counterarguments
Inquiry	To develop and support a hypothesis through research	Presents a well-formed and feasible hypothesis; uses multiple sources of evidence to support it

How does the strategy fit into unit design?
(Blueprint for Learning)

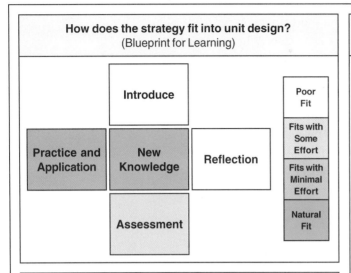

What learning styles does the strategy engage?
(Motivation/Differentiation)

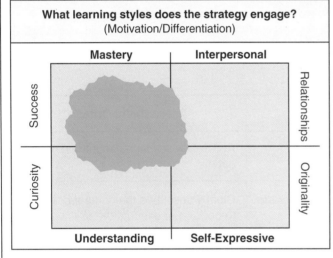

What facets of understanding does the strategy develop?
(Understanding by Design)

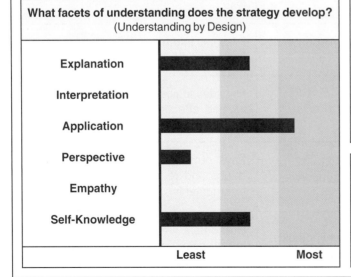

What skills does the strategy build?
(The Hidden Skills of Academic Literacy)

Read and Study
- ● Collect/organize ideas through note making
- ○ Make sense of abstract academic vocabulary
- ○ Read/interpret visuals

Reason and Analyze
- ○ Draw conclusions; make/test inferences, hypotheses, conjectures
- ○ Conduct comparisons using criteria
- ● Analyze demands of a variety of questions

Create and Communicate
- ○ Write clear, coherent explanations
- ○ Write comfortably in major nonfiction genres
- ○ Read and write about two or more documents

Reflect and Relate
- ● Construct plans to address questions and tasks
- ● Use criteria and guidelines to evaluate work
- ● Control/alter mood and impulsivity

How does the strategy incorporate the research on instructional effectiveness?
(Classroom Instruction That Works)

- ○ Identifying similarities and differences
- ● Summarizing and note taking
- ● Reinforcing effort and providing recognition
- ● Homework and practice
- ○ Nonlinguistic representation
- ○ Cooperative learning
- ● Setting objectives and feedback
- ○ Generating and testing hypotheses
- ○ Cues, questions, and advance organizers

What types of knowledge does the strategy teach?

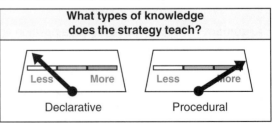

Declarative   Procedural

2

Direct Instruction

Strategy Overview

Years of advocacy for instructional approaches that emphasize inquiry, discovery, and constructivism have tarnished the reputation of more direct, teacher-driven forms of teaching. This is an unfortunate development, based on faulty "either/or" thinking. Just as certain topics lend themselves to inquiry-based learning, so do particular skills need to be mastered and used on command by students.

We have already seen how New American Lecture uses a direct instruction approach to teach declarative content. Here, we look at the application of this approach to teaching skills. Based on the influential work of Madeline Hunter (recently updated by Robin Hunter, 2004), the Direct Instruction strategy lays out a simple, four-phase process for maximizing skill acquisition.

1. **Modeling**—The skill is modeled by the teacher, who thinks aloud while performing the skill.
2. **Directed practice**—The teacher uses questions to lead students through the steps and to help them see the reasons behind the steps.
3. **Guided practice**—Students generate their own leading questions while working through the steps; the teacher observes, coaches, and provides feedback.
4. **Independent practice**—Finally, students work through more examples on their own.

The Strategy in Action

Jaidee Sakda has just posed an essential question to her 11th grade chemistry students: "How do you balance a chemical equation?" She says, "Today we're going to answer this question together, using a strategy called Direct Instruction." After explaining how Direct Instruction works, Jaidee writes down the steps in balancing chemical equations on the board. She asks students to write the steps down the left side of a clean page in their notebooks. Next, Jaidee selects an example and walks students through each step while recording her work on the board. Students listen, watch, and then perform each step, recording their work on the right side of their notebook page. During this modeling phase, Jaidee and her students produce a two-sided form, shown in Figure 2.1.

FIGURE 2.1   Direct Instruction—Balancing Chemical Equations

Step 1
Write the equation out.

propane + oxygen = carbon dioxide + steam

Step 2
Convert the chemical names to the appropriate symbols.

$$C_3H_8 + O_2 = CO_2 + H_2O$$

Step 3
Compare the number of atoms of each type on the left and right sides of the equation to check for imbalances.

Carbon - 3	Carbon - 1
Hydrogen - 8	Hydrogen - 2
Oxygen - 2	Oxygen - 3

Step 4
Balance the complex molecules first by multiplying on the appropriate side of the equation.

$$C_3H_8 + O_2 = 3CO_2 + 4H_2O$$

Step 5
Balance the elements last based on the changes you made in Step 4.

$$C_3H_8 + 5O_2 = 3CO_2 + 4H_2O$$

Step 6
Check to make sure the equation is balanced.

Carbon - 3	Carbon - 3
Hydrogen - 8	Hydrogen - 8
Oxygen - 10	Oxygen - 10

Jaidee asks students to turn to a clean sheet in their notebooks. She erases the board and writes out a new problem: *When heated, aluminum reacts with solid copper oxide to produce copper metal and aluminum oxide.* "This time," Jaidee says, "we're going to try a new example, but we're not going to have the steps listed out for us. Instead, I'm going to ask some questions that'll help us think through the process and remember the steps." To help students recall and apply each step to the new example, Jaidee uses simple guiding questions like "What is the formula for aluminum oxide?" and "OK, so now that we've written our equation, what do we do next?" However, Jaidee also makes sure to fold in questions that help students see the mathematical and scientific reasoning behind each step as well, questions such as "Why do we need to multiply the copper oxide by 3?" and "Who can tell me how this step was different when we worked on our propane and oxygen example? Do you know why?"

After running through one more example in this way, Jaidee provides students with three more examples. "What I'd like everyone to do now is to use the procedure we have just learned to solve these three examples. I want you to start by reviewing all the steps and visualizing yourself performing each step. But after that, I really want you to avoid going back to your notebook for help. Instead, if you get stuck, try to use your visualization and ask yourself questions like the ones we asked together to reason your way through the procedure." As students work on these examples, Jaidee moves around the room. She observes the students while working and provides both praise and feedback. Most important, Jaidee checks to make sure students are working through the steps correctly. When one student, Marie, skips one of the steps in the procedure, Jaidee doesn't simply correct her work. Instead, she helps Marie to get her thinking out in the open by asking, "OK, now why did you do that?" and "Why is it easiest to balance the elements after the molecules?" Jaidee also invites students to submit help cards on which they write down questions or identify the parts of the process that are giving them trouble.

As the period comes to an end, Jaidee gives students only three more problems. She also provides students with the answers to the problems. When students look at her strangely, she says, "Three problems and the answers? Have I gone crazy? No—at least I don't think so. For these three problems, I want you to do two things: First, I want you to show each step in the process. You can use the answers to check your work, but make sure you show me your work along the way. Second, I want you to write out—in your own words—what you're doing in each step of the process." The idea behind Jaidee's assignment is to keep students focused on the process so that they further internalize the steps. By keeping the assignment short, Jaidee is also positioning students to practice the skill more frequently but for short durations of time—a technique proven to maximize retention of new skills.

Why the Strategy Works

The research is clear: Teachers who spend more time demonstrating and explaining procedures and skills are more effective than teachers who spend less time doing so (Rosenshine, 1985). In addition, a large body of research supports the effectiveness of Direct Instruction as an ideal technique for teaching new skills to both general-education and learning-disabled students (Hastings, Raymond, & McLaughlin, 1989; Wilson & Sindelar, 1991; Woodward, 1991; and Tarver & Jung, 1995). However, what makes for a good Direct Instruction lesson? The successful implementation of Direct Instruction is founded on these principles:

- Effective modeling
- Emerging independence
- Learning by questioning
- Ongoing assessment

Effective Modeling

A Direct Instruction lesson begins with a good modeling session, which lays out every step in the skill and demonstrates how each step is performed. A good modeling session explains to students what outcomes they are working toward and what is expected of them as they develop the skill. Finally, good modeling means teaching both the steps in performing the skill and thinking aloud to expose the covert thinking that occurs during each step.

Emerging Independence

In teaching skills, the ultimate goal is to move students from dependence on the teacher to self-directed application of the skill. In its four-phase approach to skill acquisition (modeling, directed practice, guided practice, and independent practice), Direct Instruction nurtures learners as they move toward independence.

Learning by Questioning

Questions are integral to skill acquisition because they force students to analyze the steps in the skill. When teachers fail to incorporate questions into their Direct Instruction lessons, their students may not go through what Marzano, Pickering, and Pollock (2001) call the "shaping phase"— the critical time in the skill acquisition process when students develop a deep conceptual understanding of the skill they are learning. In the directed-practice phase of Direct Instruction, the teacher uses two distinct kinds of questions to lead students through the skill and help them "shape" their understanding:

- *Procedural questions* ask students to describe a step in the skill (e.g., "What's the next step in shooting a free throw?")
- *Conceptual questions* force students to analyze the step or explore the rationale behind it (e.g., "Why is it important to bend your knees before bringing the basketball to the shooting position? How is shooting the basketball similar to what we learned about 'setting' in volleyball? How is it different?")

Then, during guided practice, students generate questions of their own as they work through the steps of the skill with less teacher guidance.

Ongoing Assessment

When teachers emphasize performance at the expense of practice, then students tend to fixate on grades and seek to cover up mistakes rather than taking the time to learn from them. To help mitigate this problem, Direct Instruction builds in multiple practice opportunities for students to learn from their mistakes and get better at learning. Practice should be a time for students to collaborate and share ideas; the teacher should serve as a coach who guides, instructs, and provides feedback. Moreover, students should be given the criteria for successful application of the skill during practice so that they know what exemplary performance looks like and strive toward it. One teacher we know calls this ongoing assessment process the Four A's: Assess (the practice session), Analyze (according to the criteria for success), Adjust (to improve performance), and Achieve.

How to Use the Strategy

1. Select a skill and break it into a set of clear steps.
2. Model the skill by demonstrating the steps and by describing the thinking needed to perform each step.
3. Lead students through directed practice, using both procedural and conceptual questions to help them identify each step and its rationale, write out the sequence of steps, and perform the skill.

4. Before engaging students in guided practice, have them read over the sequence they wrote in Step 3 and visualize themselves performing the skill.

5. Engage students in guided practice by assigning a few tasks or examples. Encourage students to use visualizations and to ask and answer their own questions as they work through the steps. Observe, provide feedback, and coach.

6. Assign additional tasks or examples for independent practice.

7. Maximize skill acquisition by massing practice sessions at the beginning (several practice sessions lasting only a few minutes) and then distributing practice over time for periodic review.

8. Tie the skill to a performance or an assessment task so that students use the skill in a meaningful context.

Planning a Direct Instruction Lesson

When planning to teach students a skill using Direct Instruction, you will need to take the following steps:

1. **Determine the skill you would like students to master.** Direct Instruction should be used when the curriculum presents skills that students will need help developing. It is especially useful for complex skills that contain involved procedures. Skills such as constructing mathematical proofs, building literary themes, learning dance or cheerleading routines, applying the steps in an experiment, and solving analogies or word problems are all ideally suited for Direct Instruction.

2. **Identify the steps in the skill and convert the steps into focused questions.** Break your skill into a list of clear and demonstrable steps. Keep your list succinct by focusing on the critical steps and eliminating secondary ones. For example, an elementary teacher who wanted her students to learn the steps in finding the area of a rectangle listed these major steps (while eliminating secondary steps, such as spelling out what to do when dealing with values that are fractions or decimals):

- Determine or identify the length and width of the rectangle.
- Choose the proper formula ($A = lw$).
- Substitute the values for l and w into the formula.
- Solve for A.

During directed practice, you will use a set of focused questions to guide students through the steps in the skill. Questions allow students to own or shape the skill on their own terms. Questions can be procedural, requiring only that students know what to do and when to do it (e.g., "Now that we've developed a hypothesis, what is the next step in the scientific method?"), or they can be conceptual, asking students to think "behind the skill," to the motivation and rationale underlying it (e.g., "Why is it important to collect data both before and after developing a hypothesis?").

3. **Select or create examples for various stages of practice.** After modeling, you will need a repertoire of examples for guided practice and independent practice. If the skill lends itself to a range of difficulty levels, you should graduate the examples, saving the most difficult ones for later stages, after students have shown that they understand the process and can perform each step competently.

4. **Create a schedule for practicing the skill.** If you expect students to master and retain the skill fully, you must allow them time to practice after the lesson. One question to ask yourself when designing a practice schedule with your students is "How often should practice periods be conducted?" According to Marzano, Norford, Paynter, Pickering, and Gaddy (2001), the answer to this question differs over time.

In the beginning, mass the practice. This means that practice periods should be short, frequently occurring, and closely spaced, more than once daily if possible. As the material is learned over time, you can distribute the practice periods between longer periods of time. Massing practice up front makes for fast learning. Distributing practice after the skill has been learned makes for longer retention.

5. **Select or design a synthesis task that requires students to use the new skill.** Practice is not an end; it is a means toward an end. At some point, students need to apply their newly acquired skill. Make sure you give your students a chance to apply the skill to a meaningful task or performance.

Variations and Extensions

One variation of Direct Instruction is known as the Command strategy. The strategy is derived from the training practices of the military in which soldiers process commands before the commands are executed. Command allows teachers to maintain total control of student behavior in order to achieve 100 percent accuracy in completing a task or following directions. This level of control is guaranteed by leading students through a series of simple steps, one by one, on command.

Below are the steps in the Command strategy, along with an example showing how 2nd grade teacher Stacey Cancion used the strategy to conduct an interdisciplinary lesson (combining art and science) on plants.

1. **Break the task into simple steps or commands.** Stacey wants her students to be able to correctly identify, label, and state the function of the major parts of flowering plants. To make the lesson more interactive

(and therefore more memorable), Stacey decides to have the students "create" their plants by cutting out flowers, stems, leaves, and roots from construction paper and pasting them on card stock. Thus, Stacey's task breaks down into commands easily: For each plant part, Stacey will ask students to (1) cut it out, (2) paste it, (3) label it, and (4) copy a brief description of its function.

2. **Introduce the task and the command word.** "Today," Stacey says, "we are going to learn the major parts of plants and how these parts help the plant survive and help it to make more plants just like it. But we're going to do things a little differently than usual. Each of you will get four sheets of construction paper. On each piece of paper you'll find the shape of a plant part. Together we're going to take these pieces of paper and turn them into plants, one step at a time." Stacey then explains to students that she will state each step in the process and that as soon as she says the command word *plants*, students should complete that step. To help students remember their roles, she posts a code word poster in front of the room:

> **L**ook at the teacher and listen carefully to the command.
> **E**nter the command into your brain.
> **A**lways wait for the command word.
> **D**o it!
> **S**top and check to see if you've done it correctly.

3. **State the command and give the command signal.** Stacey says, "Start by finding the green piece of construction paper with the roots on it. When I give the command, I want you to carefully cut the roots out with your scissors. Ready?" Stacey then gives the command word *plants*, and students begin cutting out the roots. The lesson continues in this manner, with Stacey stating commands and students carrying out the commands, until all of the plant parts have been cut out and pasted in the appropriate places on the card stock. Stacey continues using Command to have students label—on her command—the roots, stem, leaves, and flower and then to have them write descriptions of what each plant part does. Stacey keeps descriptions short and simple. For example, for the roots, Stacey has students write, *Hold the plant in the ground and absorb water and minerals from the soil.*

4. **Observe and evaluate each student performing each command.** As students work on each step, Stacey walks around the room to make sure each student is performing the step correctly.

5. **Once the process is complete, have the students review the skill.** After all students have created their plants, Stacey explains to them that not only have they made an interesting piece of art; they have also created a great study guide. She then tells students that because labeling

and describing plant parts will be on the unit test, one of the best ways they can prepare is by covering up the right side of their plants with a blank sheet of paper and seeing how well they can label their plants and explain what each part does without looking.

3. GRADUATED DIFFICULTY

How does the strategy fit into unit design?
(Blueprint for Learning)

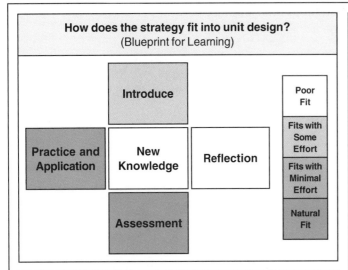

	Introduce	Poor Fit
Practice and Application	**New Knowledge**	**Reflection**	Fits with Some Effort
		Fits with Minimal Effort
	Assessment	Natural Fit

What learning styles does the strategy engage?
(Motivation/Differentiation)

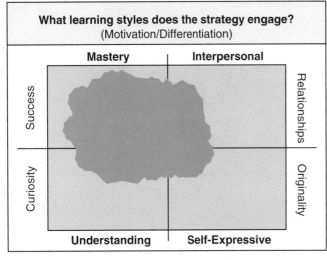

Mastery — Interpersonal
Success — Relationships
Curiosity — Originality
Understanding — Self-Expressive

What facets of understanding does the strategy develop?
(Understanding by Design)

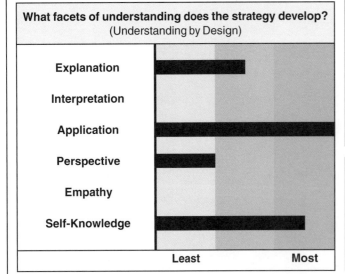

- Explanation
- Interpretation
- Application
- Perspective
- Empathy
- Self-Knowledge

Least — Most

What skills does the strategy build?
(The Hidden Skills of Academic Literacy)

Read and Study
- ○ Collect/organize ideas through note making
- ○ Make sense of abstract academic vocabulary
- ○ Read/interpret visuals

Reason and Analyze
- ○ Draw conclusions; make/test inferences, hypotheses, conjectures
- ● Conduct comparisons using criteria
- ● Analyze demands of a variety of questions

Create and Communicate
- ○ Write clear, coherent explanations
- ○ Write comfortably in major nonfiction genres
- ○ Read and write about two or more documents

Reflect and Relate
- ● Construct plans to address questions and tasks
- ● Use criteria and guidelines to evaluate work
- ● Control/alter mood and impulsivity

How does the strategy incorporate the research on instructional effectiveness?
(Classroom Instruction That Works)

- ● Identifying similarities and differences
- ○ Summarizing and note taking
- ● Reinforcing effort and providing recognition
- ● Homework and practice
- ○ Nonlinguistic representation
- ○ Cooperative learning
- ● Setting objectives and feedback
- ○ Generating and testing hypotheses
- ○ Cues, questions, and advance organizers

What types of knowledge does the strategy teach?

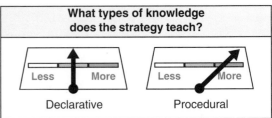

Less — More   Less — More
Declarative   Procedural

3

Graduated Difficulty

Strategy Overview

One of the most important goals of the movement for differentiated learning is the development of self-directed learning among a wide array of students. Any student who is able to analyze the demands of assigned tasks, make good decisions about how to complete that work, assess personal progress, and determine what steps are necessary to reach higher goals has obviously earned the label "self-directed learner." However, do we have the teaching strategies necessary to develop self-directed students?

Graduated Difficulty involves students directly in the differentiation process as they

- Analyze a variety of tasks at different levels of difficulty.
- Select the task that is most appropriate for them.
- Complete and evaluate their chosen task.
- Chart goals for improvement and achievement at higher levels of difficulty.

The Strategy in Action

Barb Heinzman is preparing to use the Graduated Difficulty strategy to help her 5th graders practice reducing fractions. She begins class by handing out a worksheet with three sets of problems at increasing levels of difficulty.

Sample Problems from Level 1:	$\dfrac{12}{14}$	$\dfrac{28}{42}$	$\dfrac{33}{44}$	$\dfrac{35}{10}$
Sample Problems from Level 2:	$\dfrac{12}{6006}$	$\dfrac{108}{7}$	$\dfrac{2001}{1002}$	$\dfrac{19}{209}$
Sample Problems from Level 3:	$\dfrac{606}{1616}$	$\dfrac{246}{2/3}$	$\dfrac{784}{896}$	$\dfrac{37}{0.2}$

Barb continues:

> Since we spent a lot of time talking about reducing fractions last week, I'd like to give you a chance to review and practice what we learned. You just received a worksheet with three problem sets at increasing levels of difficulty. Because everyone learns at a different pace, I will leave it up to you to decide which problem set is most appropriate for you. The only thing I ask is that you make an informed and thoughtful decision. To help you do this, I've prepared a few questions that I'd like you to consider before you make your selections.

Barb then writes the following questions on the board:

- What makes one level harder than the next?
- What skills or knowledge would be needed to complete each task?
- What level do you think will work best for you? Why?

When Barb senses that her students are ready to get started, she gives them a few final instructions:

> Remember that I trust you to make your own decisions—you are free to work at whatever level "feels best." You can ask your classmates for help if you need it, and you are welcome to check your work at any time using the answer keys posted at the front of the room. If at any point you decide that the problem set you selected is too easy or too hard, go ahead and switch levels.

Barb walks around the room as her students work. To make sure that everyone is being challenged, she asks each student who completes the Level 3 problem set successfully to develop a Level 4 problem set (along with a corresponding answer key). She then encourages these students to challenge themselves even further by "trading" Level 4 problem sets among themselves.

When her students finish working, Barb asks them to reflect on the following questions:

- What criteria did you use to select the level at which you wanted to work?

- Was your choice a good one for you? Why or why not?
- What do you need to know/do in order to work at a higher level?

Barb invites her students to share their answers with the entire class. She then uses their responses to spark a classroom discussion about the value of students making decisions for themselves, the ways in which students can evaluate and improve their decision-making skills, and the importance of setting goals.

For homework, Barb asks her students to generate "goal cards"— index cards on which they record personal goals for improvement. For example, "I need to get a better understanding of divisibility rules so that I am able to work at a higher level in the future." In an effort to encourage her students to achieve the goals they set for themselves, Barb has recently started yelling "Goooooooooooal" (with all of the enthusiasm of a professional soccer announcer) each time a student accomplishes one of the goals on a goal card. Whenever a student achieves 10 goals, Barb holds a special awards ceremony acknowledging that student's achievement. Recognizing her students' efforts and accomplishments in this way has really paid off; her students' levels of motivation have increased dramatically since the beginning of the year.

Why the Strategy Works

The Graduated Difficulty strategy is based on the work of Muska Mosston (1972), who found, long before the word *differentiation* was commonplace in education, that actively engaging students in choosing the level of difficulty of their work allowed all students to work at an optimal level of productivity. The technique also led to other significant classroom benefits, including:

- Greater opportunities for all students to succeed
- Gains in student confidence, leading them to try working at higher levels
- Decreases in disciplinary issues and improved relationships among students
- Improvement in the depth and quality of students' self-reflective and decision-making abilities

Of course, these benefits do not happen just because teachers hand out three levels of tasks. What is especially important in Mosston's work is the way it puts the learner at the center of Graduated Difficulty. Although current approaches to differentiation often place all responsibility for assigning levels and assessing the results on the teacher, Mosston proposed a collaborative relationship between teacher and student that leads to student independence over time. Students are encouraged to analyze and compare tasks, and the decisions they make about what level is best for them are their own. In this way, Graduated Difficulty enables teachers to develop a classroom culture of reflection and discussion where students look back on their work, assess their performance and their choices, and engage in regular conversations with the teacher about setting and achieving goals.

In recent years, the educational research community has caught up to Mosston and his choice-based model. New findings that support the Graduated Difficulty model have emerged from several distinct lines of research.

- **Choice Theory**—As William Glasser (1998) and Jonathan Erwin (2004) have demonstrated, choice is one of the most powerful human motivators. Classrooms that put a high premium on student choice and mutual trust between teachers and students produce students who are intrinsically motivated to learn and succeed.
- **Goal Setting in the Classroom**—Setting goals for student achievement leads to more refined and focused thinking among students. This is especially true when the teacher sets the goals but the students have the opportunity to personalize the goals and make them their own (Marzano, Pickering, & Pollock, 2001).
- **The Role of Challenge in Learning**—When tasks prove too difficult for students, they tend to give up; when tasks are so easy that they can be completed without effort, students lose interest and become bored (Jensen, 1998; Tomlinson & McTighe, 2006). Therefore, providing students with tasks at the appropriate degree of difficulty is a crucial factor in building and sustaining student engagement.

How to Use the Strategy

1. Determine the skill to be practiced or the content to be reviewed.

2. Develop a set of tasks around the selected content or skill at three (or more) levels of difficulty.

3. Make sure that your students understand the role they are expected to play in the Graduated Difficulty strategy. Then, distribute the set of tasks.

4. Encourage students to analyze all of the tasks on the list; students should determine what skills and knowledge are necessary to succeed at each level of difficulty before deciding which task they wish to complete.

5. Remind students that they are free to work at whatever level feels right and may switch levels at any time. It is important for students to recognize that you trust them to make decisions for themselves.

6. Allow students to check their work at any time. Facilitate the self-assessment process by ensuring that students have easy access to an answer key (for tasks with right or wrong answers) or an assessment rubric (for more open-ended tasks).

7. Give students time to reflect on what they learned and accomplished. Encourage them to share their thoughts and feelings with the class.

8. Work with students to help them establish personal goals for improvement; goals should be challenging but achievable.

Planning a Graduated Difficulty Lesson

Use these steps to design a Graduated Difficulty lesson.

1. **Select the skill you want students to practice or the content you want them to review and establish tasks at three (or more) levels of difficulty.** While tasks with clear right and wrong answers are well suited to Graduated Difficulty, open-ended tasks also make for great Graduated Difficulty lessons. Keep in mind that you can create levels by varying the difficulty of the content, the thinking process, or the product and performance as shown in Figure 3.1.

   In terms of establishing the degree of challenge inherent in each level, the basic guidelines are as follows:
   - Level 1 should be a relatively easy task that all students can complete; however, the task should require full demonstration of the focus skill or grasp of the focus content.
   - Level 2 should be a challenge for most of your students, but not so difficult as to scare them away.
   - Level 3 should be a challenge for all students in your class. To complete a Level 3 task, students must exhibit what you consider to be the highest levels of competence or comprehension.

2. **Develop an answer sheet, a list of criteria, or a rubric that students can use to assess their performance.** In order for students to assess their work and their choices, they must know what success looks like at each level. If your tasks have clear right and wrong answers, provide an answer sheet for students to consult. If your tasks are more open-ended or qualitative, a list of criteria for success or rubric will do the job. For example, a 6th grade teacher using Graduated Difficulty to help her students write high-level persuasive essays provided students with the rubric shown in Figure 3.2, p. 51.

3. **Think carefully about the way in which you will introduce the Graduated Difficulty strategy to your students because this level of independence and trust may be new to them.** A great way to help students understand and adjust to their roles and responsibilities in Graduated Difficulty is to create a classroom-friendly poster that guides them through the phases of the strategy. You can use the word *decide* as an acronym to help students remember the strategy.

FIGURE 3.1 Three Ways to Build Levels into Your Activities and Practice Sessions

Level of	What It Means	Examples
Content	Basing levels on the degree of rigor found in the content	A high school English teacher working to build her students' interpretive skills based her Graduated Difficulty activity on the relative difficulty of the language and ideas found in three different poems: • A short free-verse poem by William Carlos Williams (Level 1), • A slightly longer poem in rhymed couplets by Emily Dickinson (Level 2), and • A sonnet by William Shakespeare (Level 3).
Thinking Process	Basing levels on the sophistication of the thinking required by the tasks	After a set of readings on three famous dinosaurs (brontosaurus, triceratops, T. rex) an elementary teacher provided her students with a choice of these three tasks: • *Level 1 (Collecting and recording):* Fill in the provided description matrix by putting the correct information about appearance, behavior, diet, and environment in the appropriate boxes. • *Level 2 (Comparing and contrasting):* Pick two dinosaurs. Using a "top hat" organizer, compare and contrast the two dinosaurs using the criteria provided in the Level 1 task. • *Level 3 (Application):* Examine this picture of a barosaurus. Based on what you see here, can you determine whether it was a meat eater or a plant eater? Be sure to explain your thinking using details from the picture and by comparing *Barosaurus* to our other dinosaurs.
Product or Performance	Basing levels on the difficulty of the products students create or the performances they give	There are countless ways to design Graduated Difficulty around products and performances that are progressively challenging to create or deliver, but here are some general guidelines: • Lower-level products and performances stay very close to the content and ask students to restate critical information. Examples include summaries, retellings, demonstrations of a skill, graphic organizers, diagrams, and simple posters and charts. • Mid-level products and performances tend to require interpretation or synthesis on the part of the student. Examples include metaphors, poems, explanations, debates, brief essays and reports, arguments, articles, and visual icons. • High-level products and performances usually challenge students to apply their learning in a new context or to create an original piece of work. Examples include short stories, design work, inventions, real-world problem solving, fieldwork, lesson plans, and musical or dramatic performances.

How to use *decide* as an acronym for Graduted Difficulty:
- Determine what you know and understand about the content or skill to be practiced.
- Examine the levels of difficulty carefully and choose the level that is best for you.
- Check your work, change your level, communicate with others about your work, or create a new level if you are able to complete the highest level.
- Identify the criteria you used to make your choice.
- Determine if you made a good choice and decide what you need to know and understand to move to the next level.
- Establish a goal for improvement.

FIGURE 3.2   Sample Persuasive Writing Rubric

Criteria	Novice	Apprentice	Expert
How persuasive was I?	The problem and my position are confused. I didn't use much evidence, or give my reasons clearly. I didn't consider other points of view or respond to them.	I described the problem and my position. I used some reasons or evidence to support my position, though they may not be the best ones. I didn't consider other points of view or I didn't respond to them.	I described the problem and my position clearly. I used good reasons and evidence from the text to support my position. I considered other points of view and answered them.
How organized was I?	My writing is a little confusing and hard to follow. No transitions are used.	My writing has a beginning, middle, and end. I didn't use many transitions or made mistakes in using them.	My writing is clear, logical, and easy to read. I used transitions (until, however, though, because) to help my reader understand my argument.
How well did I use language?	I used only simple words and phrases. My sentences are all very similar.	I used some interesting words and phrases, and changed my sentence types occasionally.	I used rich and interesting words and phrases, and varied my sentences to keep my readers interested.
Mechanics: How correct is my writing?	I'm afraid there may be lots of errors that make my paper difficult to read.	I think I made some errors in spelling, punctuation, or grammar, but my writing can be understood.	I think I eliminated almost all the errors in my writing.

4. **Develop pre-task questions that will help students analyze the various tasks and make informed decisions.** Pre-task questions should encourage students to think about the differences between the various levels of tasks and to assess their own skills and knowledge base. Here are a few examples:

- Can you determine what makes each level progressively harder?
- What skills and content knowledge are needed to complete each level?
- What level do you think will work best for you? Why?
- What level seems to offer the proper balance of comfort and challenge?

5. **Develop post-task questions that will encourage self-reflection and analysis.** Post-task questions help students evaluate the choices they made during the lesson and establish goals for improvement. Here are a few examples:

- What did you do well? What gave you trouble?
- What criteria did you use to make your choice?
- How would you evaluate your performance? Do you feel you made the right choice? Would you make the same choice again?
- What do you need to do or learn in order to work at a higher level?
- How can you improve your performance next time?

Variations and Extensions

At its core, Graduated Difficulty is a classroom strategy that uses the naturally appealing element of choice to lead students toward learning independence. Following are some strategies and variations for getting the most out of the Graduated Difficulty structure.

Graduated Warm-ups

In many math classes, teachers begin each period with a warm-up activity to help activate prior knowledge and awaken students' minds. Warm-ups are easy to graduate by level. What's more, the inclusion of levels enriches assessment, as both the teacher and student quickly get a snapshot of how comfortable each student is with given topics. Teachers can then use this information to make decisions about how best to focus instructional time. Figure 3.3 provides an example of a graduated warm-up for solving area and perimeter problems.

Graduated Difficulty in Music and Physical Education

Graduated Difficulty is a great way for music and physical education teachers to help all learners improve performance by practicing at the

FIGURE 3.3   Graduated Warm-ups and Area and Perimeter Problems

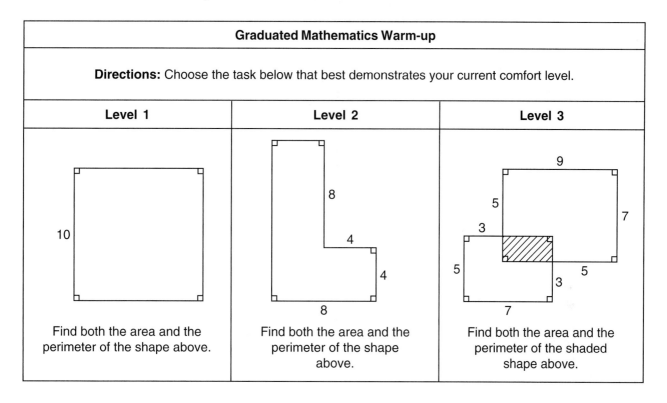

right level. For example, the strategy allows a physical education teacher to organize practice and improvement sessions around three different kinds, or levels, of volleyball serves: underhand, overhand, and jump serves. Similarly, music teachers can design lessons that allow different students to work on three increasingly difficult pieces of music simultaneously without becoming overwhelmed by an unmanageable level of individual instruction.

Assessment Menus

When it comes to assessment, providing an equal opportunity for all styles of learners to achieve can be a difficult task when everyone is not able to perform at the same level, or not interested or motivated by the same activities. The Assessment Menu strategy is designed to address this difficult problem by combining the levels of Graduated Difficulty with the variety of thinking and learning styles indigenous to the Task Rotation strategy (see pp. 241–252). In the Assessment Menu strategy, students get to develop their own portfolio of activities and performances over the course of the unit—one from each of the three

FIGURE 3.4   Bedtime Menu

Difficulty Level	Mastery	Understanding	Self-Expressive	Interpersonal
1	**Day and Night** Have students create day and night cards. Hold up pictures of routine activities. As you display each activity, have students use their day or night cards to indicate which activities are done most of the time during the day or night.	**Light and Darkness** Read aloud *Light and Darkness* by Franklyn M. Branley. Have students use a globe and a flashlight to explain why children in another part of the world are sleeping while they are awake and at school.	**Bedtime Charades** Have students pantomime a bedtime action while other students guess what they are doing. • Put toys away • Brush teeth • Put on pajamas • Read a story • Fluff up pillow • Take a bath • Climb into bed	**Bedtime Association** What do you think of when you hear the word *bedtime*? Have students brainstorm a list of words related to their feelings at bedtime and ask them to illustrate their words.
2	**Bedtime Sequence** Have students cut and arrange pictures of bedtime activities in appropriate order: • Read a book • Brush teeth • Put on pajamas • Cuddle with teddy bear • Fall asleep in bed	**Why Do You Need to Sleep?** Read aloud *Ba Ba Sheep Wouldn't Go to Sleep* by Dennis Panck. Before reading, ask students if they agree or disagree with the statements you have given them. Then after listening to the text, have students decide if they still feel the same or if they have changed their opinions. Discuss what evidence students heard in the book.	**Monsters Can't Sleep** Read aloud "Monster's Can't Sleep" by Virginia Mueller. Ask students to name all the things that were done to help the monster go to sleep. Invite students to think of some new and creative ways to help someone fall asleep. Have students illustrate their ideas and put them into a book.	**My Favorite Pajamas** Draw a picture of your favorite pajamas. Complete the following description: My favorite pajamas are_____. They have_____ _____. They feel_____ _____. I like them because _____.
3	**How Much Sleep Do You Get?** Have students draw clock hands on a clock face to show what time they go to bed and wake up in the morning. My bedtime is _____ o'clock. I wake up at _____ o'clock. I get _____ hours of sleep.	**How Do Animals Sleep?** Have students find out how different species sleep. Ask students to show that information in a picture. Also ask students to find out which species sleep in the day and work and play at night. Here are some species to start: Birds Mice Fish Horses Kittens Cows Bears Bats	**Create a Bedtime Story** A Bedtime Story by_____ Once upon a time____ _____ _____. And then something happened_____ _____ _____. They all lived_____ _____ _____.	**Good and Bad Dreams** Read aloud *Where the Wild Things Are* by Maurice Sendak. Have children discuss some good and bad dreams. Have students draw one of their favorite dreams.

levels of difficulty and one from each learning style. Figure 3.4 (p. 54) shows a sample Assessment Menu designed by a 1st grade teacher for a unit on bedtime.

4. TEAMS-GAMES-TOURNAMENTS

How does the strategy fit into unit design?
(Blueprint for Learning)

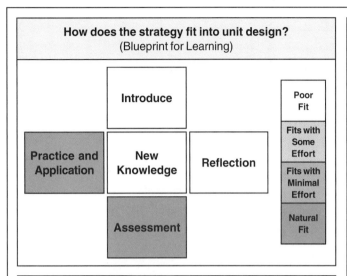

	Introduce		Poor Fit
Practice and Application	New Knowledge	Reflection	Fits with Some Effort
			Fits with Minimal Effort
	Assessment		Natural Fit

What learning styles does the strategy engage?
(Motivation/Differentiation)

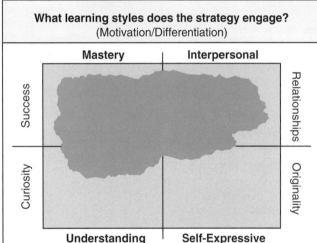

Mastery — Interpersonal

Success / Curiosity

Relationships / Originality

Understanding — Self-Expressive

What facets of understanding does the strategy develop?
(Understanding by Design)

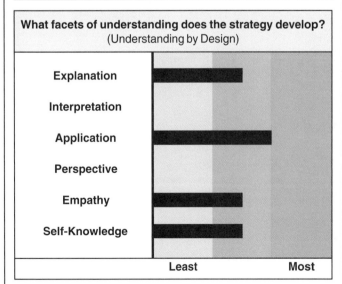

- Explanation
- Interpretation
- Application
- Perspective
- Empathy
- Self-Knowledge

Least — Most

What skills does the strategy build?
(The Hidden Skills of Academic Literacy)

Read and Study
- ○ Collect/organize ideas through note making
- ● Make sense of abstract academic vocabulary
- ○ Read/interpret visuals

Reason and Analyze
- ○ Draw conclusions; make/test inferences, hypotheses, conjectures
- ○ Conduct comparisons using criteria
- ● Analyze demands of a variety of questions

Create and Communicate
- ○ Write clear, coherent explanations
- ○ Write comfortably in major nonfiction genres
- ○ Read and write about two or more documents

Reflect and Relate
- ● Construct plans to address questions and tasks
- ○ Use criteria and guidelines to evaluate work
- ● Control/alter mood and impulsivity

How does the strategy incorporate the research on instructional effectiveness?
(Classroom Instruction That Works)

- ○ Identifying similarities and differences
- ○ Summarizing and note taking
- ● Reinforcing effort and providing recognition
- ● Homework and practice
- ○ Nonlinguistic representation
- ● Cooperative learning
- ○ Setting objectives and feedback
- ○ Generating and testing hypotheses
- ○ Cues, questions, and advance organizers

What types of knowledge does the strategy teach?

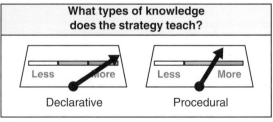

Less	More		Less	More
Declarative			Procedural	

4

Teams-Games-Tournaments

Strategy Overview

Competition and cooperation: Put these two elements together in proper balance and the human brain gets the ultimate motivational jump-start. Brain researcher Robert Sylwester (2003) explains, "We are a social species, continually cooperating and competing with one another. We are stimulated by activities that involve both—for example, in business by debate and negotiation, in play by games such as basketball and bridge" (p. 69). And we are stimulated in classrooms by strategies like Teams-Games-Tournaments.

Teams-Games-Tournaments, or TGT, optimizes content mastery through both competition and cooperation. In a TGT lesson, students at different ability levels work together in study teams to review key content and help each other shore up gaps in their learning. Students then leave their study teams to compete in an academic tournament with students from other study teams. During the tournament, students gain points for their study team by answering questions and challenging other players' answers. Thus, the study teams that are most cooperative—that do the best job of preparing all members to succeed in competition—earn the most points.

The Strategy in Action

French teacher Toni Johnson uses Teams-Games-Tournaments to help students master content and review before unit tests. Currently, Toni and her students are nearing the end of a unit on French geography and culture. For the tournament, Toni prepares the following materials.

- Several decks of question cards. Each deck contains the same 35 question cards in four separate categories: geography; cultural customs and heritage; conjugation; and translation. (See Figure 4.1 for a sampling of question cards.)
- A corresponding answer sheet, with answers cued by number to each question card.
- A review and study worksheet focused on the content of the tournament to help students prepare for the competition.

On Tuesday, Toni provides students with a study worksheet and reminds them that the tournament (and the test) will cover geography; culture; conjugation of the verbs *aller, vouloir,* and *visiter;* and simple translation. Students review the material for homework and then meet with their study teams on Wednesday. Each study team consists of four students—one high achiever, one low achiever, and two average achievers—and the teams are named after one of the five major rivers in France: la Seine, la Loire, la Garonne, le Rhône, and le Rhin. Together, each team spends the period on Wednesday responding to team members' questions and concerns, quizzing one another, and preparing all four team members for the competition.

On Thursday (the day before the unit test), members compete with players from other study teams. For the tournament, Toni sets up the competition groups so that each study team's high achiever is matched against the high achievers from the other study teams. Similarly, each study team's average and low achievers are matched against students at similar ability levels. This way, all students have an equal chance to win their tournament.

Toni reminds each competition group of the rules of tournament play, distributes a blank answer sheet to each student and a written copy of the rules to each competition group (see the following sample), and the tournament begins.

1. Decide which player will begin. The person to the left of this player is the challenger. The person to the right of the player is the checker. (To make sure the same players and challengers are not always pitted against each other, reverse assignments halfway through the tournament: challenger on the right of the player, checker on the left).

2. The player takes a card from the question deck, reads it aloud, and places it, question side up, on the table. Students at the table write down their answers on their answer sheets. Once everyone has recorded an answer, the player then turns to the challenger and asks if he wants to challenge the answer. Meanwhile, the checker finds the corresponding answer on the answer sheet.

FIGURE 4.1   A Sampling of Tournament Questions

Geography Question Cards

1.

What is the highest peak in Europe? What mountain range is it a part of?

4.

Name three countries that border France to the east.

8.

Name three regions of France that are known for their production of wine.

Culture Question Cards

12.

This region of France attracted many artists because of its sunshine. Name the region and three of the artists who visited this region to paint.

15.

What is the significance of each color of the French flag?

17.

How are Lyonnaise and Provençal cuisines different? Give three differences.

Conjugation Question Cards

21.

Spell the "je" form of the verb *aller*.

23.

Spell the "elles" form of the verb *vouloir*.

26.

Spell the "il" form of the verb *visiter*.

Translation Question Cards

30.

Translate the following into French: "We want to visit the Alps."

31.

Translate the following into French: "You (s) want to visit Bordeaux."

35.

Translate the following into French: "They (m) are going to visit the Loire River."

◦ If there is no challenge, the checker reads the answer aloud. If the player's answer is correct, the player gets to keep the question card. If the player's answer is incorrect, the correct answer should be read aloud and the question card should be shuffled back into the deck.

◦ If there is a challenge, the challenger must answer the question before the checker reads the answer aloud. If the challenger's answer is correct, the challenger gets to keep the question card. If the challenger's answer is incorrect, the challenger must surrender one of the question cards he has already won to the player. Moreover, if the player's answer was correct, the player also gets to keep the current question card. If neither the player nor the challenger answers correctly, the answer should be read aloud and then the question card should be shuffled back into the deck.

3. Play moves clockwise around the table until there are no more question cards or time runs out. Each player counts the number of cards she has accumulated. Scores are determined according to our scoring sheet (see Figure 4.2).

4. Players should return to their initial study teams and determine the team score by adding up the scores of all study team members.

Why the Strategy Works

When it came time to organize the strategies for this book according to the dominant learning style each strategy enlists, Teams-Games-Tournaments (DeVries, Edwards, & Slavin, 1978) presented a unique dilemma: Is this strategy more of a Mastery strategy or more of an Interpersonal strategy? The arguments in favor of designating TGT as an Interpersonal strategy were compelling because TGT is marked by collaborative and interactive elements that give the strategy its strong social orientation. Ultimately, however, we decided to put TGT in the section containing Mastery strategies because of its focus on review, its reliance on questions with verifiable answers, and the premium TGT places on memorizing information. The strategy turns the work of mastering critical content into an engaging and highly effective instructional technique. Here are six good reasons why TGT works.

1. **TGT incorporates the best of cooperation and competition.** Both cooperation and competition have assets and liabilities in the classroom. Competition increases motivation, but can also lead to aggressive behavior and dejection on the part of losers. Cooperative learning improves academic performance and social functioning, but teachers sometimes find it hard to manage. TGT is founded on a deep analysis of the strengths and weaknesses of both models. As a result, TGT maxi-

FIGURE 4.2   Scoring Procedures for TGT

Scoring for a Three-Player Game				
Player	**No Ties**	**Tie for High**	**Tie for Low**	**3-Way Tie**
High Scorer	6 points	5	6	4
Middle Scorer	4 points	5	3	4
Low Scorer	2 points	2	3	4

Scoring for a Four-Player Game								
Player	**No Ties**	**Tie for High**	**Tie for Middle**	**Tie for Low**	**3-Way Tie for Low**	**3-Way Tie for High**	**4-Way Tie**	**Tie for Low & High**
High Scorer	6 points	5	6	6	5	6	4	5
High Middle Scorer	4 points	5	4	4	5	3	4	5
Low Middle Scorer	3 points	3	4	3	5	3	4	3
Low Scorer	2 points	2	2	3	2	3	4	3

mizes the benefits of cooperation and competition while minimizing the drawbacks associated with each.

2. **TGT meets all the requirements of an effective cooperative learning strategy.** Most teachers have conducted cooperative learning lessons and have been disappointed by the results. A common cause of this disappointment can be traced to a lack of distinction between group work and cooperative learning. According to cooperative learning experts Johnson and Johnson (1999), five characteristics separate cooperative learning from mere group work. Cooperative learning (1) highlights *interdependence* among group members, (2) holds students *individually accountable* for their work, (3) promotes positive *face-to-face interaction,* (4) builds *small-group skills* such as communication and conflict resolution, and (5) encourages *group processing* so that students use their reflections to become better team members.

TGT meets all five of these characteristics. Interdependence comes from the notion of a team score, which motivates all study team members to help one another study and prepare. Individual accountability is guaranteed by the tournament, where each student competes against other individuals. Face-to-face interaction and small-group skills are developed over time, as study teams work with each other throughout the year. Finally, teams that engage in group processing learn how to study and prepare better—a clear strategic advantage at tournament time.

As the teacher, you should call attention to these characteristics, explain their significance, and model what they look like in the classroom. For help with this, take a look at the Cooperative Learning Troubleshooting Guide on page 193.

3. **TGT builds student learning through repetition and variation.** As brain researcher Eric Jensen (2005) tells us, "The simple fact is that repetition strengthens connections in the brain. . . . On the other hand, too much of the same thing can be boring to the learner" (pp. 38–39). Herein lies both the potential and potentially fatal flaw of learning through repetition: Repetition works, but keep on throwing those worksheets at students and their eyes will glaze over. The trick, then, to getting the most out of repetition is to marry it with an opposing force—variation. In TGT, students practice learning the same content and skills again and again (there's the repetition) in a variety of ways: independently, through cooperative study, and in a competitive tournament. The variation quotient is further increased by the integration of multiple types of questions. Rather than simple fill-in-the-blank questions, TGT questions ask students to apply a range of thinking styles and strategies to the content. (See number 6 in this list.)

4. **TGT provides the teacher with good assessment data.** Whenever a question is asked during the tournament, all students at each table write down their answers on their answer sheets before the player's answer is confirmed or challenged. By collecting each student's answer sheet after the tournament, the teacher can see how individual students fared and which items gave the class trouble as a whole.

5. **TGT uses a motivation-based scoring model.** If, during a tournament, players simply received a point for each item they answered or challenged correctly, students' motivation to succeed could be snuffed out early. One student might have 20 points to another student's two points. "Trouncing" could well become the name of the game, thereby exposing some of the drawbacks of competition. However, as Figure 4.2 (p. 61) shows, TGT scoring works differently.

By awarding points for place rather than total points earned, TGT scoring keeps students within reach of one another: No student can earn more than six points and no student comes back to the study team with fewer than two points. To keep things in ever better competitive balance, "bump" students to different tables: Move high scorers and low scorers to more or less competitive tables with each new tournament. This way, nearly every student (including your low performers) will experience winning, and nearly every student (including your most competitive learners) will experience losing.

6. **TGT incorporates a variety of question types.** Study and tournament questions need not—indeed, should not—all emphasize basic factual recall. The truth is it's easy to design questions with verifiable answers *and* have students engage in different forms of thinking—including higher-order thinking. To learn how, check out The Strategy in Action section on pp. 57–60.

How to Use the Strategy

1. Prepare short-answer objective questions and answer sheets for the tournament; prepare a study sheet to help students get ready for the tournament.

2. Assign students to study teams of three to five students. Be sure to balance teams academically so that all study teams include high achievers, average achievers, and low achievers.

3. Allow study teams time to review content and prepare for the tournament together. Remind students that the goal is to help *all* team members do well in the tournament, not just individual students. Spotlight effective teams for the entire class to use as models.

4. Assign one member from each study team to participate against other members from other study teams as part of a competition group (no more than five members). Unlike study teams, competition groups should be academically balanced (high achievers against high achievers, low achievers against low achievers, etc.).

5. Explain tournament roles (all students write their answers on their answer sheets; player answers question verbally; challenger may challenge answer; checker verifies answer) and tournament rules (see pp. 58–60).

6. Collect game scores and validate results. Allow students to discuss and reflect on the process.

7. Post results. If possible, prepare a simple tournament newsletter that celebrates the process as well as individual and team efforts.

Planning a Teams-Games-Tournaments Lesson

In planning TGT, the role of the teacher is to select the study teams, choose the content to be learned, organize the tournament, prepare the necessary materials to conduct the practice and tournament sessions, and help students process and reflect on what happened.

Begin by identifying your goals and objectives for the lesson and selecting material that is "gameable." Gameable material must lend itself to short, verifiable answers. This does not mean that all TGT questions should be of the fill-in-the-blank or true/false variety. Questions should cover the main points of the content and some should require students to demonstrate genuine understanding rather than memorization only. For example, you might include "Which one doesn't belong?" questions, categorization tasks, or any of these:

- Questions that ask students to identify similarities or differences.
  For example: *What are three differences between fables and folktales?*
- Questions in the form of a riddle.
  For example: *I am a landmass. I am surrounded by water on three sides. Florida is an example of me.*
- Questions that ask students to demonstrate a procedure or skill.
  For example: *What is the hypotenuse of a right triangle with leg measures 7 and 24?*
- Questions that ask students to develop an explanation.
  For example: *Why did Napoleon agree to sell the lands of Louisiana to the United States? Give two reasons.*
- Questions that ask students to identify a pattern or complete a sequence.
  For example: *Fill in the missing word: bat, cat, fat, _____, mat.*
- Questions that ask students to determine the validity of a statement.
  For example: *Mammals give live birth. Always true, sometimes true, never true?*

Prepare between 25 and 40 questions for a tournament along with an answer sheet or answer cards, which unlike a one-page answer sheet, eliminate the possibility of peeking at other answers during the tournament.

You'll also need to prepare practice items. Practice items should consist of sample game items, as well as parallel items that are not part of the tournament questions. Ideally, there should be a 50 percent overlap between the practice questions and the tournament items. Finally, you will need to develop a blank answer sheet so that students can write their answers to each question during the tournament.

When creating study teams, make sure you aim for balance. Study teams should have a similar mix of high, average, and low achievers so that during the tournament, competitors are evenly matched. You may also want to consider "bumping" as you hold more tournaments. Bumping means moving students who do very well or very poorly during a tournament to more competitive or less competitive tables for the next tournament. Both study teams and competition groups should be mixed with respect to gender and ethnicity.

In addition to thinking about how you will manage the TGT process in your classroom, you should also give some thought to how you can help students reflect on what happened during the lesson. Reflective writing, post-lesson discussions, and good contemplative questions will all help students become more comfortable and more self-directed as you continue to use the strategy.

Variations and Extensions

Boggle and Outburst have much in common with TGT. Both facilitate review and help students solidify their mastery over objective content. Both rely on the cooperation-competition dynamic to increase student engagement. Unlike TGT, both Boggle and Outburst require little planning on the part of the teacher.

Boggle

Use Boggle when you want students to rehearse and remember information before a test. Boggle (so called because it uses the same scoring technique as the classic word game Boggle) is quick, effective, and easy to organize in any classroom:

1. After a lecture, reading, or at the end of a unit, give students two minutes to review their notes. Remind students to focus on the big ideas and the important details.

2. Ask students to put their notes aside. Give them two minutes to "fact storm" by retrieving and writing down as many big ideas and important details as they can remember.

3. Have students meet with a review team of three to four other students. Students share their lists and add any information they did not have on their own lists.

4. Instruct students to leave their team to Boggle (compare their list against their opponent's list) with other students. Students can Boggle in pairs or trios, earning points for any idea they have on their list that their Boggle competitor doesn't have.

5. Allow students to return to their review teams and compute their team score by adding all their Boggle scores together. Collect team scores. You may choose to reward teams with outstanding scores by giving them extra credit points to add to their test scores.

6. Lead a review of the information, including those items and ideas that earned students points. Identify what is important to know and how specific information will be used on the test.

Outburst

Similar to the popular Outburst board game that lends its name to this classroom review tool, the Outburst strategy consists of teams of students competing with each other by calling out as many items as they can that fit into specific, fact-generating categories. For instance, prime numbers, reptiles, Confederate states, and Romantic poets are all examples of fact-generating categories. The twist is that the students create the Outburst items themselves, working in teams to list as many items as they can in each category before using their lists in competition. You can incorporate this fun review tool into your classroom by following these steps.

1. Break the class into an even number of teams of three to five students each. Half of the teams will be Team 1s and half will be Team 2s. Every Team 1 will be matched against a Team 2.

2. Provide four fact-generating categories to each group. For example, a teacher who was completing a unit on Ancient Egypt provided students with these categories:

Team 1 Categories	*Team 2 Categories*
Famous rulers	Egyptian gods
Advantages provided by the Nile River	Monuments
Medical innovations	Roles in society
Technological innovations	Geographic features

3. Instruct teams to list at least five items for each category.

4. Have Team 1 read one of its categories, and provide Team 2 with two minutes to call out as many items as its members can generate. Team 1 keeps track of Team 2's answers by checking off items on its list as Team 2 calls them out. After two minutes, teams review items to clarify what Team 2 said and missed. The teams then calculate their respective scores for the round using the following guidelines:

- For every item that Team 1 has listed and Team 2 calls out, Team 2 receives *one point.*
- For every item that Team 1 has listed, but Team 2 does not call out, Team 1 receives *one point* (thereby encouraging Team 1 to list as many items as possible).
- If Team 2 calls out all of the items on Team 1's list, Team 2 receives a bonus of *three points.*
- Any additional items (items that Team 2 calls out that are not on Team 1's list or items that Team 1 lists, but Team 2 doesn't call out) are then collected (or written on the board) to investigate after all of the rounds have been completed.

There are many different ways that Outburst can be set up and scored. For example, teams might have points deducted for items not called out or not listed.

5. Allow teams to continue play through three more rounds using Team 1's remaining three categories.

6. Have Team 1 and Team 2 switch roles and play for four more rounds: Team 2 now reads its four categories while Team 1 calls out answers.

7. Collect and calculate team scores and reward high-scoring teams (e.g., high-scoring teams could receive bonus points to be applied toward an upcoming test or quiz).

8. Lead a review of the information, address any relevant items that were called out but not listed by a team, and identify how the information will be included and presented on the test (e.g., match Egyptian gods to their appropriate descriptions, place famous rulers in chronological order, or write a brief essay on the advantages provided by the Nile River).

PART THREE

Understanding Strategies

Understanding strategies seek to evoke and develop students' capacities to *reason* and use evidence and logic. They motivate by arousing *curiosity* through mysteries, problems, clues, and opportunities to analyze and debate.

Strategy Chapters

5. Compare and Contrast is a strategy students use to conduct a comparative analysis using criteria to draw conclusions and infer possible causes and effects.

6. Reading for Meaning is a reading strategy that uses simple statements to help students find and evaluate evidence and build a thoughtful interpretation.

7. Concept Attainment is an in-depth approach to teaching and learning concepts based on the careful examination of examples and nonexamples.

8. Mystery is a strategy in which students interpret and organize clues to explain a puzzling situation or answer a challenging question.

How does the strategy fit into unit design?
(Blueprint for Learning)

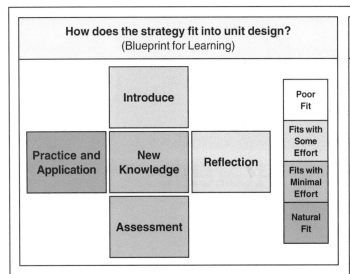

	Poor Fit
	Fits with Some Effort
	Fits with Minimal Effort
	Natural Fit

Introduce

Practice and Application | New Knowledge | Reflection

Assessment

What learning styles does the strategy engage?
(Motivation/Differentiation)

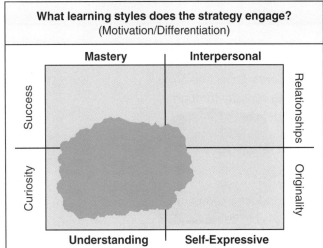

Mastery | Interpersonal

Success | Relationships

Curiosity | Originality

Understanding | Self-Expressive

What facets of understanding does the strategy develop?
(Understanding by Design)

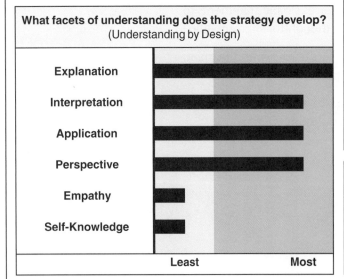

Explanation

Interpretation

Application

Perspective

Empathy

Self-Knowledge

Least | Most

What skills does the strategy build?
(The Hidden Skills of Academic Literacy)

Read and Study
- ● Collect/organize ideas through note making
- ○ Make sense of abstract academic vocabulary
- ○ Read/interpret visuals

Reason and Analyze
- ● Draw conclusions; make/test inferences, hypotheses, conjectures
- ● Conduct comparisons using criteria
- ○ Analyze demands of a variety of questions

Create and Communicate
- ○ Write clear, coherent explanations
- ● Write comfortably in major nonfiction genres
- ● Read and write about two or more documents

Reflect and Relate
- ○ Construct plans to address questions and tasks
- ● Use criteria and guidelines to evaluate work
- ○ Control/alter mood and impulsivity

How does the strategy incorporate the research on instructional effectiveness?
(Classroom Instruction That Works)

- ● Identifying similarities and differences
- ● Summarizing and note taking
- ○ Reinforcing effort and providing recognition
- ○ Homework and practice
- ○ Nonlinguistic representation
- ○ Cooperative learning
- ○ Setting objectives and feedback
- ● Generating and testing hypotheses
- ● Cues, questions, and advance organizers

What types of knowledge does the strategy teach?

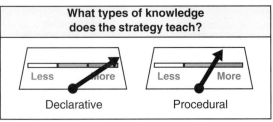

Less | More | Less | More
Declarative | Procedural

5

Compare and Contrast

Strategy Overview

Quite often, students' failures to learn are failures to recognize when their learning process has been sidetracked by those aspects of the content that are *invisible* (abstract), *confusable* (easily mixed up with other concepts), and *neglectable* (easy to overlook). When this happens, vital connections, underlying ideas, and key details escape students' attention; opportunities for insight and creative responses slip away.

How can we help our students deepen their understanding of our content and avoid falling prey to the invisible, confusable, and neglectable? The answer, as is so often the case in education, lies in a perfectly natural human capacity: the ability to compare.

The benefits of comparison as a teaching and learning process are undeniable. In fact, Robert Marzano, Debra Pickering, and Jane Pollock (2001) found that teaching students how to identify similarities and differences is the single most effective way to raise achievement. The strategy takes the natural human capacity to make comparisons and maximizes its effectiveness as an instructional technique by leading students through a process that involves

- Describing each item separately
- Identifying similarities and differences using a comparison organizer
- Forming and discussing conclusions
- Synthesizing learning by completing a task

The Strategy in Action

According to 3rd grade teacher Les Gould, one of the best things about teaching fables is that there's so much "literary payoff" in such a short time. Les explains, "Because many fables run only two to three paragraphs long and tell simple stories with clear lessons, they're perfect for conducting comparative readings. Fables give young readers the chance to conduct close and sophisticated readings, and students love them besides."

Today, Les's students are reading "The Tortoise and the Hare" by Aesop and "The Tortoise and the Antelope," a tale of the Ngoni people from southeastern Africa. In both fables, the tortoise beats its much speedier counterpart. In "The Tortoise and the Hare," the tortoise wins by moving slowly and steadily toward the finish line while the overconfident hare falls asleep; in "The Tortoise and the Antelope," the tortoise wins by developing a plan with fellow tortoises who work together to trick the antelope into thinking the tortoise is always ahead. Les gives students a simple description organizer in which students will describe each fable side by side (see Figure 5.1).

Les introduces the lesson by asking students to think about the concept of an "underdog." After a discussion in which Les and his students define and list examples of underdogs, Les tells students, "Today we are going to read two fables about underdogs. As we read, we're going to use the Compare and Contrast strategy to figure out what's similar about the fables, how they're different, and what the differences might tell us about the lesson each fable is trying to teach us."

Before having students read the two fables, Les reviews the criteria for collecting information. "What we're doing first," Les says, "is developing a really good description of each fable, which will help us make a high-quality comparison later on. Therefore, as you're reading each one, I want you to keep these four questions in your mind: (1) Who are the main characters? (2) Why do they decide to race? (3) How does the tortoise win the race? (4) What lesson do you think the fable is trying to teach us?" Students then read each fable on their own, collecting information that responds to each question on their description organizer.

Before students compare the fables, Les surveys the students and reviews the information students collected on their organizers. He then tells students, "Now we're ready to compare and contrast the fables. And with our descriptions of each fable already completed, this should be pretty easy."

Using a top hat organizer, students list key similarities and differences between the two fables. After individual work, Les and the students develop a finished top hat organizer such as the one shown in Figure 5.2.

Next, Les asks students to decide if the two fables are more alike or different and to share their conclusions with the class. To synthesize the lesson, Les has his students complete a Task Rotation. A Task Rotation (discussed fully in Chapter 20) asks students to show what they know by responding to questions in four distinct styles:

1. By "reading the lines," or retelling what happened in the story (Mastery style): *How does the tortoise beat the hare in Aesop's fable? How does the tortoise beat the antelope in the Ngoni fable?*

2. By "reading between the lines," or explaining the big ideas behind the fables (Understanding style): *What personal values does Aesop's fable teach us? What personal values does the Ngoni fable teach us?*

3. By "reading beyond the lines," or applying what they've learned in unique ways (Self-Expressive style): *Imagine you are writing a fable about a race between a fast animals and a slow animal in which the slow animal wins. Which animal would you choose? How would you make the slow animal win?*

4. By "reacting to the lines," or exploring personal responses to the fables (Interpersonal style): *Which fable do you like better? Why?*

Les uses Compare and Contrast regularly throughout the year. With each use of the strategy, Les shifts greater responsibility for applying the strategy onto his students: He teaches them how to formulate clear criteria; he teaches them how to describe items carefully; he teaches them how to create and use top hat organizers to conduct comparisons. By January, students are using the strategy without any help from Les.

Why the Strategy Works

By surveying the available research on effective classroom strategies, Marzano, Pickering, and Pollock (2001, p. 7*f*) discovered that strategies asking students to identify similarities and differences led to an *average percentile gain of 45 points* in student achievement. Marzano and his team

FIGURE 5.1   Description Organizer

"The Tortoise and the Hare"	Criteria	"The Tortoise and the Antelope"
	Characters **Why they decide to race** **How the tortoise wins** **Lesson**	

FIGURE 5.2   Top Hat Comparison Organizer

"The Tortoise and the Hare"	"The Tortoise and the Antelope"
The fast animal is a hare.	The fast animal is an antelope.
The tortoise agrees to race because the hare makes fun of him.	The tortoise agrees to race because of an argument with the antelope.
The tortoise wins because the hare is too confident and falls asleep.	The tortoise wins by working with other tortoises to trick the antelope.
The lesson is "Slow and steady wins the race."	The lesson is "Teamwork is a good way to get things done."

Similarities

Both are about a race between a slow animal and a fast animal.

In both fables, the tortoise wins the race.

Both teach a lesson that is really about people (and not animals).

further discovered that these benefits occurred across a wide range of comparison strategies. Whether the comparison activity was directed by the teacher or student; whether students represented their findings graphically, symbolically, linguistically, or in multiple forms; whether students were comparing, classifying, creating metaphors, or creating analogies, students' levels of comprehension went through the roof.

One reason that comparison strategies yield such high levels of achievement is that the human ability to compare is one of our cognitive endowments. Humans love putting things in pairs—pass us a fork and we'll look for a knife; show us a setting sun and we'll try to find the rising moon. This tendency to see the universe in sets of matching pairs has several advantages:

1. It increases our memory capacity. Two ideas linked together last longer than two ideas standing alone.

2. It lets us use old knowledge to make sense of new knowledge. For example, one way to figure out how the atmosphere works is to make a comparison by asking, "How is the atmosphere like a blanket of air?"

3. It helps us find connections and create new ideas.

4. It makes the *invisible* (or abstract) visible, the *confusable* (or easily mixed up with other content) clear, and the *neglectable* (or easily overlooked) unavoidable.

Unfortunately, as natural and helpful as comparisons can be, and in spite of all the research that points to the effectiveness of conducting comparisons as an instructional strategy, many students have a difficult time making thoughtful comparisons in school.

To understand how to achieve success when using comparison, it is important to first understand why comparison strategies often fail in the classroom. Figure 5.3, p. 76, outlines the five main causes of failed comparisons, includes suggestions for overcoming each cause of failure, and provides brief examples showing how to put each suggestion into classroom practice.

How to Use the Strategy

1. Introduce the process of comparison by first comparing and contrasting simple, everyday items that students are familiar with—cats and dogs, apples and oranges, winter and spring.

2. Choose two separate objects, concepts, or readings that students will compare and contrast.

3. Establish the purpose for comparison by answering the question "Why are we conducting a comparison?"

4. Provide students with criteria for analyzing the two items (e.g., *What do they eat? What do they look like? How do they behave?*)

5. Have students use the criteria to describe each item separately. (A two-column description organizer is often helpful.)

6. Show students how to use a comparison organizer (see Figure 5.4, p. 77, for a variety of comparison organizers) to distinguish between the two objects by recording similarities and differences.

7. Lead a discussion using synthesis questions.
    ◦ Are the two more alike or more different?
    ◦ What is the most important difference? What are the causes and effects of this difference?
    ◦ What conclusions can you draw?

8. Move students toward independence by teaching them how to formulate criteria, describe items, and determine key similarities and differences.

Planning a Compare and Contrast Lesson

When planning a Compare and Contrast lesson begin by identifying your purpose. Why have you chosen to engage students in a comparison? What insights will students gain as a result of the lesson? Students are far more likely to respond positively to the lesson if they understand what they are doing and what the benefits may be. At the beginning of any Compare and Contrast lesson, students should hear statements that sound like this: "We have read two of Shakespeare's tragedies, *Hamlet* and *Macbeth*. Let's compare the two tragic heroes to see how Shakespeare makes his characters both universal and unique."

FIGURE 5.3 Why Comparison Strategies Fail . . . and What We Can Do About It

Why Comparison Strategies Fail	What We Can Do About it	Examples
Most comparison strategies place an emphasis on evaluation by appearing in one of two settings: as end-of-chapter questions and as test items. This emphasis on evaluation reinforces students' concerns with finding the right answer, rather than discovering and analyzing.	Use Compare and Contrast as a learning strategy, and always provide students with a clear purpose for the lesson.	"People often confuse bacteria with cyanophytes: Let's compare them to make sure we're clear about how they're the same and how they're different."
Students don't have access to the information sources they might need to make an effective comparison.	Provide immediate sources of information that students can use when making comparisons.	"Look at the paragraphs describing the rules of volleyball on page 124 of your text, and the rules for table tennis on page 198."
Students don't know what they're looking for. Any two objects can be compared from an infinite number of perspectives. What aspects are critical? How will students know when they're done?	Provide or work with students to establish criteria for comparison, and keep students focused on the relevant information.	"As you describe Tutankhamen and Hatshepsut, focus in on what made each leader unique, the challenges each faced, what each accomplished, and what they were like as leaders."
Students don't know how to collect and organize their findings. As students gather information based on the criteria, they may not be collecting it in a way that will make it memorable, manageable, and useful.	Develop or help students develop a visual organizer that allows them to see the big ideas and the relevant details.	"Use this chart to describe alligators and crocodiles according to the criteria we established."
Comparison tasks often go nowhere. Disconnected from a purpose and a meaningful way to apply their work, students quickly lose their motivation to conduct thoughtful comparisons.	Allow students to discuss what they have learned and then apply their new understanding to a synthesis task.	"Now create and solve two problems like Problem 1 and two problems like Problem 2. Then, create and solve two new problems that ask you to solve for distance."

When selecting content for Compare and Contrast, look for pairs that will naturally heighten understanding when considered together. For example, if your initial concept is amphibians, you would probably select reptiles to complete the pair because of the five vertebrate families (mammals, birds, fish, reptiles, and amphibians), reptiles and amphib-

FIGURE 5.4 Organizers for Compare and Contrast

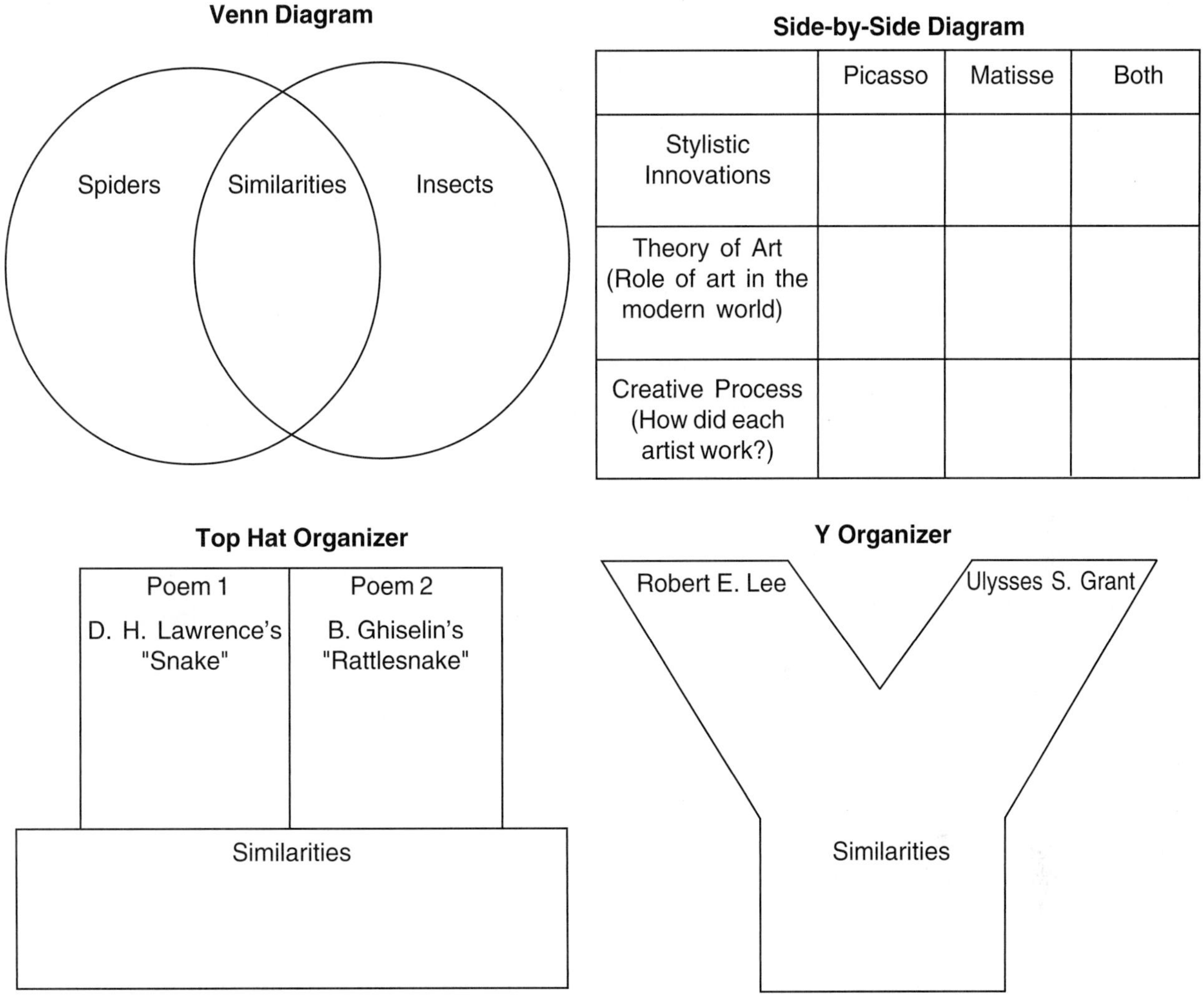

Venn Diagram

Spiders | Similarities | Insects

Side-by-Side Diagram

	Picasso	Matisse	Both
Stylistic Innovations			
Theory of Art (Role of art in the modern world)			
Creative Process (How did each artist work?)			

Top Hat Organizer

Poem 1	Poem 2
D. H. Lawrence's "Snake"	B. Ghiselin's "Rattlesnake"

Similarities

Y Organizer

Robert E. Lee / Ulysses S. Grant

Similarities

ians are most frequently confused. As shown in The Strategy in Action section and the Variations and Extensions section to follow, a comparative reading of two texts or comparative analysis of mathematical word problems also make for rich Compare and Contrast lessons.

Once you have established the purpose and selected the content, base your planning considerations on the four classroom phases that Compare and Contrast lessons follow.

• **Phase 1: Description**—Students observe and describe each item separately.
  ◦ Planning Considerations:
    What sources of information will students use? You may choose to provide students with information sources, or if you want to build

students' research skills, you may encourage them to gather information from the classroom, library, or Internet.

How will you help students identify the criteria they need to focus their description? By providing clearly defined criteria (e.g., What did T. rex and brontosaurus eat? What did each look like? Where did each live?), you help keep students focused on the pertinent aspects of the content. As students become increasingly comfortable with the strategy, teach them how to formulate criteria of their own.

• **Phase 2: Comparison**—Students use a visual organizer to identify similarities and differences between the two items.
  ◦ Planning Considerations:
    What kind of visual organizer will students use to record their comparison? Some of the most common visual organizers for comparison are shown in Figure 5.4 (p. 77).

• **Phase 3: Conclusion**—Students discuss the relationship between the items.
  ◦ Planning Considerations:
    How will you facilitate discussion and help students draw conclusions? Simple but powerful discussion questions include
    Are the items more alike or different?
    What is the most important difference?
    What causes the differences and similarities between the items?
    What are the effects of the differences?
    What can you generalize from the similarities?

• **Phase 4: Application**—Students apply what they have learned as a result of the comparison.
  ◦ Planning Considerations:
    How will students synthesize and apply their learning? There are many ways to encourage students to apply what they've learned through comparing and contrasting. A favorite synthesis task comes from a high school sociology teacher, who, after a lesson in which students used primary documents to compare a 17th century father with a 19th century father, asked students to formulate a set of ideal traits and expectations for fathers in each century. Students then had to pick two universal traits and two traits unique to the modern day to develop a want-ad for a 21st century father. One student's work appears in Figure 5.5.

Variations and Extensions

Comparison has many uses in the classroom. In this section we discuss an application of the Compare and Contrast strategy to mathematics, and we explore how you can use other strategies in this book to engage students in different forms of comparative thinking.

Comparison as Mathematical Problem Solving

In his collection of research-based strategies for improving and differentiating mathematics instruction, Ed Thomas (2003) suggests using Compare and Contrast when introducing new types of word problems to students, as a way to help students manage the abstraction and complexity found in many math problems. For example, take a look at these time-distance-rate word problems.

• **Problem 1:** Carly is running late for a meeting in Cactusville, which is 53 miles down Route 36. Carly is supposed to be at her meeting by 11:00 a.m. It is now 10:00 a.m. The speed limit on Route 36 is 40 mph. If Carly drives exactly 40 mph, how late will she be?

FIGURE 5.5   Sample of a Student's Work

**Wanted:
A 21st Century Father Who Can Wear Many Hats**

THE LOVING HAT

Responsibilities Include:
Raising children, not yelling, taking mom out to romantic dinners, listening, "being there."

Benefits:
You'll be loved right back.

THE MONEY HAT

Responsibilities Include:
Holding down a good job, making enough money to support family and pay for vacations.

Benefits:
Who doesn't want a good job? Plus, vacations with the family.

THE FUN HAT

Responsibilities Include:
Taking family to baseball games in summer, going sleigh riding in winter, being goofy, dancing.

Benefits:
What good is life if you don't have any fun? Family outings become memories that last a lifetime.

THE HANDYMAN HAT

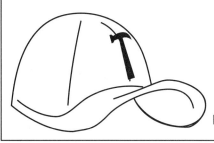

Responsibilities Include:
Taking care of the house and yard. Must know basic carpentry, landscaping, plumbing, and electrical work.

Benefits:
You'll get to have a really cool set of tools, including power tools.

• **Problem 2:** Carly is running late again. This time her meeting is down Manchester Turnpike. The meeting is 53 miles away, and it's now 10:10 a.m.. If Carly needs to be at her meeting by 11:00 a.m., how fast will she have to drive?

By having students work through the phases of Compare and Contrast, first by describing both problems, then by comparing them, then assessing the differences in how they solved each one, and finally by synthesizing their learning with a creative task, you can increase significantly students' abilities to analyze, plan for, and solve difficult problems. Figure 5.6 shows how a student worked through the first phase of this process by describing each word problem using the criteria provided by her teacher.

As students analyze and solve more problems this way they can collect their work to create a problem-solver's notebook. Then, whenever students encounter new problems, they can search through their notebooks, find past problem-solving models, and use these models to help them solve new problems.

The Many Ways to Compare

At the heart of Compare and Contrast lies one of the most essential skills needed for academic success: the ability to differentiate between items in terms of their similarities and differences. However, Compare and Contrast is only one strategy for developing this ability. In fact, when *Classroom Instruction That Works* (Marzano, Pickering, and Pollock, 2001) made it clear that the instructional category known as *identifying similarities and differences* yields the greatest gains in student achievement, the authors went on to identify a variety of effective "forms" this instructional category could take, forms such as classifying, creating metaphors, and creating analogies. Several of the strategies you'll find in this book engage students in different forms of comparative thinking. These strategies can be used to build the critical skill of identifying similarities and differences in a variety of ways to meet the unique needs of your students and your curricular objectives. Therefore, if you want students to

• Conduct a traditional compare and contrast among items	→ Use the Compare and Contrast strategy (this chapter).
• Examine characteristics closely and use them to classify data	→ Use the Concept Attainment strategy (pp. 96–105) or the Inductive Learning strategy (pp. 118–131).
• Make and defend personal decisions after comparing situations or items	→ Use the Decision Making strategy (pp. 172–181).

- Develop new insights through creative comparisons → Use the Metaphorical Expression strategy (pp. 132–141).
- Examine the design, format, or style of one item and apply it to a different item → Use the Pattern Maker strategy (pp. 142–151).

FIGURE 5.6   Student's Sample Description Organizer

	Problem 1	Problem 2
How is the problem written? (*What needs to be found out?*)	The problem is asking me to solve for *t,* or the time that Carly will arrive. Then I can figure out how late she will be.	The problem is asking me to solve for *r,* or Carly's rate of speed.
What does the diagram look like?	Leaves at 10:00 a.m. What time does she arrive? 40 mph 53 miles	Leaves at 10:10 a.m. Arrives at 11:00 a.m. What is her rate of speed? ? mph 53 miles
What is the answer to the problem?	11:20 a.m., 20 minutes late	64 mph
How did you go about solving the problem? (*Describe your thinking process.*)	I used the formula $d = rt$. If the distance is 53 miles and the rate is 40 mph, then $53 = 40t$ $t = 1.325$ hours, which you have to convert into approximately 80 minutes. This means that Carly will arrive at 11:20 a.m. or 20 minutes late.	I used the formula $d = rt$. The distance is 53 miles and the time is 50 minutes. The time needs to be converted into hours since rate is miles per hour. Converted time is 0.833 hours. So, if $53 = r \times 0.833$, then rate is 63.625, or approximately 64 mph.

Source: From *Styles and Strategies for Teaching Middle School Mathematics* by E. Thomas, 2003, Thoughtful Education Press: Ho-Ho-Kus, NJ. Adapted with permission.

How does the strategy fit into unit design?
(Blueprint for Learning)

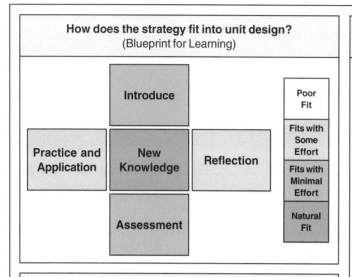

Introduce	Poor Fit
	Fits with Some Effort
Practice and Application — New Knowledge — Reflection	Fits with Minimal Effort
Assessment	Natural Fit

What learning styles does the strategy engage?
(Motivation/Differentiation)

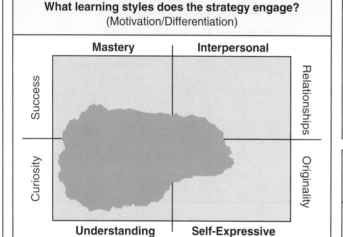

Mastery | Interpersonal

Success | Relationships

Curiosity | Originality

Understanding | Self-Expressive

What facets of understanding does the strategy develop?
(Understanding by Design)

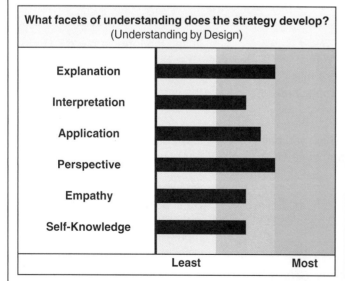

- Explanation
- Interpretation
- Application
- Perspective
- Empathy
- Self-Knowledge

Least — Most

What skills does the strategy build?
(The Hidden Skills of Academic Literacy)

Read and Study
- ● Collect/organize ideas through note making
- ● Make sense of abstract academic vocabulary
- ● Read/interpret visuals

Reason and Analyze
- ● Draw conclusions; make/test inferences, hypotheses, conjectures
- ○ Conduct comparisons using criteria
- ○ Analyze demands of a variety of questions

Create and Communicate
- ● Write clear, coherent explanations
- ● Write comfortably in major nonfiction genres*
- ○ Read and write about two or more documents

Reflect and Relate
- ○ Construct plans to address questions and tasks
- ○ Use criteria and guidelines to evaluate work
- ○ Control/alter mood and impulsivity

How does the strategy incorporate the research on instructional effectiveness?
(Classroom Instruction That Works)

- ○ Identifying similarities and differences
- ● Summarizing and note taking
- ○ Reinforcing effort and providing recognition
- ○ Homework and practice
- ○ Nonlinguistic representation
- ● Cooperative learning
- ○ Setting objectives and feedback
- ● Generating and testing hypotheses
- ● Cues, questions, and advance organizers

What types of knowledge does the strategy teach?

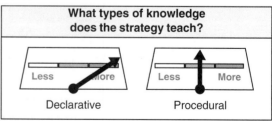

Less — More
Declarative

Less — More
Procedural

*Reading for Meaning is especially useful for building students' capacities to use evidence in their writing.

6

Reading for Meaning

Strategy Overview

At one of our recent workshops, a thoughtful and seasoned history teacher, when asked about her biggest challenge in the classroom, shared this with us:

> Reading, reading, reading. I'd love to run more lessons around primary documents and first-rate history writing, but to be perfectly honest, I'm not sure my students have the skills they need to read rigorous texts like historians that is, with a strategic approach in mind.

When we surveyed the room afterward, we found that more than 80 percent of the teachers—across all grade levels and content areas—agreed that too many of their students were having a hard time reading important texts critically.

The question then becomes, with so much of students' present and future academic success riding on their abilities as readers, how can we help all students develop a strategic approach to reading that develops their inference skills without cutting into content? One answer to this question is Reading for Meaning. In a Reading for Meaning lesson, students are provided with simple statements that help them preview and predict before reading, actively search for relevant evidence during reading, and reflect on and synthesize what they have learned after reading.

The Strategy in Action

As part of his U.S. history course, 8th grade teacher Robert Bukowski has students conduct close readings of *Texts That Changed American History*. This day, Robert and his students are studying a key document in Civil War history and perhaps the most famous presidential address ever delivered—the Gettysburg Address. Robert begins his lesson by distributing to each student a Reading for Meaning organizer (Figure 6.1), which includes five statements about the Gettysburg Address.

Robert tells students

> Tapping into their prior knowledge is something that all good historians do before they read a new text to help them get a grasp on what they're going to be reading. So, what I'd like you to do is to tap into your prior knowledge by thinking back on what you know about Abraham Lincoln, the Civil War, and the Gettysburg Address.

Robert directs students to their Reading for Meaning organizers, asking them to preview the five statements and then to use their prior knowledge to anticipate what the text might be about.

Once all students have made their predictions, they begin reading. As they read, they collect evidence on their organizer that either supports or refutes each statement. For example, Figure 6.1 shows the Reading for Meaning organizer, along with evidence that a student collected as proof against the first statement, *Lincoln believes the soldiers have died in vain.*

Afterward, Robert has students meet in their readers' groups to discuss the reading, the statements, and the evidence they collected. Students share and compare ideas and work to reach consensus on the accuracy of each statement. As students work, Robert circulates around the room to listen to group members negotiate their ideas. When disagreement occurs, Robert coaches the group in using evidence to justify opinions. After the group discussion, the whole class convenes to share insights about the content and reactions to the process. For homework, Robert asks students to develop a retelling of the Gettysburg Address that a 3rd grader could understand.

As Robert and his students continue to read *Texts That Changed American History* throughout the year, he teaches students how they can use the Reading for Meaning strategy on their own, as a way to manage difficult readings. Whenever a text becomes confusing, Robert explains and models how students can stop reading and instead focus on developing a short statement that they believe tells what the passage is about. Students can then use their statement to find out whether the reading supports or refutes their belief.

FIGURE 6.1 Reading for Meaning Organizer with Sample Student Evidence

Proof For	Statement	Proof Against
	1. Lincoln believes the soldiers have died in vain. Agree ☐ Disagree ☑ 2. Lincoln is convinced great nations survive challenges. Agree ☐ Disagree ☐ 3. Lincoln sees a clear relationship between the past and present. Agree ☐ Disagree ☐ 4. A good slogan for the Gettysburg Address would be "We can work it out." Agree ☐ Disagree ☐ 5. Lincoln's intent is to make Americans feel guilty about the war. Agree ☐ Disagree ☐	*"gave their lives that this nation might live"* *"The brave men, living and dead, who struggled here, have consecrated it..."* *"we here highly resolve that these dead men shall not have died in vain..."*

Jeffrey Berger also uses Reading for Meaning, as a way to help his 2nd graders develop the critical skill of collecting evidence and using it to support their personal reactions to literature. Today, Jeffrey is reading Arnold Lobel's short story "Dragons and Giants" from the book *Frog and Toad Together* out loud to his students. Behind Jeffrey sits an easel. On the easel are three columns: The left and right columns are labeled "Proof For" and "Proof Against." Down the center column are four statements:

1. Being brave means you are never afraid.
2. Actions are more important than appearance.

3. Frog and Toad needed each other to survive their adventure.

4. Even make-believe stories can inspire us to do great things.

Jeffrey asks students to think about these statements before he begins reading. Then, as Jeffrey reads, he stops at key points and asks students if they notice anything that might help them figure out if each statement is true or false. Jeffrey records students' ideas in the "Proof For" or "Proof Against" columns and then continues reading. Afterward, Jeffrey and his students discuss the reading, the statements, and the process they used to determine if the evidence was responsive to the statement.

Why the Strategy Works

Reading for Meaning is adapted from Harold Herber's (1970) Reading and Reasoning Guides but places much greater emphasis on developing students' inferential skills than Herber's original work. Reading for Meaning has also been updated in light of a large body of recent research into how proficient readers approach and process texts. The strategy answers the crucial question "How can we help all our students become better readers?" in two distinct ways:

1. **The strategy engages students in the process known as "strategic reading."** Research shows that a strategic approach to reading involves three phases of mental activity: pre-reading activity, during-reading activity, and post-reading activity. Young, Righeimer, and Montbriand (2002) explain that effective readers outperform ineffective readers because they use specific strategies during all three phases. For example, effective readers activate prior knowledge and clarify purpose before reading, monitor comprehension and pay attention to context clues during reading, and reflect and summarize after reading. Reading for Meaning helps students become more strategic readers by adopting this three-phase structure as follows:

   ○ **Pre-reading**—During pre-reading, students examine a set of statements about the reading before they read it, thereby helping them form an intuitive sense of the text's content and structure. The teacher may also ask students whether they agree or disagree with each statement. This serves to activate students' prior knowledge, which they use to make predictions about the text. Both of these activities—developing an intuitive sense of a text's structure and using prior knowledge to make predictions—have been shown to improve students' overall reading skills (Tierney & Cunningham, 1984).

   ◦ **Active reading**—During the active-reading phase, students' reading is filled with a sense of purpose. Because they must find and collect evidence that will support or refute their pre-reading predictions, they naturally slow down to search the text deeply for key information.

   ◦ **Post-reading**—During the post-reading phase, students reflect on their initial predictions and determine how specific evidence in the text has either confirmed or led them to revise their initial ideas about the content of the reading. Often, students will conduct this reflection session in small groups, where they must negotiate their ideas and use evidence to help the group reach consensus on each statement. Teachers usually assign a synthesis task as well, asking students to apply their learning in a meaningful way.

2. **The strategy helps readers overcome common reading difficulties.** Reading for Meaning statements are extraordinarily flexible tools for building students' reading skills. With a little practice, you can design different types of statements to address a host of critical reading issues and help students overcome common reading challenges. Ten types of Reading for Meaning statements, along with development tips and examples, follow.

Ten Types of Reading for Meaning Statements

1. **Vocabulary comprehension**—To focus students' attention on specific vocabulary words, incorporate synonyms or near-synonyms for critical words into your statement. For example, if you want 3rd graders to figure out what the word *marveled* means in the sentence "All the villagers marveled at the size of the elephant" an appropriate Reading for Meaning statement might be

   ◦ The villagers were surprised that the elephant was so large.

Vocabulary-based statements also help students use context clues to determine the meaning of academic vocabulary words, as in this statement:

   ◦ Portuguese sailors used the *astrolabe* to help them calculate where they were on Earth's surface.

2. **Forming main ideas**—To help students discover the main idea of a reading, develop statements that force them to think about the overall meaning of the entire piece:

   ◦ The author's main point is that film noir is a style, not a technique.

   ◦ A good title for this piece would be "We Can Work It Out."

3. **Building inference**—To help students discover deeper or even hidden meanings, challenge them to read between the lines with statements such as these:

- There are probably more reptiles living in Kansas than there are in Canada.
- We can tell that Pooh and Piglet have been friends for a long time.

4. **Making a case**—To help students build a case, craft your statements so that they force students to take a position:
   - Relocation is an inhumane policy.
   - Insects are more helpful than harmful.

5. **Creating mental images**—To help students visualize what they read, develop statements that draw their attention to image-laden portions of the text:
   - A good physical representation of a geometric point would be the tip of a pin.
   - The author's language helps me imagine what the inside of an aerospace laboratory looks like.

6. **Making connections between the text and other content areas**—Incorporate concepts and content from other content areas into your statements to help students make interdisciplinary connections:
   - Francis Bacon would approve of Dirty Harry's notion of private justice.
   - Teaching is more of an art than a science.

7. **Exploring metaphors and symbols**—Help students develop fresh and insightful perspectives on content with statements such as these:
   - A colony is a lot like a child.
   - A good symbol for the Mastery style of learning would be a paper clip.

8. **Appreciating style and technique**—To help students see how authors achieve intended effects, focus their attention on *how* the text is written:
   - The author of the editorial fails to anticipate possible counterarguments.
   - Lincoln's language conceals the horrors of the battlefield at Gettysburg.

9. **Empathizing**—To help students identify with other people's (or the author's) positions, feelings, and situations, create statements like these:
   - Countee Cullen was deeply hurt by the incident in the poem.
   - The author wants us to feel sorry for the mouse.
   - The Baseball Hall of Fame has treated "Shoeless" Joe Jackson unfairly.

10. **Developing a personal perspective**—To help students draw on their feelings and experiences as resources for understanding texts, write statements that invite them personally into the content:

- Emerson's feelings about personal responsibility are much like my own.
- My life would be very different if Thomas Edison hadn't been an inventor.

How to Use the Strategy

1. Provide students with (or help students create) a Reading for Meaning organizer listing four to eight statements keyed to major ideas in a reading. You can ask students to perform the following tasks.
   - Preview the statements and anticipate what the text might be about.
   - Decide whether they agree or disagree with each statement. (This option works well when your statements are not too text-specific. Text-specific statements, such as "The author wants us to feel sorry for the mouse," lead to blind guessing. More general statements, such as "Relocation is an inhumane policy," force students to call upon prior knowledge and take a position, which the reading will ultimately challenge or confirm.)
   - Determine the degree to which they agree or disagree with each statement. (For example, with a statement such as "Birds can fly" or "Polygons have four sides," you can ask students to decide if the statement is *always true, sometimes true, or never true.)*
   - Read two opposing statements ("The designated hitter is good for baseball" and "The designated hitter is bad for baseball") and choose the statement that they agree with the most.
2. Instruct students to read the text, look for evidence that corresponds to each statement, and record it on their organizer, in either the "Evidence For" or "Evidence Against" column.
3. After reading, ask students to meet with other students to discuss their evidence and to try to reach agreement on whether the text supports or refutes each statement.
4. Lead a discussion in which you survey students' positions on each statement and discuss the role of textual evidence in defending positions.
5. To extend the learning, challenge students to use their new knowledge to create a summary, develop an interpretation, or complete a synthesis task.
6. Build independent reading skills by teaching students how to develop statements and use them to verify understanding.

Planning a Reading for Meaning Lesson

Developing a Reading for Meaning lesson means answering a set of questions:

- When you select the reading, ask yourself, "What article, document, or passage needs emphasis and intensive analysis?"
- When you break the reading into essential components, ask yourself, "What themes, main ideas, and details do my students need to discover?"
- When you develop your four to eight Reading for Meaning statements, ask yourself, "What thought-provoking statements can I present to my students *before* they begin reading that will focus and engage their attention?" In developing your statements, it is also a good idea to ask, "How can I use different kinds of statements to help my students build a variety of critical reading skills?" (See Ten Types of Reading for Meaning Statements presented earlier in this chapter for help.)
- When you develop leading questions to provoke discussion, ask yourself, "What questions about the content or the process can I develop to engage my students in a discussion throughout the lesson and after the reading?" and "What kind of hook, or attention-grabbing question or activity, can I create to capture student interest at the outset of the lesson?"
- When you design a synthesis task, ask yourself, "What will my students do to apply the ideas and information they gathered from the reading?"

Variations and Extensions

In this section we explore three variations on Reading for Meaning. First, we show how Reading for Meaning statements can help students solve challenging word problems in mathematics. Next, we outline a strategy called Information Search, which uses the same three-phase reading structure as Reading for Meaning (before–during–after), but provides struggling readers with extra support in each phase. Finally, we discuss how Reading for Meaning statements can be used to build students' thesis-writing skills.

Using Reading for Meaning to Solve Math Problems

Despite their prominence on state and national tests, word problems are still one of the most commonly cited sources of difficulty and frustration for math students. Unlike other problems in math, word problems combine quantitative problem solving with inferential reading, and this combination can bring out the impulsive side in students.

Rather than slowing down and taking the time to figure out what the problem is asking them to do, many students leap to solutions. Reading for Meaning, when applied to mathematical word problems, helps reduce impulsivity and develops students' problem-solving skills through pre-solution thinking, collaborative planning, and post-solution reflection.

For example, 6th grade teacher Maggie O'Connor presents her students with this word problem:

> A train containing cars and trucks is en route to an auto dealership in Bowling Green. Before they arrive, the owner of a group of dealerships receives an invoice showing that a total of 160 vehicles will be delivered to her four locations. Unfortunately, the portion of the invoice detailing how many of each kind of vehicle is missing. Because she knows you know algebra, the owner asks for your help. The invoice states that the total mass of vehicles is 182,800 kilograms. Each truck weighs 1,400 kg, while each car weighs 1,000 kg. How many cars and how many trucks will be delivered?

Maggie has designed five Reading for Meaning statements that highlight different aspects of the problem.

- *The Facts of the Problem*
  Statement 1: Trucks have a greater mass than cars.
  Statement 2: We already know the total number of vehicles to be delivered.
- *The Process for Solving the Problem*
  Statement 3: The best way to solve this problem is to set up an equation with a single variable.
- *The Hidden Questions Embedded in the Problem*
  Statement 4: The fact that there are four dealerships is irrelevant to finding a solution.
- *The Answer to the Problem*
  Statement 5: The solution will require two different answers.

After they decide whether they agree or disagree with each statement, Maggie breaks the students into groups to discuss their responses, resolve their differences, and develop a plan for solving the problem. Students then solve the problem on their own, noting how their pre-solution plan worked or needed to be revised. Afterward, Maggie holds a discussion in which students talk about their difficulties, explore their various problem-solving strategies, and look for ideas and techniques they can apply to future word problems.

Information Search

Like Reading for Meaning, Information Search (Strong, Silver, Perini, & Tuculescu, 2002) is a comprehension-building strategy that revolves around the three phases of strategic reading. Information Search is built from the well-known strategy Know-Want-Learn, or K-W-L (Ogle, 1986), and is especially helpful with struggling readers and learners because it

- Actively engages students in assessing and organizing their memories, intuitions, questions, and feelings to build a visual pre-reading framework;
- Teaches students how to use a simple text-marking system to determine the importance of specific material in the text; and
- Harnesses the power of reflection by asking students to elaborate on how their understanding has been changed by the reading.

Information Search moves through four basic steps:

1. **Select a reading, identify the main chunks or subtopics, and convert each subtopic into a question.** For example, Wayne Cutillo is teaching a unit on exploration and wants students to explore both the tremendous accomplishments and terrible atrocities associated with the explorers known as the conquistadors. Using an article titled "Explorers or Exploiters?" Wayne converts the article's main subtopics into these four questions:
   - Who were the conquistadors?
   - What did the conquistadors accomplish?
   - How did they treat the Native Americans they encountered?
   - How should history remember the conquistadors?
2. **Ask students to identify what they know, what they think they know, what they want to know, and how they feel about each question.** Make sure students know that background knowledge is only a starting point. Encourage students to talk about what they think they know, where their natural curiosities lay, and what their personal reactions might tell them about each question. Then, using the class's input, create a comprehensive map that illustrates students' pre-reading understanding. Figure 6.2, for example, shows the map Wayne created with his students.
3. **Teach students how to use reader's punctuation to search for information and connect their reading to the map.** If possible, provide students with photocopies of the reading so they can mark it up directly. Alternatively, you may choose to provide students with sticky notes they can attach to the reading. A simple set of reader's punctuation looks like this:
   - ! This is new information.
   - = This information agrees with the information on the map.

FIGURE 6.2   Pre-Reading Map for a Reading on the Conquistadors

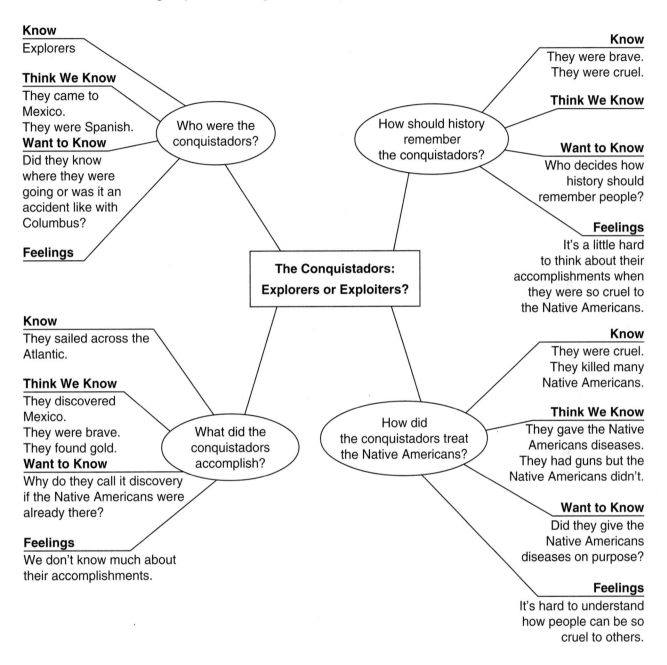

> * This information disagrees with the information on the map.
>
> ? I have a question about this. (Open questions can become the basis of further investigation, either as part of the unit or as an independent study project.)

4. **After students have read and marked the text, have them synthesize their new understanding by creating a revised map or an organizer of their own.** A post-reading task that asks students to look back on the original map, note how their understanding has changed, and then synthesize that new understanding in a comprehensive and visual way is an ideal method for helping students solidify their new learning. You may want students to create a new and revised map, or to devise a graphic organizer that suits the information from the reading. For a set of common graphic organizers, see page 30.

Thesis Writing and Reading for Meaning

Students' abilities to distinguish between essential and nonessential information, to scour readings for specific information, and to support their responses with evidence are among the most commonly assessed skills in the new state tests and assessments. For this reason, Reading for Meaning, with its emphasis on inquiry-based reading, on developing and supporting positions, and on writing carefully considered arguments, is perfectly suited to the development of thesis-style assessment tasks that will enhance students' performance on state tests. For instance, think about the skills and attitudes required for the following elementary assessment task.

> We have now been studying spiders for one week. What do you think about them? Have any of your opinions of spiders changed during this week? Below is an article that describes five different spiders and how each different type of spider affects the people, animals, and plants around it. As you read, I want you to collect evidence that proves or disproves this statement:
>
> *Spiders are more helpful than harmful.*
>
> Once you have collected evidence from the reading, you will be asked to write a persuasive essay that argues either for or against this statement.

If you know how to develop a Reading for Meaning lesson, then creating Reading for Meaning assessment tasks is easy. To develop a task, follow these four steps:

1. Select a reading or set of thematically linked readings.
2. Identify the themes, main ideas, and key details in the reading(s).

3. Develop a single Reading for Meaning statement that is central to the reading(s). Make sure the evidence you collect can support or refute the statement. The statement should be open-ended so that the student can argue either for or against it.

4. Develop assessment criteria that you and your students will use to assess their writing.

How does the strategy fit into unit design?
(Blueprint for Learning)

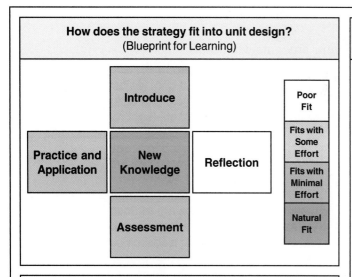

What learning styles does the strategy engage?
(Motivation/Differentiation)

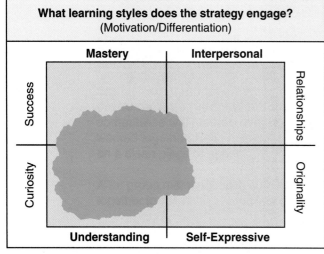

What facets of understanding does the strategy develop?
(Understanding by Design)

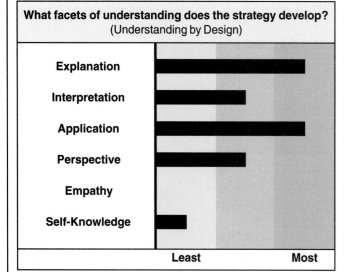

What skills does the strategy build?
(The Hidden Skills of Academic Literacy)

Read and Study

○ Collect/organize ideas through note making
● Make sense of abstract academic vocabulary
● Read/interpret visuals*

Reason and Analyze

● Draw conclusions; make/test inferences, hypotheses, conjectures
● Conduct comparisons using criteria
○ Analyze demands of a variety of questions

Create and Communicate

● Write clear, coherent explanations
○ Write comfortably in major nonfiction genres
○ Read and write about two or more documents

Reflect and Relate

○ Construct plans to address questions and tasks
○ Use criteria and guidelines to evaluate work
○ Control/alter mood and impulsivity

How does the strategy incorporate the research on instructional effectiveness?
(Classroom Instruction That Works)

● Identifying similarities and differences
○ Summarizing and note taking
● Reinforcing effort and providing recognition
○ Homework and practice
○ Nonlinguistic representation
○ Cooperative learning
○ Setting objectives and feedback
● Generating and testing hypotheses
○ Cues, questions, and advance organizers

What types of knowledge does the strategy teach?

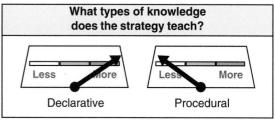

*Depending on content, Concept Attainment lessons often incorporate images.

7

Concept Attainment

Strategy Overview

Not all terms and ideas that students need to learn are equal. Some ideas rise to the level of central concepts that serve as bedrocks for future teaching and learning. When students have only a hazy understanding of key concepts like *culture* or *civilization* in social studies, *polynomials* in pre-algebra, or even *alive* in primary-grade science, much of their future learning, which rests on key concepts like these, will be hampered by that initial lack of definitional clarity.

Concept Attainment is a strategy that allows students to explore critical concepts actively and deeply. By examining examples and nonexamples of a given concept, students construct their understanding "from the ground up," testing and refining that understanding of the concept and its critical attributes until it is rock solid.

The Strategy in Action

Carl Carrozza is about to begin a lesson on predator–prey relationships. He wants his students to develop a strong conceptual understanding of what a predator is and how predators are uniquely adapted to the life they lead.

Carl begins by telling students

Today we're going to do something a little different. I'm going to hold up pictures of different animals. Some of these animals will be *yes* examples of an idea I have in mind. Some will be *no* animals. All the *yes* animals are examples of an important concept that's going to be at the center of what we study over the next few days. The *no* examples are not examples of this concept, though they may have some things in common with the *yes* examples. What I want you to do is to examine each *yes* example and each *no* example to try and figure out what the concept is. The name of the concept will be a start, but what I really want is for you to determine the critical attributes of the concept.

Carl then holds up pictures of the first three animals—cat (yes), dog (yes), rabbit (no)—and asks students to generate an initial set of attributes.

In surveying the class, Carl finds that some of the initial attributes students have come up with include *common pets, runners* (instead of hoppers), and *meat eaters.* He then presents pictures of four more animals: horse (no), lion (yes), brontosaurus (no), and velociraptor (yes).

"OK," Carl says, "so what do all the *yes* examples have in common? How are they different from the *no* examples?"

During the student discussion, students explore a number of ideas. One student notices that the brontosaurus is slow, but all the *yes* examples are fast. Another student explains how all the *yes* examples have sharp teeth and that they're all meat eaters. Carl collects the attributes students generate on the board. He then presents two more pictures—an eagle (yes) and a snake (yes).

With these examples, a student points out that the snake isn't fast, but another says, "Yeah, but it strikes fast." Other students focus on the fact that the eagle doesn't have teeth.

One student sums up, "They all have some kind of way to rip into meat. The eagle has the beak and claws; the snake has the teeth. All the other *yes* examples have claws and sharp teeth. But the *no* examples don't have these kinds of things." At this point, most of the class is reasonably confident that the concept is *carnivore* and that the critical attributes are *eats meat* and *has a way to tear into meat.* Carl then holds up one final picture of a vulture, which to many students' surprise is a *no.*

With this example, students realize that they have missed something: all the *yes* examples hunt and kill live animals, as opposed to the vulture, which eats dead animals. The class then reviews all the examples and nonexamples and, with Carl, develops a final set of critical attributes for the concept of a *predator:*

1. Hunts and kills other animals.
2. Has body parts (like claws, sharp teeth, sharp beaks) to kill and eat other animals.
3. Is fast or can use stealth to catch live animals.

After the class has worked out the critical attributes of predators, Carl presents them with pictures of various insects, birds, and fish and asks students to determine if each animal is a predator or not based on what they have learned. Later in the unit, as part of their final assessment for their portfolios, Carl will ask students to design their own predator, one that is ideally suited to an ecosystem of their choosing.

Why the Strategy Works

The Concept Attainment strategy is founded on the important work of Jerome Bruner (1973), who conducted extensive research into the psychological process known as *concept formation*. What Bruner concluded is that in order to cope with our diverse environment, humans naturally group information into categories based on common characteristics. For example, a child learns from experience that objects that have four wheels, travel on roads, and transport people belong to a category called *cars*. The conceptual soundness of the child's emerging concept of a car is then tested by SUVs, minivans, trucks, and motorcycles—and refined.

Concept Attainment draws on this powerful process of concept formation by asking students to analyze both examples (called "yes" examples in a classroom lesson) and nonexamples (called "no" examples in a classroom lesson) of a concept, group the examples into a conceptual category, test their initial categories against further examples and nonexamples and, finally, generate a set of critical attributes that define the concept they are learning. The effectiveness of Concept Attainment as an instructional strategy is further bolstered by the fact that it engages students deeply in the skills of identifying similarities and differences and generating and testing hypotheses—two of the nine instructional techniques proven to raise students' level of achievement as identified by Marzano, Pickering, and Pollock (2001).

In order to ensure that you get the most out of this tried-and-true strategy, we recommend you base your Concept Attainment lessons on three simple principles: conceptual clarity, multiple examples, and conceptual competence.

The Principle of Conceptual Clarity

Learning a concept involves more than just learning a label; it involves learning the essential attributes of a concept. To learn the essential attributes of a concept, students must be able to discriminate between examples and nonexamples. Make sure all the essential attributes are clearly present in your examples and that nonexamples embody only some of these attributes. Avoid sending students down misleading and trivial paths. For example, when presented with the set of examples shown in Figure 7.1, p. 100, students may say that the *yes* examples are shaded rather than beginning to formulate the essential attributes of a square.

The Principle of Multiple Examples

When presented with two examples, students can form initial hypotheses about a concept. However, when students see many and

FIGURE 7.1   Potentially Misleading Examples

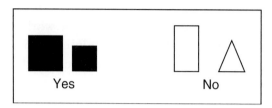

varied examples, they can define with increasing certainty the essential attributes of the concept. It is a good idea to lead with more obvious examples and then to introduce more challenging examples as you and your students progress through the lesson.

The Principle of Conceptual Competence

A concept is learned when students can list the essential attributes of the concept and when they can use those attributes to discriminate between examples and nonexamples. Never be afraid to challenge students to apply their new understanding of the concept in a variety of ways. Can they design an imaginary predator? Can they create two imaginary societies—one that fits the concept of a civilization and another that is missing one key attribute? Can they think of 10 different examples of transportation from at least three different sources (e.g., from nature, on the road, at the amusement park)?

How to Use the Strategy

1. Select a concept with clear critical attributes (e.g., tragic hero, civilization, linear equations, alive, mammals, etc.) that you want students to understand deeply.

2. Provide students with *yes* examples, which contain all the critical attributes of the concept, and *no* examples, which contain some but not all of the critical attributes.

3. Ask students to identify what all the *yes* examples have in common and how the *yes* examples differ from the *no* examples. Students should generate an initial list of critical attributes of the concept.

4. Provide more *yes* and *no* examples that students can use to test and refine their initial list of attributes.

5. As a whole class, review the *yes* and *no* examples and generate a final set of critical attributes.

6. Ask students to apply their understanding of the concept by creating a product or completing a task.

Planning a Concept Attainment Lesson

To prepare a Concept Attainment lesson, you need to take these steps.

1. **Select a concept you want your students to understand deeply and map it out.** When you have a complete understanding of the concept to be taught, it is much easier to make connections in your curriculum and extend the learning beyond the concept at hand. We suggest using a concept definition map (see pp. 102–104) at the outset of planning to clarify your concept and put it into a larger curricular context.

2. **Prepare the *yes* and *no* examples that will be presented to students.** Whether your examples are terms, pictures, poems, physical objects, or math problems, make sure they will focus students on the critical attributes and that students know that this is not a guessing game. A typical Concept Attainment lesson begins with simpler examples; more difficult examples should come later and can be used to challenge and refine students' original assumptions. For example, if your concept is mammals (warm-blooded, live birth, fur-covered bodies, live largely on land), you would be ill advised to begin your Concept Attainment lesson with descriptions of a platypus and a whale—two animals that "break the mold" of typical mammals. Examples like these should come later in the lesson, after students have solidified their basic understanding. Atypical examples can serve as the basis for rich discussions on topics like the imperfection of scientific categorization.

3. **Determine how you will assist students in processing the examples.** During the lesson, students' initial attributes should be shared and recorded. By getting students' ideas out in the open, you can help them refine and deepen their understanding of the concept. Here are some questions you might consider asking to help students articulate their covert thinking.
   ◦ Can you describe the characteristics of the positive (*yes*) and negative (*no*) examples?
   ◦ Compare the characteristics shared by positive examples. How are they similar? How do they differ?
   ◦ How can you differentiate the positive examples from the negative examples?
   ◦ Based on what characteristics would you group the positive examples?

4. **Develop a set of reflection questions.** When students are able to reflect back on what they did and learned during the lesson, they develop a deeper perspective on both the content and their own learning process. Here are reflection questions that help students look back on the *content.*
   ◦ What were the initial attributes you generated? How do your initial ideas compare with your current understanding of the concept?

◦ Did any particular example or nonexample from the lesson lead to a "conceptual breakthrough" for you?

◦ Can you think of any other concepts that might be related to this concept?

◦ How do you know when you really understand a concept?

Use reflection questions to help students look back on their *own learning process.*

◦ What happened in the activity?

◦ What did you do well? What was most difficult for you?

◦ Describe the process of making a hypothesis and your thinking process.

◦ How can you improve your performance next time?

◦ What did you learn about yourself and how you think?

5. **Design a synthesis task that allows students to apply their understanding of the concept.** The most straightforward way for students to apply their learning is to generate and explain new examples of the concept. Alternatively, you can have students try these tasks.

◦ Compare and contrast the concept to another related concept (e.g., reptiles and amphibians).

◦ Explain a given metaphor or simile. (How is democracy like a baseball game?)

◦ Develop a metaphor or simile. (Imaginary numbers are like _____ because _____.)

◦ Design an original example of the concept. (Can you invent and describe your own civilization?)

◦ Design a classification system that puts the concept into its larger context. (Can you make a "literary movement family tree" that puts Naturalism in its proper historical place?)

◦ Create and explain a visual icon, poem, or other artistic form of expression that represents the concept.

Variations and Extensions

Concepts are the building blocks of learning in any content area. This section offers you a set of classroom tools to help you teach concepts. Specifically, you'll find tools that help students map, review, and systematically analyze the critical concepts you teach.

Concept Definition Maps

Mapping concepts on paper improves students' comprehension in three ways. First, mapping teaches students the basic structure that all concepts share. Second, mapping sharpens students' analytical skills as they learn how to dissect important ideas by breaking them down into key components. Third, by placing concepts and their components into a simple visual framework, mapping provides students with a memorable record of their learning and an instant study guide for the most important terms and ideas in any unit. Figure 7.2 shows a concept definition map for the concept known as *fables*.

Here's a simple acronym-based way to teach your students how to create concept definition maps:

Make a circle at the center of the page. Write the name of the concept in the circle.

Add branches to your central concept that correspond to the following:

1. *Category*—What larger idea or unit theme is the concept part of? For example, the concept of a bicycle is part of the larger idea of transportation.

2. *Properties*—What is the important information that explains what the concept is? List each piece of information in a separate

---

FIGURE 7.2   A Concept Definition Map for Fables

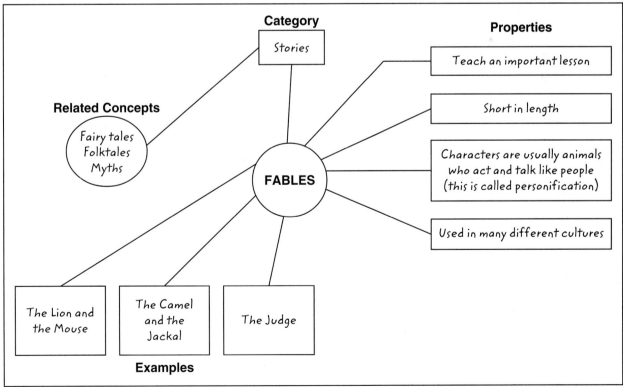

box, but make sure you choose only the most essential information. For example, for *bicycle,* you might list *two wheels, pedals,* and *rider provides power.*

3. *Examples*—Can you list any examples of the concept? For example, for *bicycle,* you might list specific models, or you might choose to list different types of bicycles, such as *racing bikes, mountain bikes,* and *two-person bikes.*

4. *Comparison*—Is there another concept that you can compare with your concept? For example, by setting another related form of transportation, such as *motorcycle* against *bicycle,* you get a clearer picture of your concept.

Put the relevant information in boxes and ovals connected to the branches.

Concept Review Game

This variation uses a guessing-game format to help students review concepts and content. To begin this review activity, the teacher tells the student that the object of the game is to figure out what the secret concept is. The teacher then provides two to four examples or nonexamples of the concept. For instance, if the secret concept is the Thirteen Colonies, the teacher might begin by telling students that Massachusetts and New Hampshire are both *yes* examples. Play then moves around the room as individual students are challenged to generate one new example, which the teacher designates as a *yes* or a *no.* If the student's example is a *yes,* the student gets a chance to guess the concept. If the student's example is a *no,* play moves on to another student. Play continues until a student guesses the secret concept.

Any of a variety of scoring and gaming procedures can make a concept review game come to life in the classroom. For example, the teacher might use a soft sponge ball to select students, throwing the ball to a particular student and then challenging the student to generate an example. The student can then throw the ball back to the teacher or to another student once the turn has ended.

Concept Analysis Matrix

For students who are just beginning to use Concept Attainment or for those who have trouble comparing examples, a concept analysis matrix (Figure 7.3) provides a systematic tool for analyzing concepts according to critical attributes. Teach students how to use a concept analysis matrix by providing them with the concept label, the critical attributes, and the examples for analysis. Students review each example against the given criteria and place a check mark in the box if the example meets the

FIGURE 7.3　Concept Analysis Matrix for Tragic Heroes

Examples: / Attribute:	Hamlet	Macbeth	Ronald Reagan	Oedipus	Superman	Rocky Balboa	Willy Loman
Prominent person	✓	✓	✓	✓	✓	X	X
Usually male	✓	✓	✓	✓	✓	✓	✓
Has a fatal flaw	✓	✓	X	✓	Not Sure (Kryptonite?)	X	✓
Brings about his own doom	✓	✓	X	✓	X	X	✓
Is graced with enlightenment before death	✓	✓	X	✓	X	X	X

criterion and an *X* in the box if the example doesn't meet the criterion. Students may also write "not sure" in the box if they're not certain whether the example meets the criterion. After initial exposure to the concept analysis matrix, teach students how to create their own as tools for differentiating among multiple examples (and nonexamples) of a given concept.

How does the strategy fit into unit design?
(Blueprint for Learning)

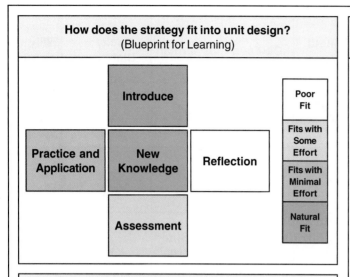

What learning styles does the strategy engage?
(Motivation/Differentiation)

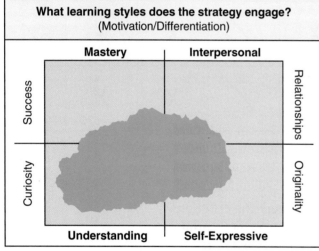

What facets of understanding does the strategy develop?
(Understanding by Design)

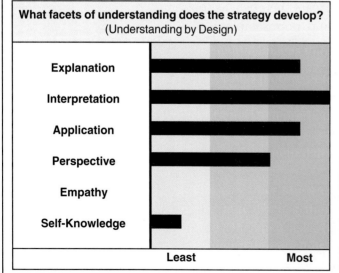

What skills does the strategy build?
(The Hidden Skills of Academic Literacy)

Read and Study
- ● Collect/organize ideas through note making
- ○ Make sense of abstract academic vocabulary
- ● Read/interpret visuals*

Reason and Analyze
- ● Draw conclusions; make/test inferences, hypotheses, conjectures
- ○ Conduct comparisons using criteria
- ○ Analyze demands of a variety of questions

Create and Communicate
- ● Write clear, coherent explanations
- ● Write comfortably in major nonfiction genres**
- ● Read and write about two or more documents

Reflect and Relate
- ● Construct plans to address questions and tasks
- ○ Use criteria and guidelines to evaluate work
- ○ Control/alter mood and impulsivity

How does the strategy incorporate the research on instructional effectiveness?
(Classroom Instruction That Works)

- ● Identifying similarities and differences
- ● Summarizing and note taking
- ○ Reinforcing effort and providing recognition
- ○ Homework and practice
- ○ Nonlinguistic representation
- ● Cooperative learning
- ○ Setting objectives and feedback
- ● Generating and testing hypotheses
- ○ Cues, questions, and advance organizers

What types of knowledge does the strategy teach?

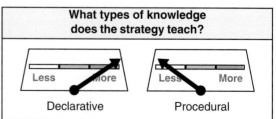

*Depending on content, Mystery lessons often incorporate visual clues, charts, and graphs.
**Mystery naturally builds students' capacities to use evidence in their writing.

8

Mystery

Strategy Overview

Doctors, researchers, scientists, lawyers, and detectives—these and so many other professions are driven by a common goal: to solve mysteries. Take any one of these professions and think about how much of the work involved revolves around gathering, organizing, and making sense of data in order to formulate solutions to puzzling questions. However, solving mysteries is not unique to the professional world. In fact, today's state tests with their emphasis on interpreting data, extracting evidence from multiple sources, and building sound cases or explanations require students to think like "mystery solvers" more than ever before.

Mystery lessons begin with a provocative question or riddle such as "Why did the Neanderthals disappear while *Homo sapiens* went on to cover the entire globe?" The teacher then provides students with a set of clues or texts that will help them solve the mystery. In working to formulate a solution, students naturally build their skills in collecting evidence, organizing and interpreting information, and developing logical hypotheses and explanations. In addition, because the Mystery strategy capitalizes on the human affinity for the intriguing and perplexing, it arouses student curiosity and increases motivation in any classroom.

The Strategy in Action

Karina Singh has just begun a unit on the Age of Exploration with her 7th graders. Today, she wants her students to explore the factors and conditions that existed in Western Europe at the time of Columbus's journey so that they develop a deeper sense of the relationship between historical forces, cultural developments, and individual accomplishment. Karina sets the tone and hooks students' interest using these statements:

> In 1960, President John F. Kennedy made an announcement that shocked the world. Kennedy claimed that the United States of America would put a man on the moon by the end of the decade. Kennedy knew he could make such a claim because he realized the conditions were right: The technology was in place, Americans supported space exploration, and brave astronauts were waiting in line to be the first humans on the moon.

> The time was also right for Christopher Columbus's famous voyage. Columbus claimed he could find a new route to the East by traveling west even though no sailor had ever attempted such a journey before. As a student of history, it is your job to figure out why the time was right for Columbus's historic journey. What conditions made it possible for Columbus to sail to the New World?

Before the teams of students start on their investigation, Karina asks them to develop a set of tentative hypotheses as to why the time may have been right for Columbus's journey in 1492. After the groups share their initial ideas, Karina presents each team with a sheet of 24 distinct "clues"—facts, quotes, and simple statements drawn from two sources: the class's textbook and an article entitled "The Time Was Right in 1492."

"What we're going to do," says Karina, "is first cut out all the clues. Once you have them all cut out, you and your team should study them and group related clues together. For example, take a look at clue 12 and clue 15. Why might they go together?"

> Clue 12: Most Spanish expeditions carried priests with them.
> Clue 15: "We have come to look for Christians and spices."
> —Quote attributed to Portuguese explorer Vasco da Gama

After establishing with students that the clues have *religion* in common, Karina continues:

> After you group your clues, devise a label for each group that describes how the clues are related. Remember that it is OK to include a clue in more than one group. You may also want to combine some of your initial groups into larger categories. Then, use your groups to draw at least three conclusions about why the time was right for Columbus's journey.

Student teams begin organizing the clues to form initial hypotheses. For example, the student team of Shane, Noelle, and Mya puts the following clues together because they all have to do with *spices:*

> Clue 3: Spices were valuable because they helped make rotten food edible.
> Clue 7: Even in wealthy homes, the meals came to the table spoiled because there was no refrigeration.

Clue 13: "The orient is dripping with spices and paved with gold."
—Quote attributed to Marco Polo

Clue 15: "We have come to look for Christians and spices."
—Quote attributed to Portuguese explorer Vasco da Gama

Clue 17: Spices came from the Spice Islands, located in the Far East.

Another student team—Judi, Dylan, and Carlos—puts these clues together:

Clue 4: The science of cartography, or mapmaking, had become sophisticated and increasingly accurate by Columbus's time.

Clue 9: New inventions like the astrolabe and mariner's compass made longer and more difficult trips possible.

Clue 20: New ships called caravels were faster and easier to navigate than any ship before.

After labeling their group *science and technology,* Judi, Dylan, and Carlos record the following hypothesis:

• New developments in science and technology led to better ships, equipment, and maps, which made a long journey like Columbus's possible.

Based on other clues, student teams form a variety of hypotheses, including these ideas:

• The only land route to the Far East was controlled by the Turkish Empire, so Europeans were traveling by sea more than ever before.

• Many powerful people, including kings and queens, merchants, and the pope were paying explorers to find new routes to China and the Spice Islands.

• There were many valuable items in the Far East such as gold, silk, jewels, and spices.

• Spices were extremely valuable because they made rotten food edible.

• King Ferdinand and Queen Isabella agreed to pay for Columbus's journey because they believed he could get to the East faster than the Portuguese if he sailed across the Atlantic Ocean.

As students work on developing and testing their hypotheses, Karina circulates around the room to help teams who are having trouble and challenge teams who seem overly confident in their hypotheses. What is most important to Karina is that students examine the evidence from all the clues and refine their hypotheses so that they are well supported.

After a round of discussion in which students share their hypotheses and the evidence they used in forming them, Karina provides students with a copy of the article entitled, "The Time Was Right in 1492." Students use the article to verify or further refine their hypotheses so that each hypothesis is historically accurate; they also use the article to complete their homework—a set of four questions:

1. Why did the Europeans want to travel to Asia?
2. Which influential groups supported this travel?
3. What was happening in the Middle East at this time?
4. What developments made it possible for Europeans to travel where they had been unable to travel before?

Using her state standards as a guide, Karina asks students to use their answers from their homework assignment to help them develop a clear and well-argued position paper that addresses this question:

• What do you think is the single most important factor that led to Columbus's voyage? Explain your position using evidence.

Why the Strategy Works

Think, for a moment, of the last suspense movie or crime thriller you saw. If you're more of a reader, try to remember your last page-turning murder mystery. What was your mind doing? In all likelihood, it was very busy, actively searching for the subtlest of clues, following the twists and turns to develop a working hypothesis as to what was happening or who was guilty, constantly refining that hypothesis in light of charged conversations and jaw-dropping revelations.

Now, compare this experience with your experiences in school. How did you learn about the American Revolution? Do you think your learning would be more memorable to you now if your teacher had begun the unit with the question "How did a ragtag militia of untrained soldiers defeat the most powerful army in the world?" and then encouraged you to solve the intriguing mystery of how the colonists overcame such a daunting military mismatch? When we compare typical information acquisition experiences in school with those that are driven by a problem to solve or a puzzling situation to figure out, the potential differences in student engagement jump out at us. Moreover, not only do mysteries grab the attention of students, but the fact is they parallel the way information is gathered through the scientific method by real-world experts and problem solvers.

Mystery is a strategy that builds on this natural affinity for intrigue and its capacity to pique our curiosity, engage us in inquiry, and satisfy us when all the pieces fall into place. The strategy is built off the work of Richard Suchman (1966) who, in developing his famous Inquiry model, found that when students investigate a problem under their own impelling curiosity, they are more likely to retain what they learn along the way because their understanding is distinctly their own. The Mystery strategy also draws power from a wide body of research showing that engaging students in the process of generating and testing hypotheses is a surefire way to increase academic achievement levels across all grade levels and content areas (Hansell, 1986; Koedinger & Anderson, 1993; Koedinger & Tabachneck, 1994; Marzano, Pickering, & Pollock, 2001).

How to Use the Strategy

1. Begin by explaining the content of the lesson and the goals of the Mystery strategy.

2. Engage student interest by presenting a problem to be solved, a question to be answered, or a situation to be explained. Encourage students to tap into their background knowledge about the topic or problem and to generate tentative hypotheses or solutions.

3. Present students with a variety of brief clues. Ask students or student teams to read the clues carefully, organize them into relevant groups, and give each group a descriptive label. Clues may be placed in more than one group.

4. Instruct students to use their labeled groups to develop hypotheses. Allow students to merge groups and refine hypotheses.

5. Hold a discussion in which students present, defend, and further refine their hypotheses.

6. Assign a synthesis task that allows students to apply what they have learned.

Planning a Mystery Lesson

Planning a Mystery lesson involves these steps:

1. **Identify a question to be answered, riddle to be solved, situation to be explained, or secret to be discovered.** Most content areas are filled with mysteries. The Mystery strategy presents students with the mystery but never the answer. Students have to discover answers for themselves. Appropriate questions for the Mystery strategy often take the form of "Yes, but why?" or "Yes, but how?" For example, "We all know that green plants take in carbon dioxide and release oxygen, whereas humans do the opposite. But why?" Questions of this nature require more than factual answers—they demand investigation and thought. Here are a few teachable mysteries:

   - How is energy from food made available to body cells?
   - Why was the death rate in the Jamestown Colony so high?
   - What happened to the dinosaurs?

Once you have formulated your mystery, ask yourself: What is the overall solution to the mystery? Identify and write out the generalizations you expect students to make in solving the mystery.

2. **Gather or develop the clues.** What sorts of clues will lead your students to the appropriate solution(s)? Make sure you develop enough clues to support each generalization you identified in Step 1. The clearer you are about the connections you want your students to make, the easier it will be for you to generate the necessary clues.

Of course, clues can take many forms. Statements, quotations, paragraphs, pictures, graphs, charts, maps, interviews, demonstrations, and even mini-experiments are all good clue candidates. For example, a 4th grade teacher we know had students conduct four separate experiments to solve the mystery of how humans hear sound. Students followed these instructions:

- Hang a clock from the ceiling and listen to it from all directions.
  (Conclusion: Sound travels in all directions.)
- Whisper to each other, with and without two cups and a string.
  (Conclusion: Sound travels through gases and solids—under certain conditions.)
- Listen to a CD of a mother whale locating her calf.
  (Conclusions: Sound travels through liquids; Sound bounces off the calf.)
- Snap a ruler over a table at various lengths.
  (Conclusion: The faster something vibrates, the higher the pitch.)

3. **Decide how students will work to solve the mystery.** How will your students work to solve the mystery? Will they work independently, in cooperative learning groups, or as an entire class? If you choose to have your students work in small groups, consider distributing the clues evenly among group members. This way, you help create a sense of interdependence among group members.

4. **Determine how you will present the clues.** Clues can be presented all at once. Students can cut them out themselves, or you can cut them up into strips, place them in an envelope, and hand them out to groups or individual students. Alternatively, you can present clues gradually. This gradual-distribution approach works especially well with students who are unfamiliar with the strategy or who have difficulty managing large amounts of information. If you present the clues gradually, you may want to create various stations around the classroom where the students go to collect the different clues.

5. **Select a format for the presentation of students' conclusions.** Students should explain and defend their solutions. This process of explanation and defense can be done as part of a synthesizing discussion or through any number of oral, visual, or written products. For example, the 4th grade teacher who had students conduct a set of experiments in order to solve the mystery of how humans hear sound asked students to create a short, illustrated pamphlet explaining and showing how sound travels from a source, through the air, and through liquids and solids, to a person's ears.

Variations and Extensions

You can use the underlying structure of Mystery to hook students' attention, engage them in a search for evidence, and ask them to generate and refine hypotheses in a number of ways in the classroom. Three variations are multiple document learning, sequencing, and problem-based learning.

Multiple Document Learning

Multiple document learning (MDL) is an important variation on the Mystery strategy. It is particularly useful in the wake of rigorous state standards and testing systems that require students to read and interpret two or more documents. Like Mystery, MDL poses an intriguing problem for students to solve by collecting evidence and forming hypotheses. MDL differs from Mystery in that students base their hypotheses on a small set of documents rather than on dozens of short clues. Here is a brief example of an MDL lesson in action:

> Meredith Hirsch is conducting a unit on the Middle Ages with her freshman class. Meredith wants to focus their attention on the economic and social arrangements between lords and vassals. Meredith designs her MDL lesson around three primary documents: a statement by a lord declaring his rights and responsibilities, a set of regulations describing the limits between a lord and a vassal, and an oath sworn by a vassal to his lord. Students collect evidence from the three documents to help them answer this question: *If the arrangements between the lords and their vassals seem to favor the lords so heavily, why did the vassals agree to the terms?* Once students have marked relevant evidence in the documents and created a set of notes, they convert their findings into a written explanation.

Sequencing

In this variation on Mystery, students put a series of elements together in a logical order to form a cohesive whole. Sequencing works well with scientific processes like the stages of mitosis, "scrambled" poems that students arrange into proper order based on elements such as narrative continuity and rhyme scheme, and even mathematical statements that students assemble to form a sound proof. For example, a middle school English teacher gave her students eight lines from Rudyard Kipling's famous poem "The Law of the Jungle." The lines were presented out of order. Using the "clues" of rhyme scheme, punctuation, capitalization, and meaning, students had to put the lines in the correct order.

Problem-Based Learning

Today more than ever, researchers, citizen groups, and business leaders criticize the difference between the nature of work in the real world and the work done in schools. While the Mystery strategy incorporates hypothesis-generating and problem-solving skills found in many professions, problem-based learning (PBL) takes the real-world connection further. In a PBL lesson or unit, students are asked to solve an authentic problem or to develop a product that addresses a real-world issue.

The heart of any PBL lesson or unit is a thinking task. A good PBL task

- Requires students to understand and apply the content and skills from your standards
  - Demands higher-order thinking
  - Involves the creation of an authentic product or performance

One simple and straightforward way to develop a good PBL task is to lean heavily on the experts. In *Classroom Instruction That Works,* for example, educational researchers Robert Marzano, Debra Pickering, and Jane Pollock (2001) describe six types of tasks found in the world beyond the classroom that engage students in the process of solving problems by generating and testing hypotheses. Figure 8.1 shows how to apply this research to the work of designing good PBL tasks. In Figure 8.1, you'll find an overview of the six types of thinking tasks outlined by Marzano and his team, along with a brief example of a PBL lesson or unit based on each type of task.

Create a problem-based unit by following these six planning and implementation steps:

1. Select a set of relevant standards and analyze the content and skills needed to meet the standards.

2. Establish a central task that will require students to understand and apply your standards, demand higher-order thinking, and involve the creation of a product or performance resembling those found in the world beyond the classroom.

3. Arrange students into teams that can work together to acquire expertise and develop a product or performance.

4. Provide lessons that model and encourage practice, research, and production skills.

5. Make sure one-fourth to one-third of unit time is set aside for coaching.

6. Design activities for reflection and celebration to bring your unit to a close.

FIGURE 8.1   Six Problem-Based Models

Problem-Based Model	Example Lesson or Unit
Systems analysis involves the careful examination of the parts and function of a system, with an eye toward how the system might respond to change or be improved.	Study the gerbil terrarium in our classroom. What are its parts? What needs of the gerbil are being met by each of these parts? What needs could be better addressed by adding new parts or changing some of the current parts?
Problem solving asks students to identify an authentic problem, determine constraints they may face in developing a solution, and then create and implement a plan that addresses the problem.	When a student at a Texas middle school suffered serious injuries in a bicycle accident, 5th graders from a nearby school took action. Upon learning that the injured student was not wearing a helmet, the 5th graders met with and wrote their city council urging council members to make bike helmets mandatory. The students were successful: Their bill was passed and their cause was widely reported by local and state media.
Historical investigation requires students to examine historical situations, documents, and data; develop a working hypothesis regarding causes and effects; and build a case that explains how and why certain events may have taken place.	In your folder you will find some numerical data, some primary documents, and some maps of the first English colonies in the Chesapeake Bay area. Use this data to explain why these colonies had higher death rates than anywhere in Europe in the 17th century.
Invention calls for students to design a product or a representation that responds to a need or solves a problem.	After studying and classifying different types of containers according to their function, a 2nd grade class was given this challenge: The local grocery store has a problem—too many broken eggs. The store has asked our class to help by submitting ideas on how the egg carton might be redesigned to better protect the eggs inside.
Experimental inquiry involves designing experiments to test hypotheses, explaining the results, and determining if more experimentation is needed to reach a conclusion.	Fourth graders spent a year studying birds in the school yard. Over the course of the year they developed hypotheses and designed experiments to investigate when and why female birds left the nest, what kinds of materials would be best for nest-building, and how human behavior affected birds' abilities to find and use resources.
Decision making entails evaluating alternatives and making a judgment as to which is most feasible, most important, or best fits a set of criteria.	Here are www.Time.com's top inventions of last year. Which three do you believe will have the greatest effect on your life? Explain your choices and the criteria you used in making your decision.

Source: The six steps in bold have been adapted from *Classroom Instruction That Works* by R. J. Marzano, D. J. Pickering, and J. E. Pollock, 2001, ASCD: Alexandria, VA.

PART FOUR

Self-Expressive Strategies

Self-Expressive Strategies

Self-Expressive strategies highlight students' abilities to imagine and create. They use imagery, metaphor, pattern, and "what if's" to motivate students' drive toward individuality and originality.

Strategy Chapters

9. Inductive Learning is a strategy in which students group and label terms to make predictions, and then verify and refine their predictions against a reading, lesson, or unit.

10. Metaphorical Expression is a strategy that seizes on the uniquely human ability to compare things that are not truly alike.

11. Pattern Maker is a technique designed to help students "see" the patterns and structures behind texts and ideas.

12. Mind's Eye is a reading strategy that teaches students the critical skill of converting the words on the page into memorable images.

How does the strategy fit into unit design?
(Blueprint for Learning)

	Introduce	
Practice and Application	**New Knowledge**	**Reflection**
	Assessment	

Poor Fit
Fits with Some Effort
Fits with Minimal Effort
Natural Fit

What learning styles does the strategy engage?
(Motivation/Differentiation)

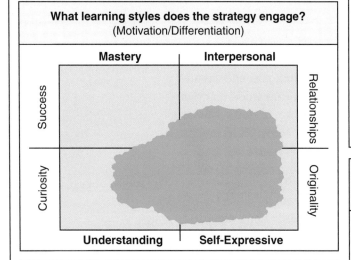

Mastery — Interpersonal
Success — Relationships
Curiosity — Originality
Understanding — Self-Expressive

What facets of understanding does the strategy develop?
(Understanding by Design)

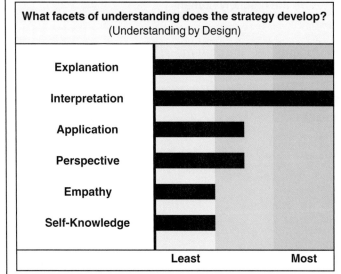

- Explanation
- Interpretation
- Application
- Perspective
- Empathy
- Self-Knowledge

Least — **Most**

What skills does the strategy build?
(The Hidden Skills of Academic Literacy)

Read and Study
- ● Collect/organize ideas through note making
- ● Make sense of abstract academic vocabulary
- ○ Read/interpret visuals

Reason and Analyze
- ● Draw conclusions; make/test inferences, hypotheses, conjectures
- ● Conduct comparisons using criteria
- ○ Analyze demands of a variety of questions

Create and Communicate
- ● Write clear, coherent explanations
- ● Write comfortably in major nonfiction genres*
- ○ Read and write about two or more documents

Reflect and Relate
- ● Construct plans to address questions and tasks
- ○ Use criteria and guidelines to evaluate work
- ○ Control/alter mood and impulsivity

How does the strategy incorporate the research on instructional effectiveness?
(Classroom Instruction That Works)

- ● Identifying similarities and differences
- ● Summarizing and note taking
- ○ Reinforcing effort and providing recognition
- ○ Homework and practice
- ○ Nonlinguistic representation
- ● Cooperative learning
- ○ Setting objectives and feedback
- ● Generating and testing hypotheses
- ○ Cues, questions, and advance organizers

What types of knowledge does the strategy teach?

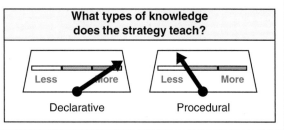

Declarative — Procedural

*Inductive Learning can be used directly as a writing strategy. See Inductive Writing, pp. 129–130.

9

Inductive Learning

Strategy Overview

Inductive Learning helps students explore topics and concepts by grouping specific terms, vocabulary words, or visual data and then classifying them according to common attributes. In creating general and more inclusive categories, students establish their own criteria for classification. For example, if given a set of geometric shapes, students might consider grouping them into a variety of categories such as circles, triangles, shapes with four sides, three-dimensional shapes, irregular shapes, shapes with right angles, and so on. The strategy does not stop at categorization, however; it also asks students to devise clear labels for their categories, and then to make a set of predictions that they can verify or revise with evidence from a reading or other activities as they progress through a unit.

The effectiveness of induction, and more specifically, Inductive Learning, lies in the way it involves students in a host of sophisticated learning behaviors. During an Inductive Learning lesson, students need to be flexible and fluent; to make associations; to identify methods of grouping; to classify; to categorize; to determine the relative inclusiveness of groups; to use categorized information to make generalizations; and to assess their own understanding of both the content and the learning process. Thus, the Inductive Learning strategy helps students develop the thinking skills they need to achieve greater independence as thinkers and learners.

The Strategy in Action

Middle school science teacher Dante Constantino says, "When students learn how scientists think, what kinds of vocabulary scientists use, and what scientists do when faced with unknown situations, then they really know what science is all about." Today is the second day of school, and Dante begins by presenting students with a list of key terms taken from an article called "How Scientists Do Their Jobs":

experiment	testing	question
hypothesis	model	controlled conditions
practice	bias	wonder
instruments	observation	previous knowledge
correct	progress	facts
interpret	preconceptions	known
refine	review	ask
gather	analyze	explain
compare	share results	examples
unknown	conclusion	wrong

Dante puts students into small teams and assigns each team the job of reviewing all of the terms on the list, looking for terms that seem to go together, and putting these common terms together into groups. As teams work to form their word groups, students follow four guidelines:

• *Think flexibly*—Never be afraid to discover new relationships between terms.

• *Change can be good*—You can always change your initial groups.

• *Word "cloning" is encouraged*—It's OK to put the same word or term into more than one group.

• *Be descriptive*—Give each group a short label that tells what the terms in each group have in common.

To make sure students are comfortable with this grouping and labeling process, Dante conducts a brief modeling session in which he puts the terms *bias, preconceptions,* and *interpret* into a group that he labels *opinion.*

Dante then gives students 15 minutes to work. He observes the students in their teams, listens in on their conversations, and helps teams that are having trouble categorizing terms. Figure 9.1 shows the results from one student team's group-and-label session.

"What we're going to do next," says Dante, "is use our labeled groups to generate some hypotheses. Take a close look at your groups and labels. What educated guesses can you and your team make about how science and scientists work?" Each team records at least three

FIGURE 9.1   Sample of Student Team's Groups and Labels

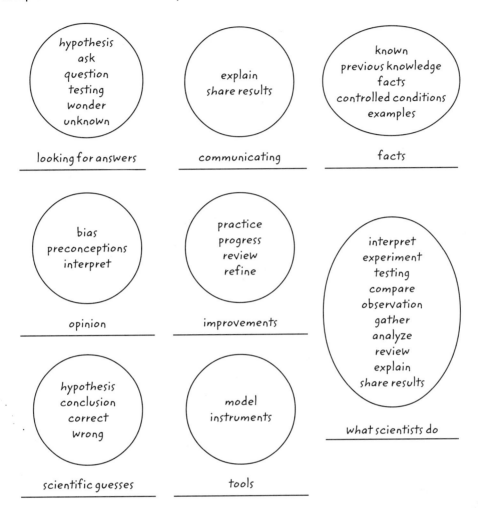

hypotheses using a support and refute organizer like the one shown in Figure 9.2, p. 122.

A few minutes later, Dante has students share their ideas, which he records on the board. Dante then hands out the article, "How Scientists Do Their Jobs." Using their support and refute organizers, students collect and record information from the article that either supports or refutes their hypotheses. Over the course of the unit, students will return to their organizers, adding new evidence to the *Support* and *Refute* columns and revising their hypotheses when presented with new evidence.

As the year goes on, Dante teaches students how to use Inductive Learning independently, as a learning and reading strategy. Dante teaches students how to skim passages to look for key ideas and vocabulary, which students can group, label, and use to help them form predictions before reading.

FIGURE 9.2   Sample Support and Refute Organizer

Evidence to support	Prediction	Evidence to refute
	Science is a way of look-ing for answers to the unknown.	
	Scientists make educated guesses and then try to test them.	
	There are many ways that scientists gather information.	
	Science tries to stick to the facts and to avoid personal opinions.	

Second grade teacher Ally Dubois also uses Inductive Learning to help her young learners develop the crucial skills of comparing, classifying, and drawing conclusions. As part of a unit on communities, Ally helps her students

• Imagine a walk through their community, during which students draw at least five things they would see there.

• Compare their pictures with other students' pictures and with a set of pictures Ally has collected.

• Group and label the pictures based on how students think different pictures go together.

• Draw three conclusions about communities based on their groupings of the pictures.

• Turn their conclusions about communities into a brief paragraph describing a community.

• Evaluate their work using a simple rubric and discuss new ideas for grouping and labeling that they can apply to the next Inductive Learning lesson.

Why the Strategy Works

Inductive Learning engages students in comparative thinking and, like Compare and Contrast, is a member of the family of strategies called *identifying similarities and differences,* which the research team of Marzano, Pickering, and Pollock (2001) have found to be the single most effective way to raise student achievement. At the heart of Inductive Learning is the principle that no idea is an island. Ideas draw their meaning from other ideas through a process of induction. Advertisers know this fact well and often use clusters of related images to sell products. For instance, a recent television commercial displays this series of pictures: A mother helping her son read, a bride and groom dancing and kissing tenderly, a nurse and an elderly man sharing a laugh, and two businesspeople shaking hands. What the creators of this commercial know is that the human brain is designed to search for patterns and assemble multiple pieces of information to form general meanings (Jensen, 1998). Therefore, in processing the specific—mother and son, bride and groom, nurse and patient, businesspeople—most viewers will come away with the larger concepts of *partnership* and *caring* or, even better from the advertiser's perspective, *caring partnerships.*

Well before the brain-based revolution in education, Hilda Taba (1971) proposed that by engaging students' natural potential for induction, educators could successfully encourage students to assume more responsibility for their learning while deepening their insight into the relationship between the big ideas and key details that make up lessons, units, and disciplines.

The Inductive Learning strategy maximizes the benefits of inductive thinking by leading students through a set of six mental operations. These operations enable students to build meaning, and eventually deep conceptual understanding, by moving step-by-step from the specific details of the content to the principles and generalizations that animate it. Figure 9.3, p. 124, outlines these six operations, the covert or "hidden" thinking associated with each operation, and a set of general focusing questions you can use throughout the lesson to help students get their thinking out in the open.

How to Use the Strategy

1. Identify and distribute key words, phrases, items, problems, or images from a reading, lecture, or unit.

2. Model the process of grouping and labeling.

3. Have students form small groups to analyze the items and to explore the different ways information can be grouped. Encourage students to think flexibly and to subsume groups into larger, more inclusive groups.

4. Ask students to devise a descriptive label for each of their groups.

5. Have students use their labels and word groupings to make several predictions or hypotheses about the reading, lecture, or unit. Students should write their predictions on a three-column support/refute organizer.

6. As students read the text, listen to the lecture, or participate in the unit, ask them to search for evidence that supports or refutes their predictions.

FIGURE 9.3   Overt Operations, Covert Operations, and Focusing Questions

Overt Mental Operations	Covert Mental Operations	Focusing Questions (General)
Examining	Review information; recall items from prior knowledge.	What do you see? Hear? Read? What did you notice?
Grouping data	Notice relationships; search for common attributes.	Which of these do you think belong together? Why do you think A, B, and C go together?
Labeling groups	Synthesize common characteristics; generate words or phrases; compare; evaluate for appropriateness.	What would be a good name for this group? Why do you think that _____ would be an appropriate label?
Subsuming groups under more inclusive groups and labels	Notice hierarchies and relationships not noted before; name or label the hierarchies or relationships.	Which of these items, now under one label, would also belong under another label? Why do you think _____ belongs under _____?
Suggesting different ways of grouping, labeling, and subsuming items based on other relationships	Actively search for and explore new ways of organizing.	Which of the items belong together for entirely different reasons? Why do you think _____ and _____ belong together? Are there any possibilities we haven't explored?
Generalizing and Predicting	Finding and applying generalized rules or principles; predicting outcomes; generating hypotheses.	What general rules or principles do your groups suggest? What predictions can you make based on your group?

7. Allow students to reflect on the Inductive Learning process and lead a discussion on what they have learned from it.

8. Over time, teach students how to generalize and conceptualize by using the inductive process to identify words, create groups, generate predictions, and then test and refine those predictions against the evidence.

Planning an Inductive Learning Lesson

To plan an Inductive Learning lesson for your students, follow these steps:

1. **Select your topic and identify the key concepts.** Inductive Learning works best when you want students to draw connections among the specific elements of the content to form generalizations and "big picture" comprehension. The strategy is especially useful for introducing new units of study, helping students organize vocabulary into meaningful categories, and reviewing previously taught material. Begin planning by selecting a topic for your lesson. Then, identify the key concepts that you want your students to understand or generalizations you want students to make upon completion of the lesson. For example, high school English teacher Justine Mueller used Inductive Learning to help her students develop an understanding of the themes of Shakespeare's *Hamlet.* She identified the following themes: madness, uncertainty, revenge/justice, and death.

2. **Select 12–40 items from the reading, lesson, or unit that support the key concepts or generalizations you want students to understand.** In selecting your items, you are not limited to words. Items can be phrases, quotations, lines of poetry, musical instruments, pictures, mathematical expressions, physical objects, or anything else that lends itself to categorization according to common attributes. For example, for her lesson on *Hamlet,* Justine selected four or five lines from the play corresponding to each theme identified in Step 1.

Regardless of your content area or the nature of the items you select, some general guidelines for selection follow:

- Items must be specific, not general.
- You need at least two (and preferably three or more) items representing each concept or generalization, otherwise no grouping is possible.
- If you are using Inductive Learning to introduce new material, select a majority of items that are already familiar to students. Students will have an easier time forming logical groups if they can connect unknown material to familiar material.

3. **Design, or teach students how to create, organizers for grouping and hypothesis checking.** Visual organizers give students a way to arrange information graphically so that it is more memorable and so that they can quite literally *see* the big idea and important details, and how they are related.

When using the Inductive Learning strategy, model the grouping process with students using a basic grouping organizer (see Figure 9.4). It is a good idea to begin the modeling process with straightforward items such as shapes, games and sports, and types of food that are easy to group. Then, introduce items linked in more subtle ways. For example, in modeling how to group lines from *Hamlet,* Justine included the grouping shown in Figure 9.4 to prompt her students to think more flexibly during the lesson.

FIGURE 9.4   Decay Imagery in Shakespeare's *Hamlet*

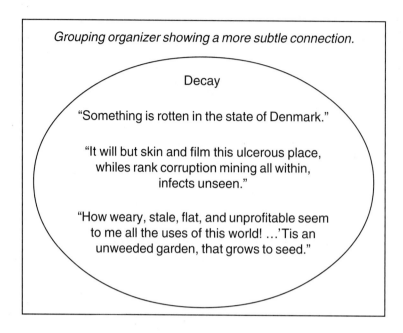

Grouping organizer showing a more subtle connection.

Decay

"Something is rotten in the state of Denmark."

"It will but skin and film this ulcerous place, whiles rank corruption mining all within, infects unseen."

"How weary, stale, flat, and unprofitable seem to me all the uses of this world! ...'Tis an unweeded garden, that grows to seed."

Hypothesis checking should also be conducted using an organizer. A three-column support/refute organizer allows students to list their hypotheses, predictions, or generalizations down the middle and record supporting and refuting evidence on either side, as shown in Figure 9.2, p. 122.

4. **Determine how students will work during the lesson.** Decide whether you want students to work individually, in small groups, or as a whole class.

5. **Consider preparing a set of "stretching questions."** Be ready to help students move beyond the obvious when they begin grouping items into categories. You can help students expand their thinking by posing "stretching" questions. When students get stuck or if they miss subtle relationships among the items, you can ask questions like these to help them move their thinking deeper:

- What other things might fit in that group?
- Can you think of a more descriptive title for that group?
- If you add _____ to your group, would it still make sense? Would you rename your group?
- Can you form some other groups?
- If you remove _____ from your group, how would that change the group?
- Why does _____ belong in the group you put it in?

FIGURE 9.5   Colonial New England Task Rotation

Directions: Choose one assignment. Read through the rubric on which you will be assessed. In your paper, provide at least three generalizations and data that support them. Compare your completed product to the rubric before you turn it in.	
Describe life in a New England town in the 1750s.	Write a letter to England from someone living in New England in the 1750s.
Compare and contrast three aspects of life in New England with life in your town today.	How was life in New England like a _____? Create a metaphor and support it.

Source: Silver, H., Strong, R., Perini, M., & Reilly, E. (2000). *Inductive Learning: Research-Based strategies for teachers*, 19. Thoughtful Education Press, LLC.

6. **Develop a synthesis task.** How will students apply what they have learned from the Inductive Learning lesson? What will students do to synthesize all of the ideas and information from the lesson? Here are some examples of good synthesis tasks:

- After reading a story based on their predictions, 1st graders are asked to draw a picture showing their understanding of the story.
- After grouping and labeling pictures to form three conclusions about communities, 2nd graders write a short paragraph describing their own community.
- After grouping and labeling words related to life in Colonial New England, forming predictions, and reading an article to verify their predictions, 5th graders are asked to complete one task from the Task Rotation shown in Figure 9.5. (Task Rotation, a strategy that allows teachers to differentiate assessment according to the four learning styles is discussed fully on pp. 241–252.)

Variations and Extensions

Though it has many uses in the classroom, Inductive Learning is most commonly used to help students organize the vocabulary for a given unit, introduce new topics or units, and review. However, a growing number of educators have learned how simple "twists" can put the power of Inductive Learning to the task of improving students' reading, writing, and mathematical reasoning skills.

Inductive Reading

By applying the Inductive Learning model to reading, you teach students how to make informed predictions about a text and then use those predictions to construct central ideas and look for relevant evidence to support their predictions. Here's how Art Quinlan uses Inductive Reading with his 3rd graders. Art begins by selecting 30 key words from a story called "Spiders and Diamonds." Working as a whole class, Art and his students form the following groups and subgroups (see Figure 9.6). Art reminds the students that words may appear in more than one group and that they should look for ways to link groups with other groups to form larger categories.

Using their groupings, students make the following predictions while Art writes them on the board:

1. The characters are a selfish man, an old man, an old woman, and a beggar.
2. The beggar needs food to eat.
3. A selfish man was mean to a beggar.
4 The people were digging in the woods for treasure.
5. The story takes place in the woods and in a house.

FIGURE 9.6   Sample Groups for Spiders and Diamonds

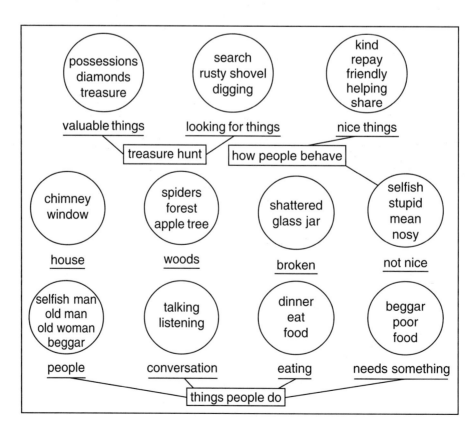

After students have made their predictions, Art gives them a copy of "Spiders and Diamonds" and instructs them to focus their reading by looking for evidence that supports or refutes the predictions they made.

Inductive Writing

"I've used Inductive Learning for years now," says elementary school teacher Michael Ledford. "What I've seen more recently is that thinking inductively is critical to the writing process. In fact, the strategy's emphasis on organizing details, finding and stating the big ideas that unite those details, and structuring large amounts of information into meaningful sets corresponds directly to the problems many of my students have when writing."

Here's how Michael Ledford conducts an Inductive Writing lesson.

• Step 1. "First, I have students generate ideas related to the assigned topic or unit. I often help students tap into their prior knowledge with prompts like, 'What do you know about _____?' 'What adjectives or descriptive words come to your mind when you think about _____?' 'What feelings do you have about _____?' Depending on what kind of writing students will be producing, I will modify my prompts. For example, if I want personal responses, I'll favor prompts designed to provoke feelings and reactions, whereas explanatory writing requires more 'How?' and 'Why?' prompts.

• Step 2. "Then, I have students group the words into related categories and assign labels, just like in a regular Inductive Learning lesson. The only difference is that I ask the students to write a sentence or a phrase for each group instead of just a label. For example, Figure 9.7, p. 130, shows how a student grouped and labeled a set of words that he brainstormed on the topic of *nighttime*.

• Step 3. "After that, I work with students to help them turn their sentences or phrases from Step 2 into clear topic sentences. Here are my student's topic sentences:

  ◦ Many things come out at night that can't be seen during the day.
  ◦ Young children are sometimes afraid of the night because it is dark and scary things happen.
  ◦ Police officers and streetlights are things that help keep your street safe.
  ◦ Children do many things at night in their homes.
  ◦ Nighttime is also a time for children to rest and go to sleep.

• Step 4. "Last, the students generate their paragraphs. The topic sentences become the first sentence in each paragraph with the items in each group to serve as the supporting details. Before they start writing, I'll have the students look over their groups and topic sentences to decide if each group is truly worthy of a paragraph. I like to model the process with my students and to 'think aloud,' showing them how I decide if each topic sentence from Step 3 is meaty enough to yield an entire paragraph. If not, I'll

FIGURE 9.7   Student's Sample Groupings

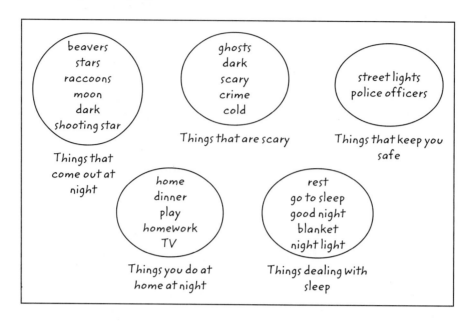

show them how I connect two separate sentences and groups to make one coherent paragraph. For example, if you look at Figure 9.8, you'll see that the student realized his third topic sentence wasn't long enough to hang an entire paragraph on, so he combined Sentences 2 and 3, along with their attending details, into one paragraph.

FIGURE 9.8   Sample Student Writing

Many things happen during the night. Because it is _dark_, things you can't see come out at night. You can see the _moon_ and the _stars_. Sometimes, if you're lucky, you can see a _shooting star_. Animals, like _beavers_ and _raccoons_, also come out at night to look for food when no people are around.

Young children are sometimes afraid at night because it is _dark_ and _scary_ and things can happen. _Ghosts_ come out at night and _black cats_ howl, which keeps you up. Animals come out at night and people need to be careful. _Street lights_ and _police officers_ help make your streets safe.

Children do many things in their _homes_ at night. They watch _TV_, eat _dinner_, finish their _homework_, and _play_ with their brothers and sisters.

Nighttime is also time for children to _rest_ and _go to sleep_. Your parents tell you when to _go to sleep_ and you sometimes argue with them because you want to watch more _TV_ or _play_. You cuddle up in your _blanket_ at night and yell "_Good night_" to everyone in your family before you _go to sleep_.

Inductive Learning and Mathematics

In applying current research-based strategies specifically to mathematics education, researcher Ed Thomas (2003) shows how to use Inductive Learning to introduce new mathematical content. The teacher provides a set of mathematical expressions to students and asks them to group and then label the expressions that seem similar. For example, for a lesson introducing the topic of factoring polynomials, the teacher would begin by selecting (or creating) examples of four different types of polynomial expressions:

Difference of Perfect Squares

$x^2 - 49$

$(x^2)^2 - (y^2)^2$

$x^4 - y^4$

$9r^2 - 4$

$1 - d^2$

$x^2 - 1$

$y^2 - 81$

$(2x)^2 - (3x)^2$

$x^2 - (1)^2$

Sum of Cubes

$m^3 + n^3$

$q^3 + 27$

$(a + b)^3 + (c \div d)^3$

Perfect Square Polynomials

$x^2 + 6x \div 9$

$x^2 - 10x + 25$

$a^2 + 2ab + b^2$

$x^2 + 14x + 49$

$x^2 - 12x + 36$

Difference of Cubes

$r^3 - (2)^3$

$r^3 - 8$

$64 - z^3$

$a^3 - b^3$

The teacher would then scatter these examples across the page, engage students in the grouping and labeling process, and then ask students to make three to five generalizations based on their groups. As students learn more about polynomials, they collect new information and use it to refine their initial groups and labels.

Part of why this process may seem foreign in math (and what may scare a fair number of teachers of mathematics from the process) can be summed up in an entirely reasonable question: What if students get it wrong? As Thomas (2003) explains, the process is not about simply getting "correct" groups. Instead, Thomas recommends basing the lesson on discussion and comparison. Students should share their groups and then work with their classmates and teacher to compare and contrast their groups and the thinking behind their groups. Then, as the unit progresses, students will revise their groups and their generalizations so that they are "actively engaged in constructing the big picture" (Thomas, 2003, p. 127).

How does the strategy fit into unit design?
(Blueprint for Learning)

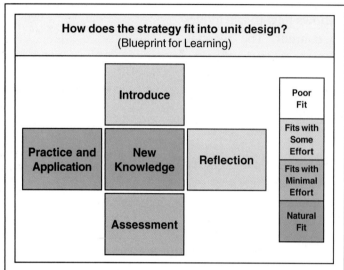

		Introduce		Poor Fit
Practice and Application		New Knowledge	Reflection	Fits with Some Effort
				Fits with Minimal Effort
		Assessment		Natural Fit

What learning styles does the strategy engage?
(Motivation/Differentiation)

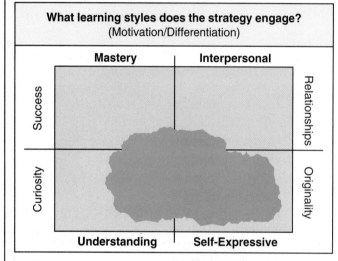

Mastery | Interpersonal
Success | Relationships
Curiosity | Originality
Understanding | Self-Expressive

What facets of understanding does the strategy develop?
(Understanding by Design)

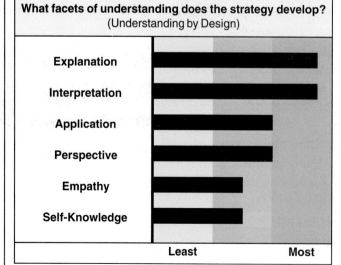

Explanation
Interpretation
Application
Perspective
Empathy
Self-Knowledge

Least — Most

What skills does the strategy build?
(The Hidden Skills of Academic Literacy)

Read and Study
○ Collect/organize ideas through note making
● Make sense of abstract academic vocabulary
○ Read/interpret visuals

Reason and Analyze
● Draw conclusions; make/test inferences, hypotheses, conjectures
● Conduct comparisons using criteria
○ Analyze demands of a variety of questions

Create and Communicate
○ Write clear, coherent explanations
○ Write comfortably in major nonfiction genres
○ Read and write about two or more documents

Reflect and Relate
○ Construct plans to address questions and tasks
○ Use criteria and guidelines to evaluate work
● Control/alter mood and impulsivity

How does the strategy incorporate the research on instructional effectiveness?
(Classroom Instruction That Works)

● Identifying similarities and differences
○ Summarizing and note taking
○ Reinforcing effort and providing recognition
○ Homework and practice
● Nonlinguistic representation
○ Cooperative learning
○ Setting objectives and feedback
● Generating and testing hypotheses
○ Cues, questions, and advance organizers

What types of knowledge does the strategy teach?

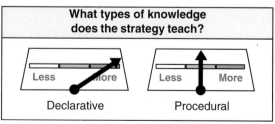

Less — More
Declarative

Less — More
Procedural

10

Metaphorical Expression

Strategy Overview

How is guilt like a stain? How is friendship like a raft? How is an equation like a tug of war? Research shows that asking students to make connections and comparisons between items that are not truly similar is one of the most effective ways to improve comprehension and foster gains in achievement. We call these kinds of comparisons metaphors and similes, and they represent one of our most colorful, creative, and enlightening forms of expression. Teachers, poets, songwriters, all of us rely on metaphors and similes to intensify what we mean or make dazzling connections between things we never before thought could go together.

The Metaphorical Expression strategy seizes on this uniquely human ability to find and make meaning through creative comparisons. By engaging students in metaphorical thinking, teachers give students the opportunity to develop their own perspective on content, paving the way for enlightening insights, powerful explanations, and the very highest levels of comprehension.

The Strategy in Action

"Metaphors and math go together better than most people imagine," says middle school math teacher Sandra Billows. "For example, I love using Metaphorical Expression to help students form a really solid understanding of mathematical concepts, like prime numbers. I also use it to help students internalize and apply key mathematical procedures."

Today, Sandra is using Metaphorical Expression with her pre-algebra students to teach them the steps in solving algebra problems. Because this is her first time using the strategy with this year's class, Sandra begins with a discussion on the use of metaphors in everyday life. Students talk about examples of metaphors in their speech, the music they listen to, movies, advertisements, even nicknames for famous people (e.g. "Air" Jordan, "The Rock" for action star Dwayne Johnson). After the discussion, Sandra reinforces the idea that metaphors make connections between two items that aren't really alike, allowing us to see both items in new, surprising, and memorable ways.

Sandra tells students that they will be creating a metaphor for the algebraic problem-solving procedure. She then works through three algebra problems, each containing one variable, with her students. Together, they extract the steps from the process and Sandra writes them on the board:

1. Read the problem carefully.
2. Convert the problem into mathematical expressions.
3. Set up the equation and follow the order of operations to solve it.
4. Use subtraction and division to simplify complex expressions.
5. Solve the equation.

Next, Sandra divides the students into groups of four and reviews with students what they know about the human digestive process. After listing the phases of digestion on the board, a few students note an immediate connection—both problem solving and digestion follow a prescribed sequence, an order of operations. Sandra shows students how they can "go deeper" with metaphors by selecting the first step in the problem-solving process and connecting it to a relevant stage in the digestive process: serving and eating the meal. With her students she creates a three-column organizer to record her comparison. Over the left column Sandra writes "Steps in Digestion"; over the right column, she writes "Steps in Solving Algebraic Problems"; and over the middle column, she writes "Sample Problem."

After modeling, Sandra instructs each group to explore the problem-solving process metaphorically by finding correlations between the steps in problem solving and the steps in digestion. As groups work, Sandra moves around the room to observe and assist students as they use their organizers to complete the metaphor and solve the sample problem step-by-step. A sample of a typical group's work appears in Figure 10.1, p. 135.

During the discussion phase of the lesson, Sandra draws out the differences in students' thinking. For example, for the second step in algebraic problem solving (*Convert the problem into mathematical expressions*), one group chooses chewing as a metaphorical counterpart, focusing on how the problem gets "chopped up into smaller pieces." Another group highlights the work of the salivary glands, comparing the way they make digestion "more manageable later on" with the way converting the problem into

FIGURE 10.1   Metaphorical Comparison of Digestion and Problem Solving

Step in Digestion	Sample Problem	Step in Solving Algebraic Problems
The meal is presented and digested.	Eighteen coins consisting of nickels and dimes have a total value of $1.25. How many dimes are there?	**Read the problem carefully:** The problem is presented and read (or "ingested").
The teeth chop the food and the salivary glands moisten it, making it easy to swallow.	Let x = number of dimes $18 - x$ = number of nickels $10x$ = value of the dimes $5(18 - x)$ = value of the nickels	**Convert the problem into mathematical expressions:** The problem is chewed on and converted into mathematical expressions, making it easier to create an equation.
The food is swallowed and follows an ordered path through the digestive tract from the mouth, to the esophagus, to the stomach, and to the intestines.	$10x + 5(18 - x) = 125$ $10x + 90 - 5x = 125$ $10x - 5x + 90 = 125$ $5x + 90 = 125$	**Set up the equation and follow the order of operations to solve it:** The equation is swallowed and follows the order of operations from parentheses, to exponents, to multiplication and division, to addition and subtraction.
Enzymes in the stomach and intestines break down the complex molecules into simple ones, which can be absorbed into the bloodstream.	$5x + 90\ (-90) = 125\ (-90)$ $5x = 35$ $5x \div 5 = 35 \div 5$	**Use subtraction and division to simplify complex expressions:** Subtraction and division are used to further break down complex expressions into simpler ones that can be absorbed and solved because the variable is separated.
The nutrients are separated and passed through the intestinal wall into the bloodstream and carried to the cells to be used for energy.	$x = 7$	**Solve the equation:** Numbers and variables are separated by an equal sign, revealing the solution, and producing mathematical energy.

mathematical expressions makes problem-solving more manageable in later stages of the process. Sandra and the class agree that both comparisons work well, and Sandra uses the opportunity to talk about the capacity of metaphors to explain complex ideas in multiple and personally meaningful ways.

At the end of the lesson, Sandra asks each student to create a new metaphor for the problem-solving process. As with the digestion analogy, students' new metaphor must mirror the problem-solving process through all its steps.

Why the Strategy Works

A metaphor is simply a comparison between two seemingly dissimilar items. What is especially amazing about metaphors—what makes them so productive in the classroom—is the way so much meaning is packed into so few words. Just think about all the possible connections implied in Shakespeare's famous metaphor "All the world's a stage," (life is like a play; humans are actors; everyone has a role to play; sometimes life is funny, other times it is sad; the list can go on and on) and you will see how just five words can produce nearly limitless pathways of meaning and expression.

Using metaphors in the classroom has been proven to raise student achievement by a number of researchers including Chen (1999), Cole and McLeod (1999), and Gottfried (1998). In fact, Marzano, Pickering, and Pollock (2001) designate metaphorical thinking as one of the surest ways to improve students' academic performance. The Metaphorical Expression strategy capitalizes on this documented ability of metaphors to enhance learning, allowing students to gain deeper insights by exploring content with "both sides of their brains" (both analytically and creatively) and through the process of "dual coding"—establishing a linguistic and visual connection to what they are learning.

The Metaphorical Expression strategy can also be used to teach new content by taking advantage of what students already know. For example, introducing the concept of a computer firewall by having students compare it to a security guard helps students in a computer class get a firm grip on the new concept of a firewall by connecting it to the well-known concept of a security guard.

Metaphorical Expression is originally based on the work of W. J. J. Gordon (1961), who found that guided creative activity, such as the creation of metaphors, naturally engages students in highly productive cognitive states. These states, which lead to breakthroughs of insight, include:

• Detachment—In looking for a creative solution, students first take a step back and detach themselves from the specific problem.

• Deferment—Rich metaphorical activity usually leads to a conscious rejection of the first, easiest, or most literal metaphor. Thus, the student tries to move beyond "Life is like a roller coaster" to more insightful and creative possibilities.

• Speculation—Once the obvious metaphors have been rejected, students begin playing with the problem by looking for new connections.

• Autonomy—Autonomy results when the student is able to think about the problem and the potential connections and solutions on his or her own terms, clearing the way for a breakthrough.

• Hedonic response—Hedonic responses are those breakthroughs, those "Aha!" moments that erupt from the unconscious. Hedonic responses are creative and tell the student that his solution is insightful or elegant. Best of all, hedonic responses feel good.

How to Use the Strategy

1. Introduce the content and set the scene using an introductory activity that hooks students' attention and helps students loosen and stretch their minds.

2. Provide a reading, lecture, or other information source(s) pertaining to the essential content of the lesson. Ask students to gather (or review) information using given (or collaboratively generated) criteria.

3. Using the provided information sources, model metaphorical thinking with students.

4. Present students with two items for metaphorical comparison, or you may choose to challenge students to develop their own metaphors. Encourage creativity and flexibility.

5. Ask students to share and explain their metaphors. Discuss variations and the ability of metaphors to explain in multiple ways.

6. Build in opportunities for students to reflect on their understanding of the content and their comfort with the process of developing and expanding metaphors.

7. Ask students to apply what they have learned in a writing activity, an oral presentation, a creative project, or another meaningful synthesis task.

Planning a Metaphorical Expression Lesson

To plan a Metaphorical Expression lesson, follow these five steps:

1. **Determine the content and purpose of the lesson.** What content do you want students to explore metaphorically? What will students get out of this lesson? Are you using the strategy to help students learn new information; spur creativity; foster empathy; develop a new perspective; explore interdisciplinary connections?

One way to think about the lesson you are planning is to ask your-self: Do I want to make the familiar strange, or do I want to make the strange familiar? *Making the familiar strange* means taking content students have already learned and having them develop new and deeper perspectives on it through metaphorical thinking. *Making the strange familiar* means relying on something students already know well and using it to make a link to new content.

To understand the difference better, think about this question: *How is a colony like a child?* Imagine first that students have already studied colonies and how they work. For these students, the metaphor will help them develop a new take on colonies, a way of thinking they hadn't con-sidered before. The familiar (colony) is being made strange, being recon-sidered through the metaphor. Now imagine students have not yet studied colonies. By having students make their initial contact with this new content through the well-known concept of a child, the teacher is taking away the strangeness, making it familiar and, therefore, easier to learn.

2. **Devise a hook or "mental stretching" exercise.** Stretching activi-ties tell the students that this lesson will take place in a loose, creative atmosphere. These activities should also draw students' attention and move their thinking in the direction of the lesson's content. If your stu-dents are new to metaphorical activity, you should consider using this mental stretching time to define and give examples of various metaphors. During this process, it is a good idea to ask questions that help students consider what metaphors are and how they work. For example:

- Why do we not rebel intellectually when people say that love is like a rose, war is hell, or the world is a stage?
- Are these statements literally true?
- What do statements like these cause our minds to do?
- Can you generate any more examples?

You may also choose to have students engage in "snap" metaphor-ical thinking by posing questions such as *How is a short story like a building? How is a mathematical proof like a machine? How is a chemical reaction like a recipe? How is an idea like a cat?*

By brainstorming metaphorical connections and then working with students to expose the thinking behind the various connections, you are preparing students to think flexibly and creatively during the actual lesson.

3. **Decide how you will establish and extend metaphorical thinking during the lesson.** Most Metaphorical Expression lessons begin with a direct analogy between your topic and something else to compare against your topic. Unlike Compare and Contrast, the two items for com-parison should not be similar in any obvious ways. Therefore, instead of comparing capitalism with socialism (as they might in a Compare and Contrast lesson), students might compare capitalism with a baseball

game or a locomotive or a bee hive. Students may be provided with both items for comparison (e.g., *How is a colony like a child? How is human circulation like a transit system?*), or you may wish to challenge students to create and develop their own item for metaphorical comparison. (*Developing an interpretation is like _____ because _____.*)

Once students have explored the central analogy of the lesson, you may wish to extend metaphorical activity to enrich student thinking. Below are some basic guidelines for extending metaphorical thinking:

- You can have students imagine they are the topic and describe themselves and how they feel (*personal analogy*). Personal analogies give students the chance to identify with the topic in the first person.
- You can introduce *compressed conflicts* (two terms that describe the topic but seem to contradict one another: e.g., *powerful* and *dependent* for capitalism) to help students explore the paradoxes and "conceptual pressure points" inherent in the topic.
- You can ask students to create new *direct analogies* to focus thinking and build new connections between ideas. (*What else can we compare to capitalism?*)

For more on how to extend students' thinking using personal analogies and compressed conflicts, see the Variations and Extensions section on page 140.

4. **Decide how students will obtain and organize necessary information.** If you are going to have students relate known material to other known material, then you may need only to review or to have students generate some of the critical attributes of the content. If you would like your students to use any new material in their metaphorical activity, then you must provide them with it. In the series of moves known as *making the strange familiar,* for example, the teacher provides students with information about whatever "strange" material students are to relate to familiar material. For example, if a biology teacher wants to introduce the circulatory system by having students compare it to a railroad, then the teacher might need to provide a handout showing and describing the parts of the circulatory system or introduce relevant information in a presentation.

Finally, you may need to provide an organizer for students to arrange the information they will use metaphorically. For a sample organizer used during a Metaphorical Expression lesson, see Figure 10.1, p. 135.

5. **Select a format for the presentation of students' ideas.** Students need opportunities to demonstrate what they know and understand as a result of their metaphorical thinking. An appropriate synthesis task is to have students generate and explain their own metaphors in any variety of formats. Possible formats include a written description, a poem, a visual representation, an essay, an art project, an oral presentation, and so on.

Variations and Extensions

Metaphors help students make connections between unfamiliar and familiar material. They can also be used to help students gain a deeper understanding of something already familiar by seeing it in a new way. So far, we have concentrated almost entirely on one type of metaphorical thinking: *direct analogies.* Direct analogies compare two objects or concepts. Most Metaphorical Expression lessons are designed around direct analogies, but two other types of analogies can also be used to unlock the great learning potential residing within this uniquely human way of thinking. *Personal analogies* describe how it feels to identify with or to be a concept, process, or living or nonliving thing. They help students build deeper and more personally meaningful connections to the topics they are studying. Examples include *If you were a type of rock (sedimentary, igneous, metamorphic), which particular one would match your personality? Why?* and *How does it feel to be a jazz composition?* Often, personal analogies are linked with free writing, in which students are asked to write spontaneously for three to five minutes. For example:

> Pretend you are a plant that has not received water for a full week. "Be" the plant. How do you feel? What do you look like? What are your prospects for survival? In your special journal that we call a Learning Log, write for five minutes without stopping. If you get stuck, write about being stuck, but don't stop writing until time is up. Let your ideas flow freely; don't hold yourself back or wait for the perfect words.

A third type of metaphor is called a *compressed conflict.* Compressed conflicts describe an object or concept using two words that contradict or "fight" each other. The two words present a paradoxical yet highly descriptive frame of meaning for the object or concept to which they refer. Examples of compressed conflicts include *How is littering passive violence? How are Romeo and Juliet trapped yet free? What is meant by catastrophic success?*

Any one of the three types of metaphors (direct analogies, personal analogies, compressed conflicts) makes for a great spot activity. Metaphors enhance any lesson because they naturally promote critical thinking, creativity, and (in the case of personal analogies) empathy among students. In addition, all three types can be used together, rather than separately, and incorporated into a single Metaphorical Expression lesson so that comprehension accumulates as students explore the concept through the various metaphors. For example, during a Metaphorical Expression lesson on the concept of democracy, a 5th grade teacher had students:

- Compare democracy with diamonds (direct analogy).
- Free-associate words and ideas connected to both democracy and diamonds and find two words from their lists that seemed at odds with one another (compressed conflict). Examples included *sensitive and strong, beautiful and never perfect,* and *hard and fragile.* Students then had to generate a list of ideas about how democracy might be said to embody this conflict.
- Pretend to be democracy (personal analogy) and free write about themselves (i.e., democracy in the first person) for five minutes.
- Write, as a synthesis task, a short, two-minute speech explaining democracy to a 2nd grader using a single metaphor of her choice.

How does the strategy fit into unit design?
(Blueprint for Learning)

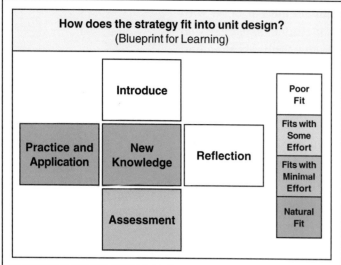

			Poor Fit
	Introduce		Fits with Some Effort
Practice and Application	New Knowledge	Reflection	Fits with Minimal Effort
	Assessment		Natural Fit

What learning styles does the strategy engage?
(Motivation/Differentiation)

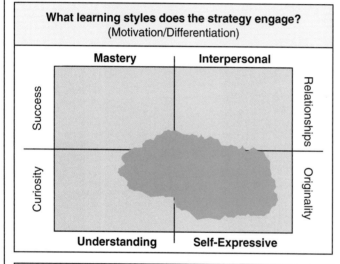

Mastery | Interpersonal
Success
Relationships
Curiosity
Originality
Understanding | Self-Expressive

What facets of understanding does the strategy develop?
(Understanding by Design)

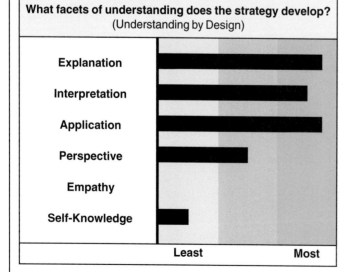

Explanation
Interpretation
Application
Perspective
Empathy
Self-Knowledge

Least — Most

What skills does the strategy build?
(The Hidden Skills of Academic Literacy)

Read and Study
- ○ Collect/organize ideas through note making
- ○ Make sense of abstract academic vocabulary
- ○ Read/interpret visuals

Reason and Analyze
- ● Draw conclusions; make/test inferences, hypotheses, conjectures
- ● Conduct comparisons using criteria
- ○ Analyze demands of a variety of questions

Create and Communicate
- ● Write clear, coherent explanations
- ● Write comfortably in major nonfiction genres*
- ● Read and write about two or more documents

Reflect and Relate
- ● Construct plans to address questions and tasks
- ○ Use criteria and guidelines to evaluate work
- ○ Control/alter mood and impulsivity

How does the strategy incorporate the research on instructional effectiveness?
(Classroom Instruction That Works)

- ● Identifying similarities and differences
- ○ Summarizing and note taking
- ○ Reinforcing effort and providing recognition
- ○ Homework and practice
- ○ Nonlinguistic representation
- ○ Cooperative learning
- ○ Setting objectives and feedback
- ● Generating and testing hypotheses
- ○ Cues, questions, and advance organizers

What types of knowledge does the strategy teach?

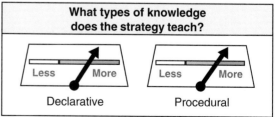

Less — More | Less — More
Declarative | Procedural

*Pattern Maker is especially useful in helping students analyze and adapt writing structures.

11

Pattern Maker

Strategy Overview

Most content that students learn has or fits into a "structure"—an organizational pattern or framework that acts as a set of orderly slots for specific pieces of information. When students have a solid understanding of structure—when they know how fairy tales are designed around a beginning, middle, and end, when they understand how the three branches of government interrelate or how protons, neutrons, and electrons make up atoms—they are not only showing "big picture" comprehension; they are ready to learn more. Pattern Maker (a.k.a. Extrapolation) is a strategy designed to help students "see" the patterns and structures behind texts and ideas. Students arrive at this big-picture understanding through the process of extrapolation; that is, students

- Closely examine known or easily understood sources.
- Extract the key structural elements from these sources.
- Put their newfound structural comprehension to work by using it to better understand a new source, create a product of their own, or make improvements to an everyday object.

The Strategy in Action

High school science teacher Claudia Geocaris was frustrated by the explanation tasks she had been assigning her students. The problem was engagement. Students were bored with the process of developing textbook-style explanations, and that boredom was coming through in their levels of participation and their written work.

During her search for more engaging ways to develop explanations, Claudia came across an unlikely source of inspiration: children's books. What she realized was that scientific descriptions in children's books are, unlike textbook descriptions, both clear and interesting. This gave Claudia an idea.

The next morning, Claudia divided students into teams and provided each team with a folder containing descriptions from a selection of children's books. She said to her students:

> Listen, our job is to explain how cells work in a clear and interesting manner. Remember, we're trying to write a textbook chapter for next year's students. We've done our homework. We know how cells work, right? Well, we're getting there. Then we studied effective explanations in the textbook and identified the key parts of a good explanation.

She placed a transparency on the overhead that summarized what they had discovered about good explanations: Good explanations (1) describe the phenomenon, (2) lay out the elements of the process, and (3) describe the process clearly.

Claudia then asked her students to look over the textbook explanations and think about two questions: (1) What are they missing? and (2) Where is there room for improvement? After a few minutes, Claudia asked students to share their ideas:

- "Well, they're pretty boring."
- "Sometimes they try to cram too much information in."
- "They can be hard to follow."
- "They don't have any—you know—style, flair."

After discussing the responses, Claudia continued:

> The problem we have is that the examples we looked at are lifeless. They're effective but not interesting, and most of the time they're too complicated to be clear. We need to do better. So we're going to do something new. We're going to study some examples of authors whose business it is to be interesting and clear—children's authors—and see if we can use them as models to help us solve our problem. Here's what I think we might do. Browse these materials in teams and, as you do, try to find answers to these questions (see Figure 11.1, p. 145). Whenever you come across an example that answers a question, make note of it. Let's see what lessons we can learn from them.

As the students studied the explanations and identified how authors make—or fail to make—their explanations appealing, clear, and insightful, Claudia circulated around the room to help students clarify their ideas. After the teams analyzed the materials, the class convened to summarize their insights. What was the result? Well, as Claudia tells it,

> When it came time for students to create their textbook chapters on how a cell works, their explanations were alive with images, metaphors, and narrative

FIGURE 11.1   Analyzing Good Explanations

How Do These Authors	List Examples
Hook their readers' interest in the phenomena they describe?	They open with a surprising question or use a simile.
Keep their readers from becoming confused about the various elements?	They make a numbered list or include a diagram.
Maintain their readers' interest and understanding as they lay out the process?	They show a practical application.

devices that revealed not only competence but also a deeper understanding of cellular structure and function than I'd ever seen with a whole class before. It was fantastic, fun, educational—anything but dull.

The previous classroom vignette originally appeared in Strong, R., Silver, H. and Perini, M. (2001, pp. 15–16). *Teaching what matters most: Standards and strategies for raising student achievement.* Association for Supervision and Curriculum Development.

Why the Strategy Works

Pattern Maker is a highly effective teaching and learning strategy for three reasons:

1. **The strategy stimulates students' curiosity and interest.** Ask any teacher or brain researcher about the role student interest plays in learning new content, and you'll hear the same things: Interested and engaged students are better and happier learners who are far more willing to attend to the complexities of challenging material. Now imagine this: You are about to begin a lesson on the Declaration of Independence. You tell your students they are going to conduct a close reading of this critical document. How many of them are ready to follow you into the world of 1776? How many are ready to wrestle with Thomas Jefferson's prose? Do you at least have their interest on your side?

Now imagine beginning the same lesson by presenting students with a short reading. The reading is not the Declaration of Independence, nor is it a section from the textbook. Instead, students are asked to read a one-page break-up letter from one partner in a relationship to another. In this letter, Marcia explains to John:

- *Why she is writing the letter:* "When two people have lived together as long as you and I have, and one of them decides to split, it's only decent to take a little time to understand the reasons for that breakup."

  ◦ *Her idea of a healthy relationship:* "In a good relationship, partners support each other, share equally in the daily tasks, and help each other grow and change."

  ◦ *Why she is breaking the relationship off:* "You never take out the garbage." "On your night to cook, you always order Chinese—and I'm allergic to Chinese food!" "When I got my promotion you sulked for a month because I was making more money than you." "When I try to talk about any of this with you, you flip on the TV."

  ◦ *What she believes the future holds:* "I will miss you. I will be lonely. But I will also be free."

Do you think this letter might help you pique students' curiosity and get their attention? Guess what? If students are asking, "This is American history?" or, "Why on earth are we reading about lovers' quarrels?" you definitely have their attention.

    2. **The strategy primes students for new learning.** In the second edition of *Teaching with the Brain in Mind,* brain researcher Eric Jensen (2005) discusses the importance and effectiveness of preparing students to learn through pre-exposure, previewing, and priming techniques. What these techniques do is maximize students' exposure to new ideas, activate their prior knowledge, and help them build onto that prior knowledge. Thus, when a new content is introduced, students are comfortable with it and ready to learn about it in greater depth.

    Pattern Maker is a strategy that capitalizes on novelty (What do lovers' quarrels have to do with U.S. history?) and on active, precontent exposure to prime the engine of deep learning. To see how, take a look back at the four structural elements in the breakup letter discussed previously. If the teacher and students work together to extract these four elements (reason for the document, principles of a healthy relationship, complaints with the current arrangement, and vision of the future), how much deeper will students' comprehension of the Declaration of Independence be when they use this same structure to analyze the "breakup" between England and its colonies as described by the Declaration of Independence?

    3. **The strategy is built on the cognitive capacity known as analogical problem solving.** In a famous and often-cited study, Mary Gick and Keith Holyoak (1980) of the University of Michigan investigated the process by which humans solve problems by analogy—that is, by applying the ideas, solutions, and structures behind known situations to new and challenging questions and dilemmas. What Gick and Holyoak did was present a "medical mystery" centered on the difficult problem of using rays to destroy tumors without destroying healthy tissue. Without help, only about 10 percent of participants could solve the problem on their own. However, when presented with and told to apply

the lessons from a seemingly unrelated story of a general who is able to take a mine-surrounded fortress by breaking his army up into small units and attacking from multiple sides, a whopping 90 percent of the participants were able to solve the medical mystery. What the story of the general did was give participants an analogous model to apply to the medical problem. Because of the general and his army, the participants figured out that the rays could be directed at the tumor from all sides but at lower intensities, thereby concentrating on the tumor at full force but not moving through any healthy tissue at full force.

Now, think one more time on the Declaration of Independence lesson. How many more students will be able to solve the difficult reader's problems posed by a challenging historical document when armed with prior knowledge from a text that is structurally analogous and easy to understand?

How to Use the Strategy

1. Introduce the purpose and content of the lesson. Discuss the value of using one information source to make inferences about another source (analogical reasoning).

2. Have students review the analog (the information source you will be using to help students understand the new content you are teaching).

3. Help students extract the structure of the analog (not the specifics!) using clear criteria. You may want to provide an organizer for this step.

4. Allow students to discuss and summarize their insights gained from the analog.

5. Present the new content to students, guiding them in applying what they've already learned about the structure of the analog to the new material. Alternately, you can have students take what they've learned from the structure of the analog and apply it to the creation of a product (e.g., creating a persuasive advertisement after studying a set of examples) or a plan for improvement (e.g., designing a better egg carton).

Planning a Pattern Maker Lesson

Pattern Maker is related to the strategy know as Metaphorical Expression and shares some of the same planning considerations; however, Pattern Maker places much greater emphasis on analysis and the extraction of defined structural elements than its more creative-minded cousin. In planning a Pattern Maker lesson, you should consider the following questions:

- What is the purpose of the lesson?
- What information sources will students use to extract key information?

- What criteria will students use to extract the required structural elements?
- Will students need an organizer to help them locate and record essential information?

What Is the Purpose of the Lesson?

Do you want students to apply the results of their analogical learning to the comprehension of new content (e.g., students apply their understanding of a breakup letter to their reading of the Declaration of Independence), to the creation of a product (e.g., students use their new knowledge of how children's nonfiction books explain difficult concepts in order to write an interesting explanation of how a cell works), or to the modification or improvement of the structure (e.g., after extracting the structure of the U.S. currency system, students identify a flaw and develop a plan to improve it).

What Information Sources Will Students Use to Extract Key Information?

How will students get the information they will need to apply later in the lesson? What text(s) or other sources will you need to provide?

What Criteria Will Students Use to Extract the Required Structural Elements?

Students' thinking during a Pattern Maker lesson should be far less divergent than the thinking typical to a Metaphorical Expression lesson, which celebrates creativity and finding as many connections as possible. With Pattern Maker, you want students to locate specific elements in one set of information that correspond predictably with the elements in some other set of information—new content, a product students will create, or the "improved version" students will develop. For example, in helping her students figure out the components common to good travel brochures (so students could produce their own), a 5th grade teacher asked her students to think about these three criteria:

- How the travel brochures grab the readers' attention on the cover.
- How the travel brochures use language to make their points quickly.
- How the travel brochures use pictures to make their message more appealing.

Will Students Need an Organizer to Help Them Locate and Record Essential Information?

A visual organizer can facilitate the lesson and concentrate students' thinking as they examine sources. Visual organizers also make it easier for students to keep track of what they learn during their initial analysis and then apply that learning to the new content or to the product they will create. A visual organizer for a Pattern Maker lesson need not be complex; a simple two-column or three-column format for collecting examples (and general principles) is usually enough. (See Figure 11.1, p. 145, for a sample organizer.)

Variations and Extensions

How are the topics that students study in school structured or designed? How does a deep understanding of the frameworks that lie behind information increase students' overall comprehension? These are the questions that animate the Pattern Maker strategy. These same questions animate the following variations on the Pattern Maker strategy.

Knowledge by Design

In 1986, David Perkins posed a challenge to educators that is as provocative and timely today as it was 20 years ago: What if we stopped teaching important ideas as information to be remembered and instead taught students to think about ideas and knowledge as *designs,* as structures adapted to meet specific purposes? By teaching students to think about the stock market, film noir, digestion, comic-book villains, pulleys, snakes, the blues, the electoral process, horror stories, Expressionist paintings, long division, advertisements using statistics, communities—almost any content will do—as designs, exciting new possibilities emerge in the classroom. Higher-order thinking becomes the norm. Lessons take on a new life as teacher and students engage in focused inquiry by asking a series of questions about the concept at hand:

- What purpose(s) does it serve?
- What is it made of? What are its structural elements or design features?
- What examples or model cases can we find that represent it?
- What are the arguments for it—and against it?

In our own adaptation of Perkins's work, we have found that we can expand opportunities for creative thinking (or Self-Expressive thinking, if learning style is the "design" that you use to make sense of the concept of cognitive diversity) by asking students to explore how the concept might be modified or improved.

Figure 11.2 shows the results of an interdisciplinary Knowledge by Design lesson on monuments developed by a middle school social studies teacher in coordination with an art teacher. The social studies teacher began by asking students to examine a picture of the Vietnam

Veterans' Memorial. After discussing the intention behind the memorial, the students brainstormed other examples of monuments, from the Statue of Liberty to the impromptu displays that grieving families create for lost loved ones. The teacher then led the class through the Knowledge by Design sequence (shown in Figure 11.2) culminating in an art project and "Gallery Walk." Note that in Figure 11.2, what is written in the *structure, purpose,* and *arguments* boxes represent the collected and synthesized ideas of the students as they worked through the lesson. The text in the *design* box shows the synthesis task designed by the teacher.

FIGURE 11.2   Knowledge by Design—Monuments

Structure (What are the design features that make a monument a monument?)	**Purpose** (What are monuments supposed to do?)
• Usually three-dimensional • Located where people can view it • May or may not be permanent • Designed to be attractive; monuments catch the eye • May use a variety of materials from stone to photographs	Monuments help us remember people, people's achievements, or important events. They are found in public places because they are for the entire public to see. Monuments are visually attractive and emotionally powerful so that everyone can understand their message.

MONUMENTS

Arguments (What are the arguments for monuments?)	**Design** (Synthesis task)
• They help people remember important people and events. (Tomb of the Unkown Soldier, Iwo Jima) • They can help people deal with grief. (Vietnam Veterans' Memorial, graveside and roadside memorials) • They keep legacies alive. (Lincoln Memorial) • They can unite many people and cultures. (Statue of Liberty) (What are some drawbacks of monuments?) • Sometimes, different people and cultures fight over who or what should be remembered in a monument. (Public displays of the Ten Commandments) • In some countries the government, and not the public, picks the people and events to be remembered in monuments. (Soviet statues of Lenin and Stalin) • Monuments can sometimes be expensive and often use public money.	You have been selected to design the next national United States monument. For your design, you must submit • One paragraph that tells who or what you have choosen to memorialize and why. • An artistic rendering of your monument (drawing, sculpture, computer design, or other medium). • A one- to two-page explanation of how it incorporates the structure, meets its purpose, supports arguments for monuments, and seeks to minimize the arguments against monuments. We will be displaying our monuments in the library, where we will have a "Gallery Walk." During the Gallery Walk, students will be able to walk around and leave comments and messages for each monument designer.

To conduct a Knowledge by Design lesson, follow these steps:

1. Select a concept (e.g., neighborhood, Newton's first law of motion), process (e.g., respiration, solving slope problems using the formula $y = mx + b$), or concrete example (e.g., a screwdriver, a deceptive advertisement).

2. Work with students to describe the purpose of the chosen topic.

3. Ask students to identify and describe the structural elements or design features that constitute the topic.

4. Ask students to consider and articulate possible arguments for and against the chosen topic. What are the pros and cons associated with the topic and its structure?

5. Encourage students to explore how they might modify or improve the chosen topic to meet its purpose better.

Extracting Principles

Sometimes, new content is difficult for students to learn because the principles that lie behind it are abstract. Yet, these abstract principles can be seen at work in concrete examples, which are often much easier for students to mentally "grip." Once students have a grip on these examples, they can use them to extract the general principles, thereby solidifying their comprehension over the abstract by way of the concrete. For example, a science teacher who wanted his students to extract the principles of the concept *osmosis* presented students with two concrete examples of osmosis and an organizer on which to draw out the overarching similarities between the two examples (see Figure 11.3).

FIGURE 11.3   Extracting Principles—Osmosis

Example 1	Similarities	Example 2
Plant absorbing water		**Capillary-cellular exchange**
1. Water in soil	*More water in one place than another.*	1. More water inside cell
2. Root hairs have less water		2. Less water in capillary
	Cells allow water in.	
3. Cell walls of root hairs are permeable to water		3. Cell membrane and capillary wall permeable to water
	Water moves from place where there's more water to place where there's less water.	
4. Water passes from soil through cell walls of root hairs into plant		4. Water passes from cell to capillary

How does the strategy fit into unit design?
(Blueprint for Learning)

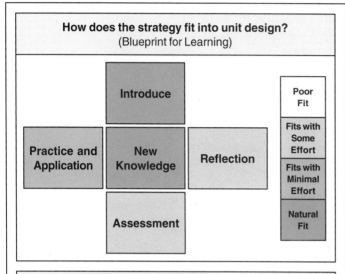

	Introduce		Poor Fit	
Practice and Application	New Knowledge	Reflection	Fits with Some Effort	
	Assessment		Fits with Minimal Effort	
			Natural Fit	

What learning styles does the strategy engage?
(Motivation/Differentiation)

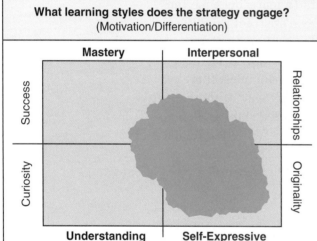

Mastery | Interpersonal
Success — Curiosity (vertical left)
Relationships — Originality (vertical right)
Understanding | Self-Expressive

What facets of understanding does the strategy develop?
(Understanding by Design)

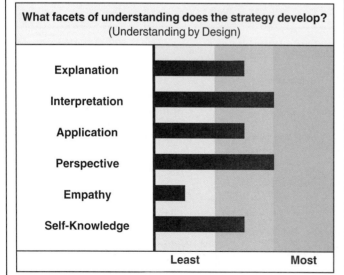

- Explanation
- Interpretation
- Application
- Perspective
- Empathy
- Self-Knowledge

Least — Most

What skills does the strategy build?
(The Hidden Skills of Academic Literacy)

Read and Study
- ● Collect/organize ideas through note making
- ● Make sense of abstract academic vocabulary
- ● Read/interpret visuals

Reason and Analyze
- ● Draw conclusions; make/test inferences, hypotheses, conjectures
- ○ Conduct comparisons using criteria
- ○ Analyze demands of a variety of questions

Create and Communicate
- ● Write clear, coherent explanations
- ● Write comfortably in major nonfiction genres*
- ○ Read and write about two or more documents

Reflect and Relate
- ○ Construct plans to address questions and tasks
- ○ Use criteria and guidelines to evaluate work
- ● Control/alter mood and impulsivity

How does the strategy incorporate the research on instructional effectiveness?
(Classroom Instruction That Works)

- ○ Identifying similarities and differences
- ● Summarizing and note taking
- ○ Reinforcing effort and providing recognition
- ○ Homework and practice
- ● Nonlinguistic representation
- ○ Cooperative learning
- ○ Setting objectives and feedback
- ● Generating and testing hypotheses
- ○ Cues, questions, and advance organizers

What types of knowledge does the strategy teach?

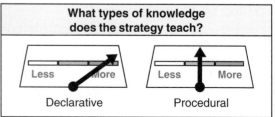

Less — More (Declarative)
Less — More (Procedural)

*Mind's Eye is especially useful for building students' descriptive powers as writers.

12

Mind's Eye

Strategy Overview

The students in today's classrooms are saturated with images. Television, movies, Web sites, magazines, billboards, comic books, even textbooks bombard students with glossy pictures and moving images that explode with color and action. However, reading works differently. Most texts don't show readers pictures. Instead, readers must supply their own images by actively converting words on the page into realistic settings, flesh-and-blood characters, and dynamic scenes or, in the case of nonfiction, memorable representations of essential content.

This ability to "see" a text unfold in the mind is essential for deep reading, yet it is a skill that many average and below-average readers lack. Mind's Eye is a strategy that builds students' capacity to create mental images from texts by:

- Drawing their attention to key image-laden words in a text
- Encouraging them to make predictions about a text based on the images they create
- Allowing students to process their images and share their predictions with other students through a product of their choice
- Engaging them in active reading by having them test their predictions against the actual text
- Teaching them how to use image making independently

The Strategy in Action

High school English teacher Robin Cederblad is frustrated by the way in which her students are responding—or rather, failing to respond—to Charles Dickens's novel, *A Tale of Two Cities*. Robin has been discussing the novel with her students for over a week, but almost none of them seems to know (or care!) what is going on. Because Robin is convinced that her students would really enjoy the novel if she could just get them to visualize the rich story that is hidden under the old-fashioned vocabulary, she decides to give the Mind's Eye strategy a try.

Robin begins by telling her students that she is going to read them a list of key words from the next chapter in *A Tale of Two Cities*. After she reads the first word on her list, she asks her students to "create a picture of the word in their minds." When everyone has generated a mental image of the word *storms,* Robin continues. She reads each word on her list slowly and with extra emotion:

storms	courtyard
child	carriage
recklessness	screaming
silent	killed
eyes	coin
purse	contemptuous
horses	escaping
dispersed	knitting
watchfulness	

As she reads each new word aloud, Robin encourages her students to alter their mental pictures accordingly; she wants them to create a "snapshot" or "movie" that illustrates what they think is going on in the chapter. When Robin finishes reading, she allows her students to process their mental images in one of four ways:

1. Draw a picture of the image they generated.
2. Develop a question that they hope the chapter will answer.
3. Generate a prediction about the chapter.
4. Describe the personal feelings that were evoked as they constructed their mental images.

Robin gives her students time to share their products with their classmates and discuss their ideas about how the chapter might actually unfold. She then asks her students to read the chapter on their own. When her students finish reading, Robin encourages them to discuss the ways in which their initial ideas and predictions were (or were not) borne out by the actual text. She also asks them whether the pre-reading activities—making images and developing predictions—affected the way in which they read the text or their attitude about the text. Robin is pleasantly surprised by her students' animated responses:

- "It was cool when all of a sudden, the part that had to do with my drawing came up, and I could really see what it meant."
- "The words that you read really stood out for me when I came across them in the chapter."
- "The chapter was like a movie this time. I mean, I really saw the action."
- "It was exciting when my prediction turned out to be right. I already have some predictions for the next chapter—I can't wait to see if I'm right about those, too."

Over the course of the next few weeks, Robin continues to help her students build their image making skills. Once her students are comfortable with Mind's Eye, Robin tells students:

> In order for you to be able to use this image making and predicting technique independently, we're going to work on how to select image-rich words. I'm not going to give you a list this time. Instead, I'm going to show you how I choose words, and then you're going to try it out on your own.

Using image-rich passages from various texts, Robin models the way in which she focuses in on key words and phrases and then uses those words to help her form images. Robin then gives her students time to practice this new type of image making in small groups. After several practice sessions, Robin conducts mini-conferences with student groups to determine who needs more practice and who is ready to work independently.

Why the Strategy Works

Mind's Eye is a strategy whose overall benefits on reading comprehension can be traced through three distinct lines of research.

Research Line 1: Proficient Reader Research

Beginning in the late 1970s and the early 1980s, reading researchers began investigating a new question: What do proficient readers do in their minds while reading that makes them better readers than their peers?

What this research shows is that the ability to construct images in the mind is one of the key reading skills that proficient readers employ spontaneously and that separate them from their average and below-average counterparts (Keene & Zimmerman, 1997; Pressley, 2002). The good news for average and below-average readers (and their teachers) is that students as young as 3rd graders can be taught how to create images in less than an hour (Pressley, 1976; Gambrell & Bales, 1986). In addition to image making, proficient readers also activate prior knowledge and use it to make predictions about a text (Pressley, 2002)—another key skill highlighted in the Mind's Eye strategy. Finally, Mind's Eye is built on the three-phase reading approach that all proficient-reader research identifies as critical to students' comprehension: pre-reading (preparing for the reading), during-reading (reading actively and purposefully while monitoring comprehension), and post-reading (reflecting on the reading process).

Research Line 2: Dual Coding

Mind's Eye also has roots in a well-known psychological principle called "dual coding" (Paivio, 1990), which tells us that storing information in two ways—through language and through images—makes learning deeper and easier to remember. Sadoski and Paivio (2001, 2004) have since advanced dual coding as a general theory of reading that emphasizes concrete language and multisensory processing as keys to making meaning. The value of a dual coding approach to reading is borne out by studies showing that teaching students how to construct mental images while they read enhances their abilities to make inferences, make predictions, and remember what they have read (Gambrell & Bales, 1986; Sadoski & Paivio, 2004).

Research Line 3: Field Research

Research shows that developmental and remedial reading programs based on dual coding have led repeatedly to increased reading comprehension inside schools and in clinical studies (Lindamood, Bell, & Lindamood, 1997). A recent and ambitious example comes from Sadoski and Willson (2006), who undertook a large-scale study of a dual-coding-based reading program and its effects on Pueblo School District 60—a heavily minority urban district in Colorado with a high concentration of Title I schools. Sadoski and Willson tracked reading achievement levels in Grades 3–5 across 28 schools, including 18 Title I schools, from 1998 to 2003. When Sadoski and Willson analyzed the results, they found that reading comprehension scores improved across the board, with Pueblo's students significantly outperforming students from comparable Colorado districts and Title I schools.

How to Use the Strategy

1. Select 20–30 key words from the text.

2. Explain to students that you will be reading words from the text aloud while they will "create movies in their minds." Ask students to consider whether they are most likely to draw a picture, ask a question, make a prediction, or describe their feelings in response to the words you will read. Instruct students to use their chosen "end product" (picture, question, prediction, or description of feelings) as a frame of reference for their visualizations.

3. Read the words slowly to students, one at a time and with emphasized feeling. Ask students to create movies or mental images as you read the words and to add to and refine their images with each new word. Allow students to develop their end products and share them in pairs, in small groups, or with the whole class.

4. Instruct students to read the text, comparing their initial ideas with what they discovered while reading.

5. Encourage students to reflect on the process and the types of thinking they are most comfortable using (visualization, questioning, exploring feelings, or predicting).

6. Teach students how to use the strategy independently, modeling how you select key words, make images, form predictions, and read actively to confirm your predictions.

Planning a Mind's Eye Lesson

Mind's Eye is a strategy with a big payoff, yet it requires only a small amount of planning. Before using Mind's Eye in the classroom, you will need to choose 20–30 key words or phrases from your selected text. Because the terms you select will become the basis for your students' images and pre-reading predictions, it's important to choose carefully. Consider the following questions before making each selection:

- Is this particular word or term especially important to the selected text?
- Does this word offer information about the text's meaning, setting, themes, and so on?
- Does this word or term contain visual or other sensory information that can help students form rich images?

Before you develop your list of terms, ask yourself whether the words, when taken together, will provide students with enough information to make quality predictions about your selected text. After you complete your list, organize the terms on the list in the order that you will read them to your students—remember that the order in which you read the words can have a significant impact on the images your students create.

As you help students develop their independence as image makers, you will need to think about how you will guide their learning and assess their proficiency in image making. Silver, Strong, and Perini (2000) describe four simple "moves" you can make to help your students become better, more independent image makers:

1. **Begin with simple, nontextual image making.** Students can learn to apply the skill of image making more effectively if you begin with simple, everyday objects. Ask students to visualize an apple, a crowded beach, an aquarium. Work in other senses as well using examples such as a coyote howling at midnight and the sight, feel, taste, and smell of a slice of pepperoni pizza. Have students "layer" their visualizations and sensations, for example, by having them first "taste" chocolate, then adding in nuts, and then raisins. Add in a sour taste and watch their faces; if they wince or frown, then you know their minds are busy replicating sensations. During these initial imaging sessions, ask students, "What do you see? What do you hear, smell, taste? How do you feel?" Students should practice making images for short periods of time over the course of several days.

2. **Show students how to pre-read passages.** Model with students how they can skim readings and identify the key words needed to create good images. Make sure students know they need to be economical, focusing specifically on words and phrases that hold essential visual or sensory information.

3. **Work with students in small groups.** It is always a good idea to ask students to read passages aloud and talk about how they selected key words and developed their images.

4. **Use conferences to assess students' proficiency in image making.** If students are struggling, provide further assistance and coaching. Students who are proficient in image making should be encouraged to work independently.

Variations and Extensions

The basic psychological principle behind Mind's Eye is simple: Information that is stored in the memory in more than one way—through words as well as through visual images or other sensory pathways—is more memorable, easier to access when needed, and forms a more solid foundation for future learning. This idea is known as "dual coding" (Paivio, 1990) and it has many applications in the classroom.

Etch-a-Sketch Notes

In their book *Tomorrow's Classrooms Today,* Brownlie, Close, and Wingren (1990) explore a variety of note making strategies that combine words and images in the name of deeper and richer learning. One such strategy adapted from Brownlie, Close, and Wingren's work is known as Etch-a-Sketch Notes (see Figure 12.1). In using Etch-a-Sketch Notes, the teacher begins by presenting students with a brief overview of a text, lecture, or presentation. The teacher then presents the information to students, speaking slowly and with emphasized emotion while students draw three to five sketches or icons that represent their

FIGURE 12.1 Etch-a-Sketch Notes

Source: From *The Interactive Lecture: Research-Based Strategies for Teachers* (p. 55), by H. Silver, R. Strong, M. Perini, and E. Reilly, 2001, Ho-Ho-Kus, NJ: Thoughtful Education Press. Used with permission.

understanding of the content. Students meet with one another, guess what each other's drawings mean, and work together to capture the big ideas and critical details from the presentation. The teacher surveys students' ideas and continues with the lecture or presentation. At the end of the presentation, students synthesize their ideas in writing, a visual format, or a combination of the two. Figure 12.1, p. 159, presents a set of Etch-a-Sketch Notes created by a high school student while listening to her teacher read Jonathan Edwards's famous Puritan sermon, "Sinners in the Hands of an Angry God."

Visualizing Vocabulary

As a way to boost vocabulary comprehension, the principle of dual coding also lies behind such strategies as

- **Visualizing vocabulary**—Creating visual images, sketches, or icons for key words with one-sentence explanations to demonstrate understanding.
- **Deep processing**—Exploring the meaning of important terms deeply by putting the definition in one's own words, creating a simple visualization, using the hands or body to make a physical representation, or describing the feelings one associates with the term.

Math Notes

Dual coding is also a great way to improve students' mathematical problem-solving skills. The strategy known as Math Notes (pp. 212–213) helps students use both written description and visual representation to analyze and solve complex math problems.

PART FIVE

Interpersonal Strategies

Interpersonal Strategies

Interpersonal strategies concern themselves with fostering students' need to relate personally to the curriculum and to each other. They use teams, partnerships, and coaching to motivate students through their drive for membership and *relationships*.

Strategy Chapters

13. Reciprocal Learning is a strategy that increases the power of practice and learning by establishing partnerships in which students coach their peers through the learning process.

14. Decision Making is a highly personal form of comparison in which students use their own criteria and values to evaluate and make decisions.

15. Jigsaw is a cooperative strategy in which students form expert groups to conduct research on a particular area of the content, then return to their original team to teach their findings to one another.

16. Community Circle is group discussion strategy designed to build a sense of classroom togetherness, mutual respect, and emotional openness.

How does the strategy fit into unit design?
(Blueprint for Learning)

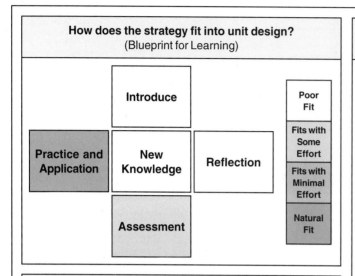

	Introduce			Poor Fit	
Practice and Application	New Knowledge	Reflection		Fits with Some Effort	
	Assessment			Fits with Minimal Effort	
				Natural Fit	

What learning styles does the strategy engage?
(Motivation/Differentiation)

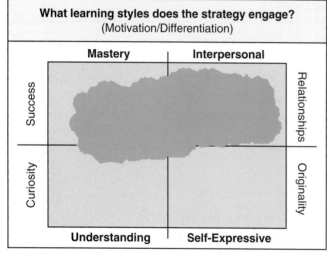

Mastery   Interpersonal

Success   Relationships

Curiosity   Originality

Understanding   Self-Expressive

What facets of understanding does the strategy develop?
(Understanding by Design)

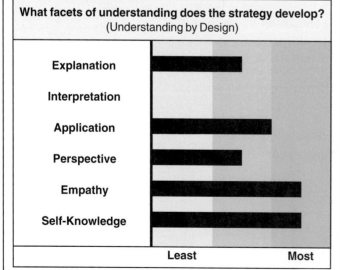

- Explanation
- Interpretation
- Application
- Perspective
- Empathy
- Self-Knowledge

Least   Most

What skills does the strategy build?
(The Hidden Skills of Academic Literacy)

Read and Study
- ○ Collect/organize ideas through note making
- ○ Make sense of abstract academic vocabulary
- ○ Read/interpret visuals

Reason and Analyze
- ○ Draw conclusions; make/test inferences, hypotheses, conjectures
- ○ Conduct comparisons using criteria
- ● Analyze demands of a variety of questions

Create and Communicate
- ○ Write clear, coherent explanations
- ○ Write comfortably in major nonfiction genres
- ○ Read and write about two or more documents

Reflect and Relate
- ○ Construct plans to address questions and tasks
- ● Use criteria and guidelines to evaluate work
- ● Control/alter mood and impulsivity

How does the strategy incorporate the research on instructional effectiveness?
(Classroom Instruction That Works)

- ○ Identifying similarities and differences
- ○ Summarizing and note taking
- ● Reinforcing effort and providing recognition
- ● Homework and practice
- ○ Nonlinguistic representation
- ● Cooperative learning
- ● Setting objectives and feedback
- ○ Generating and testing hypotheses
- ● Cues, questions, and advance organizers

What types of knowledge does the strategy teach?

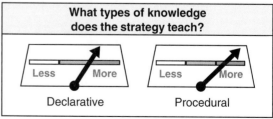

Less More	Less More
Declarative	Procedural

13

Reciprocal Learning

Strategy Overview

Think back on a great coach you have had or seen at work. How did this coach get the most out of each player? How did the players respond to the coach? Reciprocal Learning is a student-pairing strategy designed with the principles of effective coaching in mind. During a Reciprocal Learning lesson, two students form a learning partnership committed to helping each other reach a particular learning goal. Each student in the partnership plays two roles: As a *player*, each student works to complete an activity or solve a problem while "thinking out loud"; as a *coach*, each student observes the player's work and listens to the player's thinking while providing praise, feedback, and clues that help the player complete the activity. Because each student plays both roles in the partnership, the power of the learning is effectively doubled. In addition, students also develop the dispositions and skills of first-rate coaches: patience, active listening, constructive feedback, and the ability to praise and critique performances.

The Strategy in Action

Second grade teacher Raphael Figueroa knows how important reinforcing recently learned information is for his students. That's why Raphael likes the Reciprocal Learning strategy. According to Raphael, having students work as coaching and learning partners often has three major benefits:

1. It helps Raphael get a good sense of where students are with the lesson—what skills they have learned, what skills they need to better develop, and how the content has been received thus far.

2. It fosters students' mastery of key concepts and skills.

3. It sets a tone and a pace for the school year. Consistent use of Reciprocal Learning lets students know that the classroom is a place for collaboration, mutual respect, and helping each other learn.

Today, Raphael is conducting a review of what the class has learned about fractions and how they can be represented visually and mathematically. He begins the lesson by asking students to think about and share an experience when someone helped them learn something important. Students share stories about how they learned to ride a bicycle, throw and catch a baseball, and read and write. Raphael then asks students to think about the people in their stories, and how the "coach" in their stories helped them and how they responded during the process. He then writes two questions on the board: "What does a good coach do to help someone learn? What does a good learner or a good player do while being coached?"

Students gather in small groups to discuss the questions and generate responses, and then Raphael compiles student responses on the board. After a few minutes, Raphael and his students have a list of behaviors shown by good coaches and good players.

Next, Raphael explains to students that today they will be playing the role of both a coach and a player while working with another student. Raphael divides students into pairs and distributes the Reciprocal Learning worksheets (see Figure 13.1). To help students get a clearer understanding of how partnerships work, Raphael has two students—Ian and Li—model the process for the class. Raphael draws attention to what each partner does during the lesson.

Next, Raphael walks around the room while students work in their partnerships. He pays particular attention to players who are struggling. Raphael reminds players to talk out loud to expose their thinking processes, and he reminds coaches to provide praise, review the part-to-whole relationships with their players, but not give answers. For students who finish early, Raphael provides a cooperative challenge, which pairs must solve together as a team:

> Joe owns the most popular pizzeria in town, and his new Super Square pizza is everyone's favorite. The Super Square pizza is normally cut into nine square slices. After a soccer game on Saturday, Christine and Elizabeth go to Joe's for a pizza. They want to share a Super Square pizza. How can you help Joe cut the pizza so that both Christine and Elizabeth get an equal amount of square slices with no slices left over?
>
> (*Hint:* Start by drawing the regular nine-slice Super Square pizza and then try cutting it in other ways.)

FIGURE 13.1 Sample Reciprocal Learning Worksheets—Fractions

Sample Reciprocal Learning Worksheets

Notice how the answers to Player A's questions are on Player B's worksheet and vice versa. This is because while Player A is working, Player B is using his worksheet to coach Player A toward the answers. (Also, notice how the worksheets provide coaches with a clear method for helping players arrive at their answers rather than simply providing answers; coaches can help the players by keeping them focused on the number of total parts and the number of shaded parts).

Player A's Worksheet

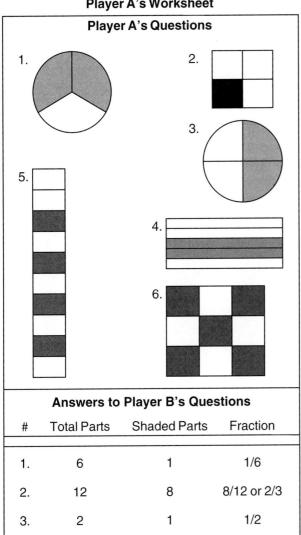

Player A's Questions

Answers to Player B's Questions

#	Total Parts	Shaded Parts	Fraction
1.	6	1	1/6
2.	12	8	8/12 or 2/3
3.	2	1	1/2
4.	4	1	1/4
5.	3	1	1/3
6.	8	4	4/8 or 1/2

Player B's Worksheet

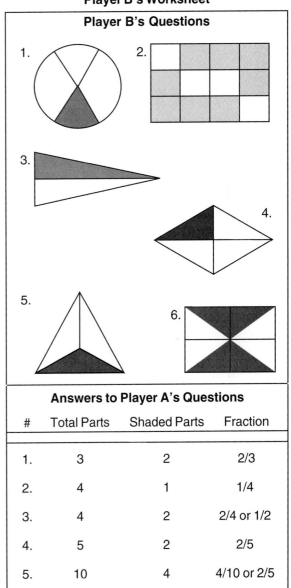

Player B's Questions

Answers to Player A's Questions

#	Total Parts	Shaded Parts	Fraction
1.	3	2	2/3
2.	4	1	1/4
3.	4	2	2/4 or 1/2
4.	5	2	2/5
5.	10	4	4/10 or 2/5
6.	9	5	5/9

When all students have completed the worksheets, Raphael leads a classroom discussion. He encourages students to reflect on the relationship between fractions represented visually and fractions represented mathematically, the cooperative challenge, as well as what they learned from the process of coaching and being coached. Raphael ends the lesson by asking students to respond by writing in their Learning Logs. The writing prompt is *What can you do to improve as a coach and as a player? Give yourself at least two suggestions for improving as a coach and two suggestions for improving as a player.*

Why the Strategy Works

The benefits of student learning partnerships are numerous and compelling. Among the findings

* Student partnerships improve students' social interactions (Butler, 1999).
* Student partnerships lead to deeper and more substantive classroom discussions (Hashey & Connors, 2003).
* Student partnerships increase students' academic intensity without adding instructional time (Fuchs, Fuchs, Mathes, & Simmons, 1997).
* Students will spend more time on a task when working with a partner than they will when working independently (King-Sears & Bradley, 1995).
* Students who work in peer partnerships make measurable academic gains and develop more positive attitudes toward subject matter (King-Sears & Bradley, 1995).
* Student partnerships lead to more productive, more genial classrooms where students are more self-directed and less dependent on the teacher (King-Sears & Bradley, 1995).
* When applied to reading, student partnerships enhance decoding skills, deepen comprehension, and help students learn how to read difficult, information-rich texts (Hashey & Connors, 2003).

Reciprocal Learning maximizes the learning and retention potential of student partnerships by asking each student to play two separate roles. As a *player,* the student attempts to complete an activity or solve a problem provided by the teacher. In this role, the student should try to think out loud—to expose his or her internal thinking process to the coach while completing the exercise. As a *coach,* the student listens to the player and provides encouragement, praise, feedback, and clues for answering questions when the player gets stuck. The coach must not provide answers. Rather, coaches should think of themselves as "thinking coaches" working to help players think out loud while leading them to the answers. This assumption of two roles on the part of each student—a player committed to mastering concepts and skills and a coach committed to shaping the player's thinking and increasing the player's proficiency—results in two times the learning. It also develops students' perspective on the dynamics and behaviors associated with successful learning and teaching.

How to Use the Strategy

1. Create a set of Reciprocal Learning sheets to distribute to each student pair.

2. Break students into pairs and model the cooperative skills needed to play the roles of coach and player.

3. Instruct Player A to work through the exercises on his sheet, while the coach uses the "Coach's Hints" on her sheet to help Player A to the answers.

4. Help the coach, not the player, if the partnership is experiencing difficulties.

5. Have students reverse roles. Player A becomes the coach, while the coach becomes Player B. Player B then works through the exercises on her sheet while Player A coaches her.

6. Include a cooperative challenge for students to solve together after they have both served as player and coach.

7. Help students reflect back on the lesson and their own roles as player and coach.

Planning a Reciprocal Learning Lesson

Putting Reciprocal Learning to work in your classroom means thinking through four planning steps:

1. **Select or design the exercises or activities.** Because most Reciprocal Learning lessons are used to review content and practice skills, the best items tend to have clear right and wrong answers. For this reason, Reciprocal Learning is ideally suited to applying spelling and grammar rules in English or any world language, solving analogies and math problems, reviewing critical vocabulary terms in a unit, and reviewing key historic and scientific concepts and facts. Reciprocal Learning can also be used to improve reading comprehension and develop problem-solving

skills. For more on these "higher-order" applications of Reciprocal Learning, see the Variations and Extensions section on page 169.

2. **Develop answers and hints.** The hints you provide coaches are entirely up to you. You can provide memory refreshers (Do you remember when we dissected the frog? Can you visualize what its heart looked like? Can you describe that?), content-oriented hints (This president also served as a general for the Union during the Civil War), or the steps in an algorithm or process (Remember: Order of Operations follow the steps in the acronym "Please Excuse My Dear Aunt Sally"). Encourage coaches to be creative and develop clues of their own as well.

3. **Design the worksheets students will receive.** Whether you choose to put each student's questions and answers on one sheet or multiple sheets, remember this simple rule: Player A gets a set of questions/activities and the hints and answers to Player B's questions and activities. Players B gets a set of questions/activities and the hints and answers to Player A's questions and activities.

Try to include a "cooperative challenge" question at the bottom of each worksheet. The two students can work on the cooperative challenge together (no more coach, no more player—partners on equal footing) while they wait for other pairs to finish the initial exercises. Cooperative challenges tend to require more effort and more analytical thinking than the regular activities on the worksheets. Cooperative challenges can be short-answer questions, challenging problems, or mini-synthesis tasks. For example, after using Reciprocal Learning to review the imperfect and subjunctive tenses, a Spanish teacher posed this cooperative challenge to student pairs:

- How does the past tense differ from the imperfect and subjunctive tenses?
- Now, translate your answer into Spanish.

4. **Decide how you will assign partners and arrange the classroom.** You should probably establish partnerships randomly to eliminate the chances that a student will feel left out because no one picked him or her as a partner. Plan to have students change partners frequently as you continue to use the strategy. Changing partners establishes an important message about your expectations for cooperation: In your classroom, everyone works together.

As teachers, we sometimes assume that students know each other just because they are members of the same class, but this is not usually the case. Plan to help partners get to know each other. You might want to design a simple warm-up question (Whom do you most admire? What foreign country would you most like to visit?) to allow the partners to interact before starting the lesson.

Some other considerations include time (How long will students work in partnerships?) and the seating plan for the lesson. Because students feel more like members of a team when they sit side-by-side, the ideal seating arrangement has players sitting next to their coaches. In this position, the coach is able to observe the player's work clearly. When students sit opposite each other, the atmosphere seems more adverse, and the player may feel that the coach is correcting and judging rather than helping.

Variations and Extensions

In its most traditional form, Reciprocal Learning serves as a review and practice strategy with activities designed around objective exercises or the demonstration of a particular skill. However, both research and classroom practice demonstrate that the strategy has a significant impact when applied to building reading comprehension and developing problem-solving skills. In this section, we discuss two variations of Reciprocal Learning dedicated to reading and solving difficult problems— Peer Reading and Peer Problem Solving.

Peer Reading

Research shows that when applied to reading, Reciprocal Learning can play a major role in helping students read and summarize difficult passages (Hashey & Connors, 2003). This application of the strategy is called Peer Reading, and it is especially useful in helping students overcome the reading challenges typically associated with textbooks and dense nonfiction writing: too many details, difficulty in separating the essential from the nonessential information, or no sense of the overall structure of the text.

Peer Reading involves seven steps:

1. Select a reading and break it up into manageable sections.
2. For each section, create a question or a set of questions that will require a pair of students (Reader A and Reader B) to summarize the section. For example, 4th grade teacher Paul Costas developed this set of questions for a reading called "Surviving Everest."
   - Section 1 Questions (for Reader A)
     What factors make Mount Everest so dangerous to climb?
     How do climbers survive with so little oxygen?
   - Section 2 Question (for Reader B)
     What are the effects of the jet stream on climbers who reach the top of Mount Everest?

- ◦ Section 3 Question (for Reader A)

  What can climbers do to prepare for the extreme cold and high winds?
- ◦ Section 4 Questions (for Reader B)

  What happens once a climber reaches the Death Zone?

  Why is it more dangerous to climb down Mount Everest than to climb up it?

3. Divide students into pairs. Distribute the reading and the summarizing questions to students.

4. Ask students to read the first section, mark their text, and then review and summarize in coaching partnerships (Reader A puts her reading away while the coach asks the summarizing questions and uses his marked text to coach Reader A to a more complete answer).

5. Instruct students to continue reading the text in sections, reversing roles as reader and coach for each section.

6. When they have finished reading, have students use the questions and their marked texts to create a summary together.

7. Encourage student independence by modeling and coaching students through the process of breaking readings into manageable chunks and creating summarizing questions to test comprehension.

Peer Problem Solving

As Whimbey and Lochhead (1999) have shown, student partnerships are also a great way to build students' skills as problem solvers. In a Peer Problem-Solving lesson, each student is given a challenging, nonroutine problem to solve. For example, the two students in a Peer Problem-Solving pair might receive the two problems shown in Figure 13.2. Each student is also provided with the answer to the other partner's problem, along with a set of tips for coaching the partner to the answer. Answers and tips are shown in Figure 13.2.

Before meeting in player–coach partnerships, all coaches (remember: every student is a coach) meet in small groups with other coaches. These coach's groups solve their player's problem cooperatively and generate any additional clues that they think might be useful in helping their players solve the problem. Then, students form the partnership, and one student becomes the problem solver. The problem solver's job is to solve the problem while describing his or her thinking process out loud. The other student is the coach. The coach's job is to keep the problem solver talking, listen carefully to what the problem solver says, and use what has been learned in the coach's groups to provide hints and help clarify the problem solver's thinking. Roles are then reversed for the second problem.

FIGURE 13.2   Sample Peer Problem Solving Problems

Partner A's Problem

A farmer has some land that is to be divided equally among his four children into four parcels. His land is shown below. The parcels must be the same shape and size. Draw the four parcels on the figure below.

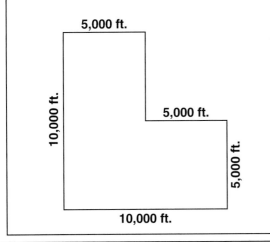

Partner B's Problem

You have eight balls, all of which look exactly the same. Seven of them weigh the same, but one is slightly lighter than the others. You have a scale to balance the balls. How can you find out which is the lighter ball in only two weighings?

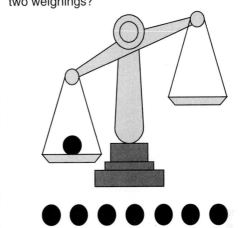

Hints and Answers to Partner A's Problem

Hints

A. Suggest that your partner consider dividing the property into three equal parts.

B. Then, divide each of three parcels into four smaller parts.

C. Have your partner count the total number of smaller parts (there should be 12). Next, tell your partner to divide the 12 parts by 4 since there are 4 children.

D. Finally, have your partner arrange the little parts in such a way that all of the children receive a parcel of the same shape.

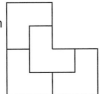

Hints and Answers to Partner B's Problem

Hints

1. Most people try to weigh all eight balls at once.

2. How can you figure out which is lightest if you only have three balls?

Answer

1. Weigh six balls (three on each side).

2. If they weigh the same, then the lighter ball must be one of the two balls not weighed. Weigh the remaining two balls to see which is lighter.

3. If the three balls from Step 1 are of different weights, weigh two of the three balls that were on the lighter side. If they weigh the same, the ball that is left is the lighter ball. If one weighs less, you have found the lighter ball.

Source: From *Teaching Styles and Strategies* (pp. 207–210), by H. Silver, R. Hanson, R. Strong, and P. Schwartz, 2003, Ho-Ho-Kus, NJ: Thoughtful Education Press. Adapted with permission.

How does the strategy fit into unit design?
(Blueprint for Learning)

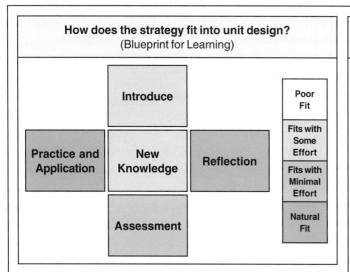

	Introduce	Poor Fit
Practice and Application	New Knowledge	Reflection	Fits with Some Effort
		Fits with Minimal Effort
	Assessment	Natural Fit

What learning styles does the strategy engage?
(Motivation/Differentiation)

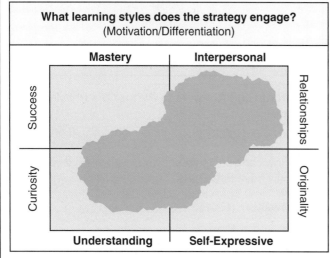

Mastery | Interpersonal
Success
Relationships
Curiosity
Originality
Understanding | Self-Expressive

What facets of understanding does the strategy develop?
(Understanding by Design)

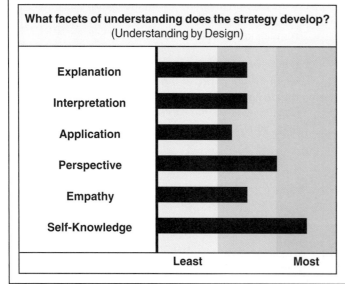

Explanation
Interpretation
Application
Perspective
Empathy
Self-Knowledge

Least — Most

What skills does the strategy build?
(The Hidden Skills of Academic Literacy)

Read and Study
- ● Collect/organize ideas through note making
- ○ Make sense of abstract academic vocabulary
- ○ Read/interpret visuals

Reason and Analyze
- ● Draw conclusions; make/test inferences, hypotheses, conjectures
- ● Conduct comparisons using criteria
- ○ Analyze demands of a variety of questions

Create and Communicate
- ○ Write clear, coherent explanations
- ● Write comfortably in major nonfiction genres*
- ● Read and write about two or more documents

Reflect and Relate
- ○ Construct plans to address questions and tasks
- ● Use criteria and guidelines to evaluate work
- ● Control/alter mood and impulsivity

How does the strategy incorporate the research on instructional effectiveness?
(Classroom Instruction That Works)

- ● Identifying similarities and differences
- ● Summarizing and note taking
- ○ Reinforcing effort and providing recognition
- ○ Homework and practice
- ○ Nonlinguistic representation
- ○ Cooperative learning
- ○ Setting objectives and feedback
- ● Generating and testing hypotheses
- ○ Cues, questions, and advance organizers

What types of knowledge does the strategy teach?

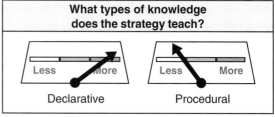

Less — More   Less — More
Declarative   Procedural

*Decision Making builds students' capacities on writing tasks that ask them to make and justify personal decisions.

14

Decision Making

Strategy Overview

Decision making is a skill that is at once highly personal and deeply analytical, academic and integral to everyday life, easy to take for granted and critical to individual success. We are all forced to make decisions every day, from the little decisions in the grocery store aisle to the far-reaching decisions that affect our lives, our careers, and our families.

The Decision Making strategy hones this critical skill by providing students with a unique opportunity to become personally involved in what they are studying through questions such as these:

- Who was the most influential president of the United States?
- If you were in the position of Tim from *My Brother Sam Is Dead,* whose side would you take in the argument between Sam and Father?
- Based on statistics, which player would you want to shoot a free throw with the game on the line?

In addition to inviting students "into" the content, where they are more likely to develop powerful insights, Decision Making also teaches students a strategic approach to making informed decisions, which they can apply to other content, controversial topics, and their lives beyond the school walls.

The Strategy in Action

High school science teacher Maya LeVond thinks most students take science for granted. According to Maya:

Too many students aren't making the connection. They text-message each other on their cell phones, they surf the Internet, they download thousands of songs and videos on their MP3 players, and then they grumble through their science classes. They forget how much science has affected their lives, how much we all depend on it every day.

A few years back, I came to the conclusion that students weren't paying attention to the connection among science, technology, and their own lives because no one was asking them to explore that link. So, I decided to make more time to engage students in thinking about science personally, as something they should reflect on and make decisions about. The Decision Making strategy is a great way to get students involved in science—without sacrificing either content or careful thinking to the personal.

Today, Maya is using Decision Making to help her students analyze the impact of some of the most far-reaching scientific developments of the last 100 years. After breaking students up into groups of four, Maya provides each group with a manila folder containing the following items:

• **A hook to the lesson.** For its annual "Ranking the Greats" series, Public Airwaves Inc. wants to produce a documentary on the five most influential scientific developments of the last 100 years. From the millions of scientific inventions, discoveries, ideas, and contributions, the production company has selected five for your consideration: *global communication, atomic theory, air travel, genetics,* and *computers.* However, the committee is uncertain about how to rank these selections and has hired your firm, Scientific Perspectives, to develop a system for ranking the five selections.

• **A case study showing how an expert uses criteria to make decisions.** Maya distributes a section from the introduction to historian Michael Hart's 1992 book, *The 100: A Ranking of the Most Influential Persons in History,* in which Hart describes the criteria he used to make his selections. As students review Hart's criteria, Maya makes it clear that students are not to copy them. Rather, the groups review Hart's criteria and justifications so that they can see what well-formulated criteria look like and "hear" the thinking that goes on during the selection process.

• **A set of five "briefs" discussing the origins and influence of each of the five scientific developments under consideration.** For example, an excerpt from the brief on air travel appears in Figure 14.1, p. 175.

Students read the five briefs twice. The purpose of the first reading is to allow students to become familiar with the content so that they can formulate a list of criteria for ranking the five scientific developments. Each student group must agree on four criteria and provide a justification for each of their selections. The second reading is a closer reading, during which students use their criteria to help them decide how to rank the five developments.

• **A Comparative Decision Making Matrix to help students rank the developments systematically (see Figure 14.2, p. 176).** As student groups discuss their thinking and negotiate their selections, Maya sits in

FIGURE 14.1   Air Travel

Air Travel

In an average year, a modern airport can move more than 1.5 million metric tons of freight and service over 70 million passengers. Air traffic has increased greatly in recent years, and the demands on air travel continue to grow. Manufacturers are looking to design new airplanes that can carry more people and travel longer distances. The newest and largest airplane is the Airbus 350, which has a wingspan that is nearly the length of a football field. The airplane has two decks, four aisles, cocktail lounges, and business conference rooms. The Airbus 350 can carry 555 passengers with half the noise and greater fuel efficiency than its closest competitor, the Boeing 747.

---

on various groups, helping them to cite evidence, draw conclusions, and reach consensus on their rankings. Once students have developed their criteria and applied them by completing the matrix, Maya gives them their synthesis task:

> Now that you've all ranked our five developments, you will need to make your recommendations to the production committee. Each of you must write a brief letter to the committee. Make sure your letter tells the committee about your group's process for developing criteria, the justification behind your rankings, and a special explanation as to why you think the development you chose to top your list is particularly influential.

Why the Strategy Works

Of all the forms of comparative thinking (comparison, classification, metaphors, analogies, etc.), decision making is the most personal and perhaps the most engaging. The Decision Making strategy requires students to examine a problem or situation, and then make and justify a decision. In making their decisions, students become personally connected to the content they are studying. The strategy helps students recognize the value of a systematic way of examining alternatives and helps them gain confidence in their own decision-making abilities.

Recent research makes clear both the value and benefits of classroom decision-making strategies. The work of Jimenez-Aleixandre and Pereiro-Munoz (2002) shows that learning through decision making leads to higher levels of conceptual understanding because it lets students access and manipulate content through the lens of their own personal value system. Other researchers, including Rowland and Adkins (1992) and Naftel (1993), stress the importance of providing students—who are in the process of developing their own set of ethics to guide real-life decisions—with opportunities to practice making decisions and evaluating the results in the safety of the classroom. What these researchers have found is that students who are encouraged to develop good decision-making skills and habits carry those skills and habits into their lives beyond the classroom.

FIGURE 14.2   Comparative/Decision Making Matrix

For each criterion, rank each development 1–5 (1 being the development that most fits that criterion). For example, if one of your criterion is *most people affected by the development*, you might rank global communication 1, computers 2, air travel 3, atomic theory 4, and genetics 5. The lowest score at the end will be your most influential development. In case of a tie, establish other criterion and use it to break the tie.

How does each development meet your criteria?
(Rank 1–5: 1 fits criterion most, 5 fits least)

	Criterion 1:	Criterion 2:	Criterion 3:	Criterion 4:
Global Communication				
Atomic Theory				
Computers				
Air Travel				
Genetics				

SCIENTIFIC DEVELOPMENT

Depending on your content and objectives, Decision Making lessons can be designed to highlight different forms of thinking, from developing a personal ranking system (*Who is the greatest U.S. president?*), to wrestling with ethical and moral dilemmas (*What do you think of George's decision to shoot Lenny at the end of* Of Mice and Men? *What would you have done if you were George?*), to analyzing data (*After analyzing each computer's "spec sheet," decide which computer is the best value*). Regardless of the thinking they emphasize, all good Decision Making lessons revolve around four principles: background knowledge, alternatives, criteria, and reflection.

The Principle of Background Knowledge

The more students know about a situation, the better they are able to understand the alternatives that are available to them. Good decision making requires a broad base of knowledge from which to extract relevant information. By providing students with good background information, you help them develop a deeper and more comprehensive perspective, and you enable them to eliminate particularly unfeasible alternatives.

The Principle of Alternatives

Decision making means choosing among alternatives. Students need options in order to make choices. By exploring given alternatives or establishing their own, students see the range of possibilities and learn that many different solutions are possible.

The Principle of Criteria

Decisions are based on criteria, implicit or explicit. The more students are able to articulate the criteria, the easier it becomes to analyze the alternatives. Clearly stated criteria help students to weed out impractical or weak alternatives. In addition, when students select or create criteria, they naturally align them with their own value systems.

The Principle of Reflection

By examining their own and others' decision-making processes, students are able to refine their decision-making skills. Because decision making is a lifelong process that is constantly tested under new circumstances, active reflection becomes a crucial tool in adapting the decision-making process to varying situations.

How to Use the Strategy

1. Introduce the lesson and its purpose, and explain what students will do during the lesson. To hook students' interest, you may want to lead a discussion in which students recall their own decision-making experiences.

2. Provide or present students with the background information or information sources they will need to conduct a thorough analysis of the situation and the alternatives. Clarify questions and review critical issues and concepts with students.

3. Present, or generate with students, the alternatives and the criteria for analyzing the alternatives.

4. Instruct students to compare the alternatives, take notes, and make a decision.

5. Allow students to communicate their decisions and their justifications in small groups, as part of a whole-class discussion, or through a synthesis task.

6. Provide time for students to reflect and share their personal thoughts and feelings about the content and their decision-making process.

Planning a Decision Making Lesson

To plan a Decision Making lesson for your classroom, follow these steps:

1. **Determine the content you would like students to explore and make decisions about.** Decision Making can be applied to three different types of content:
   - Moral and ethical dilemmas (e.g., evaluating the political, ethical, and human implications in using the atomic bomb during World War II).
   - Content that includes several alternatives (e.g., analyzing systems of garbage disposal and deciding which is the best for the town).
   - Data analysis (e.g., examining a wide range of statistical data to decide which basketball player is the most accurate and dependable shooter).

While most decision making involves all three of these elements—moral and ethical dilemmas, several alternatives, and data analysis—most lessons emphasize one over the others. This means that shaping your lesson is generally a matter of focus:
   - Is the moral angle the most essential to your content?
   - Is the careful consideration of alternatives and their implications at the center?
   - Is the analysis of hard data the critical element?

2. **Decide how the question, dilemma, or situation and the alternatives will be presented to students.** It is always a good idea to present the lesson to students in a way that is interesting and authentic. For example, the teacher who designed a Decision Making lesson on finding the best system of garbage disposal placed students within the context of a community dispute between townspeople, taxpayers' organizations, contractors, and environmental agencies. Thus, students were challenged by an authentic context containing varying sets of interests and demands that led them to consider the issue more deeply.

You should also look for ways to link the issue at hand to your students' genuine interests or concerns. For example, by placing students in the context of a close basketball game where a free-throw shooter has the chance to tie or win the game, a math teacher can create a realistic and engrossing situation. This identification with the context facilitates the lesson process, as students will begin examining rather complex statistical data with greatly increased interest.

Once you have thought about how you want to present the situation, it's time to consider how you will present the various alternatives. Possibilities include presenting the alternatives yourself, allowing students to conduct research and generate their own alternatives, and working with students to generate the alternatives together.

3. **Decide if students will be decision makers or decision evaluators.** Although the roles are similar, decision making (e.g., selecting the best

garbage disposal system) fosters greater personal identification with the content, because it requires students to project themselves into the role and to make decisions on their own. Decision evaluation (e.g., evaluating Truman's decision to use the atomic bomb) implies greater distance from the material in that students are examining the decisions of others, rather than making their own decisions. You may also want students to play both roles and to reflect on the differences between the two.

4. **Identify the information sources students will need to make an informed decision.** Both decision makers and decision evaluators require information to begin their exploration of content. In designing your lesson, make sure you identify what sources of information students will need to make a thoughtful decision. Are their notes, memories, and class texts enough, or will supplementary sources be needed? Remember that supplementary sources need not be books and reference texts. Videos, lectures, experiments, demonstrations, maps, graphs, Web sites, and many others are all great sources of information.

5. **Select or develop the criteria that students will use to compare and contrast alternatives.** Criteria provide students with explicit guidelines for judging how positive or negative the outcomes of each alternative might be. Depending on your purposes and the roles students will play, you may establish criteria for your students or encourage them to design their own. Criteria may also be weighted according to importance.

6. **Decide how the decision will be communicated.** Decision Making lends itself to a variety of product formats. Students can communicate their decisions and the thinking process they used in making those decisions through oral presentations, persuasive essays, debates, role playing, legal briefs, or other synthesis tasks.

Variations and Extensions

The techniques you will find in this section serve two purposes. First, they can be used "on the fly" as tools to engage students in active learning and build decision-making skills. In addition, these techniques can be planned into Decision Making lessons, where they can enhance student learning in alignment with your larger goals and objectives.

Physical Barometer

Physical Barometer gives students an opportunity to take a public position on a particular issue, to see where others stand on the same issue, and to discuss their points of view with those who hold similar and opposing views. When using this technique, the teacher designates areas of the room to represent different opinions or the relative strength of students' opinions. For example, five different areas of the classroom could represent five different strengths of opinion: strongly agree, agree, neutral (or need to know more), disagree, and strongly disagree. Once room sections have been assigned, the teacher makes a statement such as, "Hunting black bears is a humane way to control their population and protect people." Students move to the area of the room that reflects their opinion on hunting.

Next, the teacher asks the students in each area to discuss with the others standing with them the reasons for their position. Each group explains its position to the entire class. After the explanations, the groups can ask questions of one other. At the end of the activity, students may change their positions provided they explain what influenced them to do so.

Priority Pyramid

Thoughtful decision making often requires us to reflect on our own priorities and values. Priority Pyramid helps students build this reflective capacity by presenting them with a set of items, which they must prioritize according to personal importance. Students are then asked to explain how they made their decisions. For example, students might be asked to use a pyramid-shaped organizer to prioritize the following items: education, friends, financial security, job satisfaction, health, vacation, and house. Students would then write a brief justification for their top choice.

Consensus Building

In group decision making, members must have a thorough and open discussion regarding alternatives in order to make the best possible decision. Only when all possibilities are exposed and examined can we assume that all the information needed to make a decision is on the table. In addition, only when every member of the group has had an opportunity to express his or her recommendations and rationale should group members be willing to consider other points of view. When modeling Consensus Building, the teacher should provide students with a written copy of its rules. Even better, post the rules in the classroom:

1. Work in groups of four to five students each.
2. Remember that every student in the group gets an equal opportunity to share information, ideas, and concerns.
3. Keep in mind that exploring different opinions helps foster discussion and leads to more innovative and effective solutions.
4. Work through the impasse by looking for the most acceptable outcome for everyone. Don't give up on your positions simply to avoid conflict.
5. Avoid taking the easy way out through arbitrary techniques like flipping a coin, picking an idea out of a hat, or taking a straw poll.

Rank Order

In the Rank Order technique, students examine and rank objective data according to specified criteria.

> Rank these countries first in terms of population and then in terms of landmass: China, Japan, Indonesia, United States, Nigeria, and Brazil. Use your rankings to determine which country has the most pronounced population problem.

After students complete their ranking, they should explain and justify their reasoning. The teacher should discuss with students the criteria they used to rank their choices and the importance of using a logical process when making decisions.

Decision Making Matrix

The Decision Making Matrix is a tool used by students to systematically analyze and choose among alternatives. With the Decision Making Matrix, students make decisions by devising a mathematical rating system. Across the top of the matrix, students list the alternatives that will be analyzed. Down the left side of the matrix, students list the attributes they will consider in choosing among the alternatives. For each attribute, students determine its importance by assigning it a numeric "weight" (3 = very important, 2 = important, 1 = unimportant). Once the rows and columns of the matrix are complete, students analyze each alternative against the attribute listed, also through a simple numerical system (3 = meets the attribute completely, 2 = meets the attribute to a great extent, 1 = meets the attribute somewhat, 0 = doesn't meet the attribute at all). Students multiply the numbers, tally the results, and use the totals to make the decision. Figure 14.3 shows how a student used a Decision Making Matrix to choose the best MP3 player.

FIGURE 14.3   Student's Decision Making Matrix for MP3 Players

Attributes	Importance 3 = Very Important 2 = Important 1 = Unimportant	Manufacturers of MP3 Players		
		iRiver	Creative Labs	Apple
		These MP3 players meet each attribute: 3 = Completely 2 = Considerably 1 = Somewhat 0 = Not At All		
Price	3	2 x 3 = 6	3 x 3 = 9	1 x 3 = 3
Storage Capacity	3	2 x 3 = 6	2 x 3 = 6	3 x 3 = 9
FM Tuner	1	3 x 1 = 3	3 x 1 = 3	0 x 1 = 0
Screen (Size & Color)	2	2 x 2 = 4	1 x 2 = 2	3 x 2 = 6
Battery Life	1	3 x 1 = 3	3 x 1 = 3	2 x 1 = 2
Colors & Accesories	2	2 x 2 = 4	3 x 2 = 6	2 x 2 = 4
Total Score		26	29	24

Based on my analysis, the Creative Labs MP3 player is the best choice for me.

How does the strategy fit into unit design?
(Blueprint for Learning)

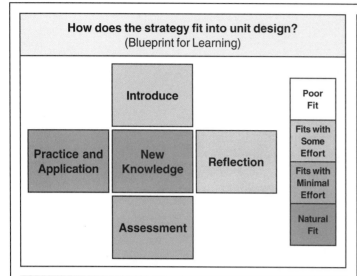

Introduce	Poor Fit
Practice and Application	Fits with Some Effort
New Knowledge	Fits with Minimal Effort
Reflection	Natural Fit
Assessment	

What learning styles does the strategy engage?
(Motivation/Differentiation)

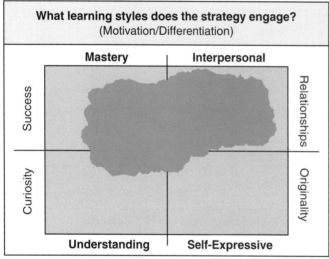

Mastery — Interpersonal
Success — Relationships
Curiosity — Originality
Understanding — Self-Expressive

What facets of understanding does the strategy develop?
(Understanding by Design)

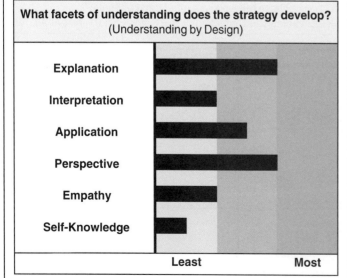

- Explanation
- Interpretation
- Application
- Perspective
- Empathy
- Self-Knowledge

Least — Most

What skills does the strategy build?
(The Hidden Skills of Academic Literacy)

Read and Study
- ● Collect/organize ideas through note making
- ○ Make sense of abstract academic vocabulary
- ○ Read/interpret visuals

Reason and Analyze
- ● Draw conclusions; make/test inferences, hypotheses, conjectures
- ○ Conduct comparisons using criteria
- ● Analyze demands of a variety of questions

Create and Communicate
- ● Write clear, coherent explanations
- ○ Write comfortably in major nonfiction genres
- ○ Read and write about two or more documents

Reflect and Relate
- ● Construct plans to address questions and tasks
- ○ Use criteria and guidelines to evaluate work
- ● Control/alter mood and impulsivity

How does the strategy incorporate the research on instructional effectiveness?
(Classroom Instruction That Works)

- ○ Identifying similarities and differences
- ● Summarizing and note taking
- ● Reinforcing effort and providing recognition
- ○ Homework and practice
- ○ Nonlinguistic representation
- ● Cooperative learning
- ○ Setting objectives and feedback
- ○ Generating and testing hypotheses
- ○ Cues, questions, and advance organizers

What types of knowledge does the strategy teach?

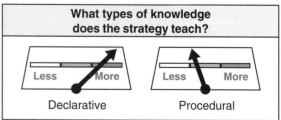

Less — More | Less — More
Declarative | Procedural

15

Jigsaw

Strategy Overview

Many of today's most successful companies have rejected "cubicle culture" and instead restructured their workforces into self-managed teams. What these businesses have learned is that when employees collaborate in pursuit of a common goal, worker satisfaction, company morale, and productivity increase across the board. The same idea holds true in school: Students who are well versed in the skills of cooperative learning—skills like active listening, effective communication, consensus building, and conflict resolution—are better able to solve challenging problems, formulate clear and cogent opinions, and produce first-rate work. Moreover, as the workforce of the future, students who can understand and work effectively with their peers hold a significant advantage over students whose academic life is marked largely by independent seatwork.

In this chapter, we explore the strategy known as Jigsaw, a highly effective cooperative learning strategy. Jigsaw teaches research, communication, planning, and general cooperative skills by having students

• Join a "Jigsaw Team" comprised of three to five students, each of whom takes responsibility for becoming an expert in one aspect or subtopic of the content.

• Join an expert group to conduct research on their assigned subtopic.

• Work with their expert groups to develop a plan for teaching what they have learned back to the Jigsaw team.

• Collaboratively construct the "big picture" by teaching their subtopic to the Jigsaw team and learning about the other subtopics from other members of the Jigsaw team.

The Strategy in Action

"Jigsaw is a real workhorse," says middle school science teacher Carl Carrozza:

> It builds research skills. It builds communication and reporting skills. It builds interpersonal and cooperative skills. It allows students to acquire and master a large amount of information in a relatively short time. But what I've discovered over the years is that it's more than just a strategy for teaching a particular lesson. In fact, I like to design mini-units, say three to five days in length, around Jigsaw.

Carl is beginning one such mini-unit on reptiles. After an introductory activity in which students were asked to consider how a frog would need to adapt or evolve if it were to live on land (in effect by "becoming" a reptile), Carl delivers a New American Lecture on reptiles. The lecture is built on students' already-acquired knowledge of amphibians and, after a basic overview of reptilian characteristics, follows a comparative structure outlining the similarities and differences between reptiles and amphibians.

The next day, Carl explains to his students that they will be responsible for learning and teaching the key content of the rest of the unit using the Jigsaw technique. During the unit, students will seek answers to two essential questions:

- What kinds of reptiles are there?
- How do reptiles adapt to their environment?

Once he sets up his unit in this way, here's how Carl uses Jigsaw to implement the remainder of the unit:

1. First, he breaks students up into Jigsaw teams of four and provides each student with a general research organizer that divides the content into clear chunks (see Figure 15.1, p. 185). Carl then reviews the Jigsaw process with students, reminding them that each member of the team will become an expert in one major aspect of the content and will teach that aspect back to the Jigsaw team.

2. Carl then has each Jigsaw team decide which students will develop expertise in which topics. However, to ensure that experts do not conduct their research too narrowly by focusing on only one order of reptile and perhaps lose sight of the bigger picture of adaptation, Carl establishes the topics for expertise around each of the four adaptations. Thus, each member of the Jigsaw team becomes one of the following: a food expert, a temperature and water expert, a survival expert, or a child-rearing expert. This way, students have to search for relevant information across all four orders of reptiles.

3. Experts in each topic meet with the experts in the same topic from the other Jigsaw teams. Together, experts search for the relevant information and collect it on their experts' research organizer (see Figure 15.2, p. 186). Carl uses two different organizers because he has learned that the general grid organizer helps students see the content at a glance, but a separate, question-based organizer for the experts spurs students to go deeper in their search for answers. This organizer also keeps students focused on the ultimate goal of their research: presenting the answers they find back to their Jigsaw teams.

4. For their research, expert groups begin by consulting their textbooks. However, Carl also talks with students about the potential shortcomings of research driven by a textbook only, and he encourages students to consult a range of resources from around the room, including books, articles, and the Internet. After the expert groups agree that they have collected all of the necessary information, they develop a plan for teaching what they have learned back to their Jigsaw teams. As expert groups plan, Carl meets with the expert groups to help them develop sound and engaging plans that are organized around the big ideas and relevant details. Finally, all expert groups must submit three suggested test questions based on their topic—two short-answer questions and one constructed-response question that members believe captures the most important idea in their topic.

5. Experts return to their original Jigsaw teams. Experts take turns teaching their lessons to the members of the Jigsaw team, who record the information in the appropriate grids of their general research organizers (see Figure 15.1). During this "lesson day," Carl circulates around

FIGURE 15.1   General Research Organizer—Reptiles

	Food	Temperature/ Water	Survival	Child Rearing
Lizards				
Snakes				
Turtles				
Crocodiles or Alligators				

FIGURE 15.2   Experts' Research Organizer—Reptiles

Food Experts:	Child-Rearing Experts:
What kind of food is eaten and how is it caught? Lizards: Snakes: Turtles: Crocodiles or Alligators:	What are the patterns of reproduction, nesting, and child care? Lizards: Snakes: Turtles: Crocodiles or Alligators:
Temperature and Water Experts:	**Survival Experts:**
How are reptiles adapted to life on land? How do reptiles react and/or adapt to temperature variations? Lizards: Snakes: Turtles: Crocodiles or Alligators:	What kind of defense is used by each type of reptile for survival? Lizards: Snakes: Turtles: Crocodiles or Alligators:

the room and observes the lessons in progress. After all of the lessons have been presented, Carl conducts a follow-up lesson in which experts are called upon to act as leaders in a discussion focused on the most important topics.

6. To complete the unit, Carl

- tests students' understanding through a mastery test based on the expert groups' suggested questions. To ensure both individual and group accountability, Carl gives students an individual grade, Jigsaw teams a team grade, and bonus points to the expert group that did the best job of teaching its material (as revealed by all students' test scores). For example, A.J. received 89 points for his individual score; because A.J.'s Jigsaw team got the second-highest overall score, A.J. received another 2 points; and because the class as a whole "aced" the section of the test related to A.J.'s expert-group subtopic, A.J. received an additional bonus of 1 point. Group scores are posted on a leader's board at the front of the room.

- holds a discussion in which students reflect on and evaluate the Jigsaw process and their own performance. In their Learning Logs, students record their thoughts and questions, and make suggestions to themselves for improving their performance next time.

- gives students an opportunity to apply their new learning creatively and comprehensively by asking them to return to their

Jigsaw teams to complete a synthesis task involving a real-world context (e.g., Design a reptile that could live in a cold climate for the Natural History Museum's new exhibit teaching the public about adaptation).

Why the Strategy Works

Of all the instructional methods teachers use in their classrooms, cooperative learning is probably the most thoroughly researched. Marzano, Pickering, and Pollock (2001) include it in *Classroom Instruction That Works* as one of the nine instructional methods proven by research to make a significant difference in student performance. Ellis and Fouts (1997) claim that, of all the educational practices backed by research studies, cooperative learning has the "best and largest empirical base" (p. 173). In addition, citing their meta-analysis of over 375 studies, Johnson, Johnson, and Holubec (1994) show that cooperative learning consistently yields higher levels of achievement than either competitive or independent learning.

The research backing cooperative learning is not only exhaustive; it is also eye-catching in terms of its benefits. Among the findings

- Cooperative learning leads to peer norms that promote academic excellence. This is critical because peer norms drive adolescent behavior (Slavin, 1995).
- Teachers that employ cooperative learning regularly report increases in student motivation, peer cooperation, and academic performance (Slavin & Cooper, 1999).
- Cooperative learning leads to increased student capacity for demonstrating high-level reasoning, generating new solutions, and applying learning in new contexts (Johnson & Johnson, 1999).
- Cooperative learning nurtures the development of peer relationships among diverse students (Johnson & Johnson, 1999).

Jigsaw is one of the most well-known and most effective of all cooperative learning strategies. In the original version of Jigsaw (Aronson et al., 1978), students work together in heterogeneous Jigsaw teams to learn content that has been broken up into chunks (for example, a primary teacher might break a lesson on seasons up into winter, spring, summer, and fall). Each member of the Jigsaw team is assigned one of these chunks to master. Members from each Jigsaw team who have been assigned the same chunk form expert groups that help each other learn (or research) the material and develop a plan to teach it back to their original Jigsaw teams. Experts then return to their Jigsaw teams and take turns teaching their area of expertise to the members of the team. For evaluations of learning, the teacher gives students a quiz, and grading is based on individual performance.

More recently, Robert Slavin (1986) developed Jigsaw II. Jigsaw II strengthens the connection between group effectiveness and individual performance by introducing a group reward structure. Students receive an individual grade and a team grade determined by adding the test scores of all members of each Jigsaw team. Team scores then serve as the basis for a competition among the Jigsaw teams. While both methods have been shown to improve students' self-esteem, relationships with other students, motivation, and academic performance, Jigsaw II tends to yield better results (Slavin, 1995). To get even better results, we also suggest giving a bonus score to some of the expert groups to promote quality teaching: When students perform well on the portion of the test that corresponds to an expert group's subtopic, it signals that members of the expert group have done a good job teaching its content back to the Jigsaw teams.

How to Use the Strategy

1. Divide students into heterogeneous Jigsaw teams of three to five students each. Each Jigsaw team member will be responsible for one subtopic of the content. Provide an organizer that makes these subtopics clear.

2. Allow students from each Jigsaw team to meet with students from other Jigsaw teams who are responsible for the same subtopic.

3. Instruct the members of these expert groups to use the provided resources to conduct research on their subtopics. After individual research, expert group members assemble to review, discuss, and determine the most important concepts.

4. Work with expert groups to develop a plan to teach their subtopic back to the Jigsaw team, and have all expert groups draft a set of questions related to their subtopic for use on the test.

5. Reassemble Jigsaw teams. Have experts take turns teaching their subtopic while the other Jigsaw members record key information on their organizer. Circulate and observe these student-led discussions to ensure key ideas are being covered.

6. Lead a discussion or follow-up session covering the entire topic.

7. Develop a quiz or test based on the questions submitted by expert groups. Provide students with two grades—an individual grade and a team grade (found by adding the test scores of all the members of the Jigsaw team). Provide bonus scores to any groups whose subtopic content was "aced" by the class. To increase the sense of competition, post team scores and provide recognition for high-achieving Jigsaw teams and expert groups.

Planning a Jigsaw Lesson

In planning a Jigsaw lesson, you will need to consider the questions on the following pages:

1. **What topics lend themselves to the Jigsaw format?** Typically, Jigsaw lessons are designed around topics with three to five natural divisions or subtopics: the three branches of government, the four main parts of speech (noun, verb, adjective, and adverb), or the four major U.S. coins. Of course, many other creative divisions within any content are possible. For example, in order to teach students about the consequences of the American Revolution while working to develop students' skills in interpreting different forms of historical data, high school history teacher Sherry Gibbon developed a Jigsaw lesson around Howard Gardner's model of multiple intelligences (Gardner, 1999):

- The *Eyes-On Team* studied a portfolio of maps (spatial intelligence).
- The *Personal History Team* studied excerpts from diaries and personal biographies (intrapersonal, linguistic intelligence).
- The *Policy Team* studied excerpts from policy documents (logical-mathematical, linguistic intelligence).
- The *Accounting Team* studied tables, charts, and graphs (logical-mathematical, spatial intelligence).
- The *Arts Team* studied representations of the war and its aftermath in the visual arts and poetry (spatial, linguistic intelligence).

Finally, in thinking about your topic, you will need to decide whether you are developing a basic one-period lesson, a mini-unit such as the one created by Carl Carrozza in The Strategy in Action section (see p. 184), or something in between.

2. **How much support will students need?** A class that has already demonstrated positive working relationships, supportive attitudes, and solid work habits will be ready to study a sophisticated, challenging topic. A class that needs work in these areas is probably better served by a carefully chosen topic with plenty of teacher modeling built into the process. For help in supporting students as they work through the challenges of working cooperatively, see The Cooperative Learning Troubleshooter's Guide in Figure 15.4, p. 193.

3. **What resources will students need in order to gather the appropriate information?** A simple Jigsaw lesson can be designed around a single textbook section or an article divided into sections. More involved lessons that stress research can involve multiple sources including texts, articles, primary documents, essays, visual materials, Web pages, and even hands-on learning activities that are set up as learning centers.

4. **How will Jigsaw teams and expert groups be organized?** In deciding on Jigsaw team and expert group membership, consider the particular strengths of individual students. Cooperative groups work best when they are composed of students who bring different talents (e.g., conceptualizing, creative thinking, organizing information, tending to details) to the learning process.

5. **What kind of organizer will you design to help structure and organize student learning?** The most typical organizer is a simple grid or

matrix that reveals the larger structure of the topic and gives the student room to write about each subtopic. However, many different organizer formats are possible. For some ideas, take a look at the sample organizers associated with New American Lecture (Figure 1.3, p. 30).

6. **How will you ensure the quality of student lessons?** Because students depend on other students to learn critical information, it is important that the lessons the students teach back to their Jigsaw teams are clearly organized and contain all the necessary information. Here are some tips for helping the expert groups plan and deliver high-quality lessons:

- Create a separate research organizer or worksheet for each expert group like the one Carl Carrozza created for his lesson on reptiles (see pp. 184–187).
- Meet with expert groups to make sure they have collected all the necessary information. Then, work with each group to develop a lesson. Provide suggestions, coaching, and examples from your own teaching.
- Have the students in the expert groups generate and reach consensus on the one or two key questions their lesson must answer. Coach them through the process of aligning their lesson with their question(s).
- Listen in on the lessons. Praise good teaching. For student-teachers who have trouble delivering the lesson, use focusing questions that point them to the main ideas and essential details.

7. **How will you assess student learning and performance?** In the improved version of Jigsaw known as Jigsaw II (Slavin, 1986), students are tested and the results are compiled in two ways. First, to ensure individual accountability, students will be given an individual grade. In addition, students receive a score based on the overall score of all the members in their Jigsaw team. This adds a competitive element to the lesson and motivates students to work as productively as possible with their team members. In designing your test, consider having the expert groups generate the questions. Finally, if your Jigsaw lesson is involved and carries a significant content load, you may want to design a synthesis task that requires students to apply their learning in a new context.

8. **How will you help students process the lesson and their roles in it?** One of the most important aspects of a strategy like Jigsaw is its hidden goal of helping students learn how to learn. Be sure to give students time to discuss and reflect on the process using questions such as:

- What did you like best and least about this lesson? Why?
- What kinds of information were hardest for you to remember?
- What information was easiest to remember?
- Did working with your expert group make research easier for you? How?
- What did you learn about yourself as a researcher? As a teacher? How might you improve next time?

Variations and Extensions

In this section, we provide you with an innovative cooperative learning strategy and a tool for improving the levels of cooperation in any classroom. The strategy, Learning by Committee, uses the authentic context of news committees to motivate students to work together to produce a high-quality product. The Cooperative Learning Troubleshooter's Guide (see Figure 15.4, p. 193) is a tool that offers a host of practical suggestions for overcoming the most common classroom challenges associated with cooperative learning lessons.

Learning by Committee

Learning by Committee (Silver, Strong, & Perini, 1999) is a cooperative strategy that helps students create original work while highlighting the essential content from a particular unit of study. The strategy revolves around the real-world context of newspaper production committees who must develop and implement a plan for production. In a typical Learning by Committee lesson, students break up into four groups:

- The **current events committee** is responsible for "fast-breaking" stories. Each group member chooses one topic and independently drafts a historically accurate news story about the event or topic.
- The **editorial page committee** focuses on a controversial issue. Two members of the group draft opposing editorials, while the other members each draft a letter in response to one of the editorials.
- Members of the **feature article committee** select a person to interview or choose important places or ideas to write about. Each member should draft a human interest feature article that explores the content in depth.
- Members of the **graphic design committee** work with the other groups to create appropriate visuals for the newspaper. Visuals may include graphs, charts, maps, time lines, diagrams of battles, political cartoons, and so on.

While students are working, the teacher monitors progress and levels of cooperation. When a group has difficulty, the teacher should advise members on how to work cooperatively and use other groups as models of effective collaborators. When students complete their drafts and visuals, group members work together to revise and edit their own and each other's work for accuracy, coherence, and clarity. After all students produce a final draft of their work, the class convenes to arrange the written and visual elements together to create the newspaper. Figure 15.3 (p. 192) shows how a high school teacher used the Learning by Committee strategy with her students.

FIGURE 15.3   Sample Learning by Committee Task

Read All About It!

As you now know, the Middle Ages was one of the most dynamic periods in all of human history. It was a time of kings and queens, lords and ladies, long-suffering peasants, and wily craftsmen. It was also a time of plots and ploys for power when popes and kings played chess with ideas and real-life knights in their quest for empire. Within this time, Europeans faced a plague that wiped out one-third of the population, planted the seeds of democracy, developed the concept of nationhood, and launched the first international war.

As reporters for *The Middle Ages Chronicle*, it is your group's job to capture the essence of this dynamic period in a newspaper format. After our class discussion, the class will break up into groups and form committees:

- A current events committee
- An editorial page committee
- A feature article committee
- A graphic design committee

Each group will be responsible for studying the essential elements of its reporting format and then using the group's research to create individual drafts. The group members should help each other revise and refine drafts through feedback on accuracy, coherence, and clarity. The committees will also be evaluated according to how productively they worked together. Each member will be responsible for a final draft written on a clean piece of paper.

After group members have completed their final drafts, the class will come together to assemble a complete edition of *The Middle Ages Chronicle*.

The Cooperative Learning Troubleshooter's Guide

In spite of all the benefits suggested by the research on cooperative learning, most teachers have experienced cooperative learning lessons that seem to fall flat or disappoint in terms of their outcomes. One common reason for these failures lies in a lack of distinction between group work and cooperative learning. Cooperative learning is much more than clumping students into groups and telling them to work together. In fact, successful cooperative learning lessons are designed around five principles for success, which are adapted from the work of Johnson and Johnson (1999). The Cooperative Learning Troubleshooter's Guide (Figure 15.4) outlines these five principles of effective cooperative learning lessons, lists potential signs of trouble that result when particular principles are not in effect, and provides troubleshooting tips on how to restore each principle and improve current and future lessons.

FIGURE 15.4   The Cooperative Learning Troubleshooter's Guide

Principle	Signs of Trouble	Troubleshooting Tips
Interdependence: Positive interdependence is the perception among students that they are linked so that one student cannot succeed unless the others succeed as well.	• Factions within group • Group members pursuing independent paths • Noncooperative dividing—"You do Part A, I'll do Part B, and Seth can do Part C."	• Remind groups that the work of all members is inextricably linked. • Use two-tiered grading that rewards contributions to the group as well as individual effort. • Highlight the work of effective groups so other groups can see a model.
Individual accountability: All students must know that they are responsible for their own work and that there is no "hitchhiking" on the work of others.	• Unequal contributions among group members • Some students "loaf" while conscientious students work harder	• Circulate around the room while groups work to observe individual and group effort. • Allow students to evaluate group functioning confidentially. • Use two-tiered grading that rewards individual and group effort.

Face-to-face interaction: Cooperative learning implies proximity; students must know how to work productively and positively with fellow group members face-to-face.	• Resistance, hostility, name-calling
	• Negative criticism
	• "My way or the highway" attitude
	• Failure to recognize the efforts of others
		• Model with students positive group behaviors such as praising, applauding effort, active listening, and so on.
		• Teach students the rules of consensus negotiation:
		  1. Avoid win-lose situations.
		  2. Avoid quick and simple solutions.
		  3. Make sure all positions use evidence.
		  4. Stay positive and constructive.

Interpersonal and small group skills: Learning groups are not productive unless members are skilled in cooperating with one another.	• Group impasse • Little rapport or trust among group members • Off-task behavior	• Keep groups small in size (3–5 students). • Select a focus skill (e.g., conflict resolution, decision making, communication) and build cooperative learning sessions around different skills. • Model effective interpersonal skills.
Group processing: Effective groups discuss how well group members are learning and maintaining productive relationships.	• "All business" attitude—little recognition of group process • Sitting around once the work is complete	• Build in time for reflection and discussion. • Provide specific prompts and questions to guide reflection and discussion (e.g., Did the group come to an impasse? What did you do to overcome it?). • Remind students to think about what happened during the lesson when they process content.

Note: The principles are based on Johnson & Johnson (1999).

How does the strategy fit into unit design?
(Blueprint for Learning)

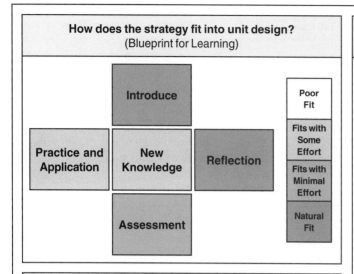

Introduce	
Practice and Application	New Knowledge
Reflection	
Assessment	

Poor Fit

Fits with Some Effort

Fits with Minimal Effort

Natural Fit

What learning styles does the strategy engage?
(Motivation/Differentiation)

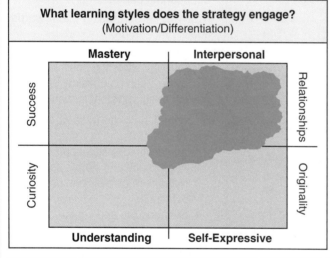

Mastery · Interpersonal
Success · Relationships
Curiosity · Originality
Understanding · Self-Expressive

What facets of understanding does the strategy develop?
(Understanding by Design)

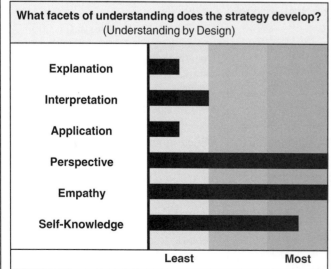

Explanation

Interpretation

Application

Perspective

Empathy

Self-Knowledge

Least — Most

What skills does the strategy build?
(The Hidden Skills of Academic Literacy)

Read and Study
- ○ Collect/organize ideas through note making
- ○ Make sense of abstract academic vocabulary
- ○ Read/interpret visuals

Reason and Analyze
- ● Draw conclusions; make/test inferences, hypotheses, conjectures
- ○ Conduct comparisons using criteria
- ○ Analyze demands of a variety of questions

Create and Communicate
- ○ Write clear, coherent explanations
- ○ Write comfortably in major nonfiction genres
- ○ Read and write about two or more documents

Reflect and Relate
- ○ Construct plans to address questions and tasks
- ○ Use criteria and guidelines to evaluate work
- ● Control/alter mood and impulsivity

How does the strategy incorporate the research on instructional effectiveness?
(Classroom Instruction That Works)

- ○ Identifying similarities and differences
- ○ Summarizing and note taking
- ● Reinforcing effort and providing recognition
- ○ Homework and practice
- ○ Nonlinguistic representation
- ● Cooperative learning
- ○ Setting objectives and feedback
- ● Generating and testing hypotheses
- ○ Cues, questions, and advance organizers

What types of knowledge does the strategy teach?

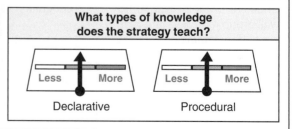

Less — More
Declarative

Less — More
Procedural

16

Community Circle

Strategy Overview

In an educational climate marked by rigorous standards, high-stakes testing, and accountability laws, it can be tempting to overlook the less "testable" areas of a student's education. A sense of belonging, the personal feelings and values of students, the development of a learning community—these are the things too often sacrificed in the name of the test. Yet, not only do these sacrifices violate our own natural sense of what constitutes good teaching, but they also lead to the exact opposite of their intended effect: A wide and ever-growing body of research shows that when emotional and communal well-being are surrendered to content coverage, student learning suffers dramatically.

Community Circle is a strategy that develops students' awareness of themselves, their feelings and values, and the feelings and values of their fellow students. By organizing discussions around a nonhierarchical circle in which the teacher and students all share (or choose not to share) their personal experiences and emotional responses as equals and without fear of judgment, the strategy builds each student's self-concept and fosters a classroom culture of togetherness and respect for differences.

The Strategy in Action

Meyer Sharmat is beginning an autobiography unit with his 4th graders. Today, Meyer wants two things to happen in his classroom. First, he wants students to get an initial sense of how most autobiographical writing works—how it tells the story of an individual overcoming an obstacle in a first-person narrative. Second, he wants students to draw deeply on their personal experiences, memories, and feelings and to share that rich autobiographical material with each other as a way to begin the process of crafting their own autobiographies.

After having students arrange their desks to form a circle, Meyer asks them to close their eyes and listen carefully as he reads an excerpt from Jackie Robinson's autobiography, *I Never Had It Made.* In the excerpt, Jackie Robinson

- Describes being heckled by fans and other players, and how "mischief-makers" tried to goad teammate Pee Wee Reese into rejecting Jackie as a teammate.
- Describes two different incidents that show how Pee Wee Reese supported Jackie Robinson.
- Explains how his friendship with Pee Wee Reese helped him overcome his obstacles and succeed under difficult circumstances.

After reviewing the reading and emphasizing its structure (obstacle–incident(s)–how the obstacle is eventually overcome), Meyer asks students to think about a similar episode from their own lives. "What obstacle or challenge did you face? How did you overcome it? What were some of the steps or incidents along the way that were important in this process of overcoming your obstacle?" he asks students before giving them silent time to think about his questions. Meyer encourages students to close their eyes and to visualize their experiences, remembering everything they can about the events, settings, feelings, and associations that make up those experiences.

Before asking students to share their experiences, Meyer reminds students that in a circle, every person gets an equal chance and time to share, that a student may choose not to take a turn, and that everyone must listen actively to the person who is sharing without interruption. Meyer then begins the circle process by describing how he learned how to hang glide, despite his fear of heights.

As the conversation moves around the circle, all but two students—Kim and Mikhail—share their experiences. During this process, Meyer nods encouragingly and provides praise by saying things like "That's a great story, Cammie." After all students have had an opportunity to share their episodes, Meyer and his students review what was said. Meyer helps students compare and explore the patterns in their responses with statements and questions:

Adil's story about moving reminded me a little bit of Rachel's story about summer camp. Adil, did you notice any similarities? How about you, Rachel? Did Adil's story remind you of your own experiences? Were any other stories about adjusting to new places or people?

Meyer is especially careful to avoid coming across as judgmental toward any student's contributions.

After all students have had an opportunity to share their episodes, Meyer asks them to "circle" again, this time focusing specifically on the feelings they experienced during their episode. Again, Meyer gets the circle started by relating the way his knees used to buckle with fear each time he looked over the edge of a cliff; the slow emergence of hope as he learned to hang glide, first close to the ground and then at higher and higher altitudes; and finally, the elation he felt while soaring over the trees like a bird in flight. When students share around the circle this time, three things happen.

First, Meyer does far less talking and allows for more silent time. Second, when students look to Meyer to fill the silent time or make a connection, Meyer encourages them to take over the discussion and to act as temporary leaders if and when they would like. Third, during this round of circling, both Kim and Mikhail make small contributions to the discussion. When the circle is complete, Meyer and his students review, compare responses, and identify a common theme—negative emotions becoming positive emotions.

Next, Meyer moves the lesson toward synthesis by making the following statement: "It has been said that all autobiographies are really emotional journeys, and that the best ones show us how people are able to turn negative emotions, like fear and anger, into positive emotions." Meyer then gives students a few moments to reflect on the statement before posing his synthesis questions for discussion:

- What do you think of this idea?
- What from today's lesson seems to fit this idea?
- What still seems to challenge it?

Once again, Meyer allows students to control the discussion, getting involved only once when three students all try to talk over one another. After drawing attention to what happened and providing students with tips on how to avoid this common pitfall of talking at the same time, Meyer lets the discussion resume, with the highest levels of participation that he has ever seen from the class.

Why the Strategy Works

One of our most fundamental needs as humans is to belong, to feel valued and appreciated as part of a community. Nowhere is this truer than in school. The school years make up a critical and formative time during which students develop the social identity they will carry with them for the rest of their lives. When schools and classrooms fail to pay attention to this crucial fact, students pay a heavy price. Barbara Given

(2002) explains: "for those groups of students where socially appropriate membership is out of reach, primitive instincts and drives tend to surface and produce aggression and other undesirable behaviors" (p. 44). By deliberately setting up a discussion culture based on mutual respect, equality (between the teacher and students as well as among the students), and an awareness of personal commonalities and differences, Community Circle is a strategy that carries an important lesson about how learning (and human) relationships should work.

However, good relationships are only half the story behind Community Circle. The other half lies in the way the strategy reaches out to the emotional interests and passions of the students. What's the educational benefit of engaging students emotionally in what they're learning? While most teachers have known the answer to this question for years, brain researchers struggled with it until quite recently. In fact, until the 1990s, most neuroscientists steered clear of the "dark" and "mysterious" realm of human emotions, focusing instead on the mechanisms of memory and critical thinking, thereby creating an implicit separation between the cognitive and affective sides of learning. Today, we know that this was an artificial separation; cognition and emotion cannot be thought of as dueling sides, and emotions are at the core of learning. Here's what we have learned since the welcome "affective revolution" began:

• Emotions are distributed across the brain and influence nearly all acts of learning (Kolb & Taylor, 2000).

• Emotions are strongly linked to better recall and more vivid memories (Cahill, Prins, Weber, & McGaugh, 1994).

• Emotions tell learners when to pay attention and when to withdraw (LeDoux, 1994).

• Emotions help us organize new experiences and make sense of the outside world (Damasio, 1994).

• Positive emotional states lead to better behavior, greater adaptability, and increased receptiveness to new learning (Ashby, Isen, & Turken, 1999).

• Social problem solving, attention priorities, and the passion for learning are all mediated by the emotions (Jensen, 2005).

• Positive emotional experiences in the classroom boost students' confidence and improve their self-concept (Sousa, 2001).

Community Circle is a strategy designed to strengthen student learning through the development of a positive learning environment and through strong emotional connections to content. By celebrating students' feelings and emotional responses, and by allowing students to share those feelings and responses in a communal and nonjudgmental learning environment, Community Circle leads to great benefits in any classroom. Students' attention; receptiveness; self-concept; sense of belonging; and ability to process, store, and make meaning of new content all get a size-able boost.

How to Use the Strategy

1. Select or have students select a topic for discussion.

2. Arrange students in a circle. Ideally, a Community Circle should contain approximately 10 students. Larger groups are fine, but will make the lesson longer.

3. Allow each student a chance to speak by moving the discussion around the circle. Students are not obligated to speak. You may circle several times, but make sure students have the opportunity to express feelings and personal values or responses at some point during the discussion.

4. After each circle is complete, conduct a review of what has been said. Encourage students to compare responses and look for patterns.

5. After all circling is complete, help students make conclusions and extend their thinking using synthesis questions. Help them reflect on the process and their own behaviors using reflection questions.

6. Help students assume leadership over future discussions by drawing attention to positive and negative behaviors and by modeling and suggesting how to avoid common discussion pitfalls.

Planning a Community Circle Lesson

Community Circle is a strategy that requires little in the way of designing or planning ahead of time. The main considerations

- What topic will lend itself to this kind of open-ended discussion?
- Who is involved (smaller group vs. whole class), and how can they be arranged in a circle?
- How will you incorporate students' feelings and personal values into the discussion?
- How will you and your students review what has been said and look for similarities and differences?
- How will you and your students draw conclusions from the discussion, extend learning, and reflect on the process?

A basic assumption of the Community Circle strategy is that, given the opportunity and training, every student has the ability to lead the group. Therefore, a final consideration involves your role in the lesson: How much of a role will you play and what steps can you take to transfer leadership to students? You may choose to train student leaders once group members are comfortable with one another and procedures are familiar.

During Community Circle lessons, especially initial ones, it is a good idea to model good leadership behaviors, as follows:

- **Focus-setting behavior** involves presenting a topic for discussion or recognizing an appropriate student-presented topic: "One thing we might want to think and talk about is 'Why does Huck let Tom Sawyer mistreat Jim at the end of the novel?'"
- **Structuring behavior** involves establishing ground rules for the lesson by explaining the format, and students' and teachers' roles: "Just a minute, Chris, only one person at a time. Everyone has the right to an opinion."
- **Accepting behavior** involves acknowledging ideas and opinions neutrally, without judging or valuing them. Accepting responses include "OK," "Yes," "Could be," or "That's possible."
- **Clarifying behavior** involves clarifying or amplifying a student's statement or question when it is ambiguous: "You've mentioned several things, Kelly. Are you saying that people are the problem, or are you saying that we need to change the laws concerning gun possession?"
- **Responding to the student's data** involves taking action, if feasible, to help the student to obtain better data: "Ray, according to the information contained in one study, more than half of students who smoked reported they started because all their friends smoked. Let's see if we can find that study on the Internet after this lesson."
- **Teacher silence** involves empowering students to choose a course of action or develop their own conclusions by remaining silent at decision times.

Variations and Extensions

One idea at the heart of Community Circle is the idea of togetherness, of the ties that bind individuals into a community of learners with common goals and personal differences. In this section, we explore three small-group techniques that draw on students' natural social needs and collaborative inclinations: Literature Circles, Shared Interest Groups, and Writer's Clubs.

Literature Circles

Sometimes, we forget just how personal the act of reading and responding to literature is. All readers bring their own experiences, feelings, and prior knowledge to bear on a text. Questions about rich literary topics like Hamlet's state of mind, or the ending of *Huckleberry Finn,* or Charlotte's motivation in *Charlotte's Web* can give rise to dozens of insightful interpretations—from students and literary critics alike. Nevertheless, thinking in isolation can only take a reader so far. Literature Circles give students the opportunity to reflect on and talk about their own and others' post-reading responses by participating in what Peterson and Eeds (1990) call "grand conversations" about literature. Grand conversations focus on big ideas and "juicy" topics as well as the different ways that students interpret these ideas and topics. In this way, a Literature Circle functions much like a Book Club, with a small and intimate group exploring both the text and personal reactions to what the text says.

Peterson and Eeds (1990) suggest that students in the Literature Circle abide by only two rules:

1. Always respect the interpretations of other students, and help them develop their interpretations whenever possible.

2. Try to enter every Literature Circle without a preconceived plan in mind. Spontaneity, listening, and responding are the fuel for new insights.

A Literature Circle can be greatly enhanced when participants have access to a question menu. A question menu contains a set of questions that encourage students to explore the reading and others' responses from multiple perspectives. For example, students in a Literature Circle can keep their discussions lively and dynamic by referring to a question menu that encourages them to think literally, analytically, creatively, and personally about literature:

- **Literal Questions**
  - Who are the main characters?
  - What are their traits?
  - What is the setting?
  - What is happening in the story?
- **Analytical Questions**
  - What is the significance of a particular quote?
  - Why does a particular character do or say _____?
  - How do you interpret _____?
  - What evidence can you find for your position?
- **Creative Questions**
  - What do you predict will happen next?
  - What images or symbols stood out for you?
  - What do you imagine a particular character is thinking?
  - How is _____ like _____? (Create and explain a simile.)
- **Personal Questions**
  - How does _____ make you feel?

- ○ Has something like this ever happened to you or someone you know?
- ○ How can you relate you personal experiences to the reading?
- ○ Do you like or dislike a particular character? Why?

Shared Interest Groups

In a Shared Interest Group, students are asked to select a certain aspect of the content that interests them and to work cooperatively with others who share similar interests. The technique enables students to improve cooperation and problem-solving skills, while giving them a means to share their preferences for particular topics or content.

Teachers may divide content up in a variety of ways: by level of difficulty, by theme, by stylistic variations (e.g., different styles of writing or art), by the kind of thinking required to solve particular problems, by perspective (e.g., a set of opinions on the issue of human cloning), by natural "chunks" or aspects inherent in the material (e.g., the three branches of government), or by the different learning styles or multiple intelligences embedded in the content or activity. Students preview the selections and then decide which appeals to them most. For example, a middle school English teacher might provide her students with the first 100 words from five different short stories, while an elementary math teacher might provide students with five different kinds of "part-to-whole" problems: a fraction problem, a problem involving decimals, a percentage problem, a ratio problem, and a problem dealing with a proportion. Once students select their favorite, they form a group with students who selected the same favorite. Student groups, now organized by common interest, begin in-depth work on their chosen material.

Writer's Clubs

Polished writing requires feedback from fellow writers who help their colleagues weed out weaknesses and fine-tune their craft. The Writer's Club is a support and feedback group for writers composed of fellow writers and students.

Writer's Clubs can be set up in many ways. Members can read their pieces aloud and then receive feedback from other members. Members can read other writers' pieces in order to help fellow writers notice where their own writing causes the reader to falter. Another option uses a moderator structure and a menu of activities and questions designed to help writers develop greater insight into their own compositions. The rules and a sample activity menu for this moderator-based option are shown in Figure 16.1.

FIGURE 16.1   Moderator-Based Writer's Club

Literal Questions	**Personal Questions**
• Summarize the piece. • Give the main points. • Give a headline or title to this piece.	• How did this piece affect you? • What feelings did this piece arouse in you?

Rules of the Writer's Club

1. Everyone reads.
2. Listeners respond to questions chosen by the moderator.
3. Writer listens to responses and does not defend self or piece.
4. When the moderator reads, someone else moderates.

Interpretive Questions	**Creative Questions**

• What stood out for you?
• What's the most important part of this piece?
• If this piece were yours, how would you change it?
	• If this piece were a kind of
	   - clothing
	   - music
	   - period of history
	   - weather
	what would it be?

Source: From *Tools for Promoting Active, In-Depth Learning* (p. 85), by H. Silver, R. Strong, and M. Perini, 2001, Ho-Ho-Kus, NJ: Thoughtful Education Press. Adapted with permission.

PART SIX

Four-Style Strategies

Four-Style Strategies

Four-style strategies engage multiple styles simultaneously, thereby encouraging students to develop a balanced and dynamic approach to learning.

Strategy Chapters

17. Window Notes is a strategy that employs note making techniques and tools that build reflection skills and value students' own ideas, feelings, and questions.

18. Circle of Knowledge is a set of discussion techniques that ensure high levels of participation, a content-driven focus, and active, in-depth thinking on the part of students.

19. Do You Hear What I Hear? is a comprehensive approach to teaching rigorous content while building students' skills as readers, writers, listeners, and speakers.

20. Task Rotation is a strategy that provides teachers with a manageable and classroom-friendly framework for differentiating instruction and assessment by learning style.

How does the strategy fit into unit design?
(Blueprint for Learning)

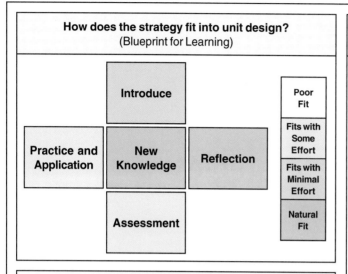

Introduce	Poor Fit
	Fits with Some Effort
Practice and Application — New Knowledge — Reflection	Fits with Minimal Effort
Assessment	Natural Fit

What learning styles does the strategy engage?
(Motivation/Differentiation)

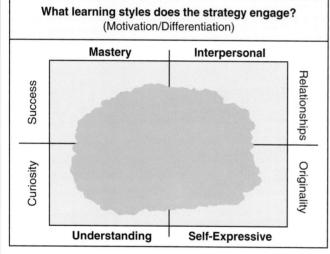

Mastery | Interpersonal

Success — Curiosity

Relationships — Originality

Understanding | Self-Expressive

What facets of understanding does the strategy develop?
(Understanding by Design)

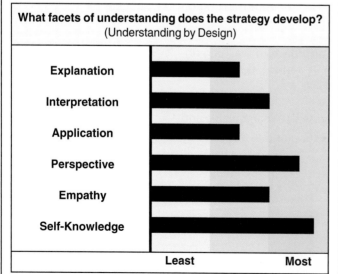

- Explanation
- Interpretation
- Application
- Perspective
- Empathy
- Self-Knowledge

Least — Most

What skills does the strategy build?
(The Hidden Skills of Academic Literacy)

Read and Study
- ● Collect/organize ideas through note making
- ● Make sense of abstract academic vocabulary
- ○ Read/interpret visuals

Reason and Analyze
- ● Draw conclusions; make/test inferences, hypotheses, conjectures
- ○ Conduct comparisons using criteria
- ○ Analyze demands of a variety of questions

Create and Communicate
- ○ Write clear, coherent explanations
- ○ Write comfortably in major nonfiction genres
- ○ Read and write about two or more documents

Reflect and Relate
- ○ Construct plans to address questions and tasks
- ○ Use criteria and guidelines to evaluate work
- ● Control/alter mood and impulsivity

How does the strategy incorporate the research on instructional effectiveness?
(Classroom Instruction That Works)

- ○ Identifying similarities and differences
- ● Summarizing and note taking
- ○ Reinforcing effort and providing recognition
- ○ Homework and practice
- ○ Nonlinguistic representation
- ○ Cooperative learning
- ○ Setting objectives and feedback
- ○ Generating and testing hypotheses
- ● Cues, questions, and advance organizers

What types of knowledge does the strategy teach?

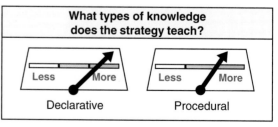

Declarative | Procedural

17

Window Notes

Strategy Overview

Most adults can remember being asked as students to copy notes from the board or to arrange ideas and information according to the rules of the traditional Roman numeral outline. Tasks like these often obscure the amount of genuine thinking necessary to create good and useful notes. Window Notes are different. The Window Notes strategy provides students with a powerful notemaking framework that helps them

- Deepen comprehension by thinking as they read and learn.
- Develop the capacity to reflect on and improve their performance as readers and learners through metacognition.
- Capture and put to use their own ideas, feelings, questions, and associations.

The Strategy in Action

DaShawn Lewis's freshman English students are about to begin reading J. D. Salinger's *The Catcher in the Rye*. DaShawn explains to students that for today's lesson, students will be reading the first chapter of Salinger's classic novel while paying close attention to the narrator, Holden Caulfield. DaShawn tells students:

> One of the things that's so interesting, so amazing about this novel is the way we learn so much about the narrator simply by the way he tells the story. We touched upon this idea a little bit before when we read some short stories by Edgar Allen Poe, but with *The Catcher in the Rye*, we're going to pay much closer attention to what Holden's words and private thoughts tell us about his character.

DaShawn then instructs students to turn to a clean page in their notebook and to divide the page into a four-quadrant Window Notes organizer. At the top of each quadrant, students write the words *Facts, Questions, Ideas,* and *Feelings.*

DaShawn tells students,

> To begin our novel-long exploration of Holden Caulfield's character as revealed by his narration, we're going to use a new note making technique called Window Notes. Window Notes provide us with a great way to collect and organize our ideas about literature because they allow us to record not only the facts, but also our own personal questions, ideas, and feelings about what we read.

Before asking students to make Window Notes about the very short first chapter of *The Catcher in the Rye,* DaShawn models the process with his students, showing them how to use the Window Notes technique by applying it to a specific day in his own life: yesterday. Using an overhead projector, DaShawn reads facts as well as questions, ideas, and feelings about his day (see Figure 17.1). DaShawn then allows students to practice the technique by taking five minutes to write up a set of Window Notes about their day yesterday.

Using the modeling and practice sessions to guide them, students read the six pages that make up the first chapter of *The Catcher in the Rye.* As they read, students make a set of Window Notes about Holden Caulfield and what they can figure out about his personality. A sample of one student's notes is shown in Figure 17.2.

As students read and create their Window Notes, DaShawn circulates around the room to catch a glimpse of students' minds at work while processing, interpreting, and reacting to literature.

DaShawn gives students 15 minutes to complete the reading and their notes before collecting their ideas on the board in a Window Notes organizer. If a student offers up a fact, he writes it in the Facts quadrant; if a student offers up a question, it goes in the Questions quadrant, and so on. With each new offering from students, DaShawn connects the responses back to the question under investigation: "What does this piece of information tell us about Holden?"

Before the period ends, DaShawn gives students a homework assignment: *Write a one-page letter to Holden telling him what you find likeable about him and advising him about which of his personality traits you think might get him into trouble.*

Throughout the reading of the novel, DaShawn's students use Window Notes three more times, as a tool for getting a handle on key chapters and sections and continuing their investigation into Holden's personality. After a few times of using the strategy, students' preferences for different kinds of notes start to become noticeable. DaShawn has students add up their totals for each kind of note (*Facts, Questions, Ideas,* and *Feelings*) and engages them in an ongoing discussion about how they

FIGURE 17.1   Teacher's Mode Window Notes

Facts	Feelings
• I got a haircut. • My wife and daughter thought my haircut was too short. • I spent an hour and a half planning for today's classes.	• It's a great feeling to come home to my family—even if it's just to be teased. • I had a hard time sleeping last night because I was excited about starting The Catcher in the Rye with the class.
Questions	**Ideas**
• Why do my wife and daughter always tease me about my haircuts? • Will the Dolphins' big comeback in last night's game be the turning point of the season?	• Maybe if I just let my hair grow out for a whole year, my wife and daughter will beg me to get my hair cut next time. • Thank goodness my barber isn't a Jets fan.

FIGURE 17.2   Student's Sample Window Notes

Facts	Feelings
• Holden was kicked out of Pencey Prep School. • Holden visits a teacher of his, Mr. Spencer. • Holden is very intelligent.	• I'm very confused about Holden. Just when I think I like him he says something that makes me mad. • To me, Holden seems a little too smart for his age.
Questions	**Ideas**
• What happened in Holden's family life that his parents would have "two hemorrhages" if he told anyone? • Why does Holden have such a connection with Mr. Spencer? • Why does Holden seem to hold a grudge against everyone?	Holden reminds me of my Uncle Phil. Uncle Phil sits around at holiday dinners and makes comments. Sometimes his comments are clever, but sometimes they hurt people, too.

learn and how they use their own preferences to interpret literature. By the second use of the strategy, DaShawn and his students are exploring questions such as these:

- How might Window Notes act as a window into your mind?
- What if you had the kind of mind that paid attention mostly to facts? Why might that be a good thing when reading literature?

- If you kept your eye on feelings, what skills might that give you?
- What if you were a questioner or an idea maker? Why would it be good to be either of those?
- How might you use this technique on your own or in other classes?

Why the Strategy Works

The evidence is irrefutable: Students who know how to take good notes outperform their peers significantly and consistently. Meta-analytic research covering dozens of individual studies compiled by Beecher (1988), Kiewra (1985), Marzano, Pickering, and Pollock (2001), and Kobayashi (2006) all reveal the wide-ranging benefits of teaching students how to take notes.

While the effectiveness of notes may be a given, what is not so clear is how teachers can get their students interested in the process. Many students take great pride in how their notebooks look on the outside, but only a select few (usually the best students, which is no coincidence) enjoy taking care of what's inside. Aversion to taking notes is not limited to students; ask a few adults to share their experiences as note takers and you're likely to hear about the hours they lost copying from the board, the drudgery of paraphrasing encyclopedia entries, or the cramped wrists they got while trying to keep up with a professor's monotone delivery. Even teachers, well versed in the value and benefits of note-taking, often use words like *joyless* and *struggle* when talking about their experiences in helping students become better note takers. The source of all this reluctance and resistance can be summed up in one word: boredom.

The Window Notes strategy has grown out of the work of Richard Strong, Harvey Silver, and their colleagues (Strong, Silver, Perini, & Tuculescu, 2003). During their investigation into the causes of student boredom, Strong and his team found that boredom is rooted in the failure to engage natural student drives in school. Specifically, students withdraw from learning and become bored when the drives associated with mastering competencies, making sense and meaning out of ideas, expressing the unique aspects of their personalities, and relating personally to learning are neglected in the classroom.

Strong and Silver developed Window Notes by applying this research on boredom specifically to the act of taking notes. The idea behind the strategy is simple: Because notes are so critical to student success, we need to stop treating them as repetitive and routine tasks. If we expect students to be actively engaged in collecting and recording their ideas, then we need strategies that teach students how to *make* notes rather than *take* notes—strategies that treat notes as deep and dynamic forms of thinking, as personal and creative acts.

Aside from its general positive effects as a research-based note making strategy, Window Notes has two added benefits. First, it has proven especially effective with reluctant and at-risk learners. Why? Strong (2005) explains:

> Reluctant learners believe no one's interested in what they think. . . . [Window Notes] asks them what they think and lets them have their own opinions. Kids get bored when what they're learning doesn't relate to their lives or isn't deep enough. . . . Window Notes challenge [students] to go beyond the basic facts of what they're learning and push further, into self-discovery. The window-shaped structure explicitly lays out what they need to share.

Second, the strategy provides teachers with deep insight into how each student's mind works. By observing and discussing students' preferences for different kinds of notes, teachers learn which drives and learning styles are most developed and least developed in their students. Armed with this information, teachers can work collaboratively with students to capitalize on learning strengths and minimize weaknesses.

How to Use the Strategy

1. Introduce and model Window Notes by showing students how you collect facts, questions, ideas, and feelings related to a particular topic or text.

2. Ask students to divide a blank sheet of paper into a window-shaped organizer of four quadrants. Students should label the quadrants *Facts, Questions, Ideas,* and *Feelings.*

3. Introduce the text or topic to be learned. Have students collect different kinds of notes and responses on their organizers as they read the text or learn about the topic.

4. Invite students to share their notes with the class, and conduct a discussion on what students have learned about the content and about their personal preferences as notemakers.

5. Assign a task that requires students to use their notes.

6. Over time, teach students how to use the strategy independently, as a way to help them break new learning up into meaningful sets of information and as a way to help them pay attention to the inner workings of their own minds.

Planning a Window Notes Lesson

Window Notes carries a fairly light planning load. Some of the key questions you should consider before putting a Window Notes lesson into action in your classroom include:

- Why are students creating Window Notes? (What is the purpose of this lesson?)
- How will I model the Window Notes process for my students?
- How will I collect students' responses and connect those responses back to the purpose guiding the lesson?
- How will students apply their notes to a meaningful task?
- How will I encourage student independence in using Window Notes as a learning and note-making tool?
- How can I use the different styles of thought embedded in Window Notes (finding facts, asking questions, investigating ideas, and exploring feelings) to help students pay close attention to their preferences and potential liabilities as learners?

Variations and Extensions

Window Notes helps students (and teachers) make the leap from *note taking* to *note making*. Moreover, the clear window-shaped structure of Window Notes gives students a visual map revealing the complex relationship between the content and their own personal learning process. In this section, we present two more strategies that adopt this same window-like approach to note making: Math Notes for solving mathematical word problems and Four Thought for essay planning and developing layered interpretations.

Math Notes

Word problems in math can be frustrating for students and their teachers. Unlike other kinds of math problems, word problems require both reading and math skills. Math Notes teaches students how to use notes to manage both sets of skills by systematically breaking word problems down into these steps:

- The facts of the problem, including what is missing.
- The main question that needs answering, along with any hidden questions that lurk beneath the problem.
- A visualization that represents the problem in nonlinguistic terms.
- A set of action steps that can be used to solve the problem.

A sample set of Math Notes is shown in Figure 17.3. One great added benefit of Math Notes is that as students build up a notebook of problems solved using the technique, they can use their notebook as a reference tool, searching for past problems and solutions that they can apply to new problems. For example, in solving the problem shown in Figure 17.3, many students looked back on models they had developed weeks earlier, when they were working on problems related to grouping.

Four Thought

Quality interpretations have layers—they can describe, explain, critique, investigate ideas, explore solutions, and even discuss personal reactions

FIGURE 17.3 Student's Sample Math Notes

> **The Problem:** There are three 5th grade classes going on a field trip. Two classes have 22 students, and one class has 21 students. The elementary school wants to purchase a juice box for each student going on the field trip. Juice boxes are sold in nine-packs or four-packs. How many juice boxes does the school need? What is the fewest number of packs the school needs to buy so that every student gets a juice box and the school has the least possible number of leftover juice boxes?

The Facts	The Steps
What are the facts? • Large packs contain nine juice boxes. • Small packs contain four juice boxes. What is missing? • Number of students in the 5th grade classes. • Number of juice boxes the school should buy.	What steps can we take to solve the problem? • Find out how many students are going on the trip. That's how many juice boxes we need. • See how many sets of nine I can get out of the number of students. • I know I can't get any more sets of nine when I have a number lower than nine left. • When I get to a number lower than nine, see if it is better to buy a nine-pack or a four-pack.

The Question	The Diagram
What question needs to be answered? • How many nine-packs and four-packs does the school need to buy? Are there any hidden questions that need to be answered? • How many people are going on the trip? • Is there more than one right answer?	How can we represent the problem visually?

all in the space of a single essay. Yet for many students, these layers are invisible. When students are unable to differentiate among the various layers that constitute high-quality interpretations, one of two results tends to occur in their own interpretive writing:

- They produce simple summaries, or "single-layer" interpretations.
- Their writing tends to wander "all over the map"—here a little critique, there some description, here a brief rant, none of which is carried through to a meaningful end.

In these cases, the students may be aware that interpretations have layers, but show no sense of how to manage the layering in their own writing. What makes this common difficulty especially troubling for teachers and students is that open-response items on state tests take the ability to manage multiple layers for granted.

Four Thought (Silver, Strong, & Perini, 2001) guides students through the process of developing high-quality, multilayered essays and interpretations in six steps:

1. Present students with a topic and have them generate their initial ideas and associations.

2. Show students how to describe, analyze, propose solutions, and react to the topic using a Four Thought organizer. One 6th grader's completed Four Thought organizer on the topic of Hurricane Katrina is shown in Figure 17.4.

3. After students have completed their organizers, allow them to meet in small groups to share and compare their responses.

4. Teach students how to use their Four Thought responses to develop a first draft of an essay on the topic.

5. Allow students to meet in Writer's Clubs (see p. 202) to provide feedback on one another's essays. Feedback should be focused on:
  ◦ Use of powerful words
  ◦ Clarity of ideas
  ◦ Incorporation of Four Thought stems into writing
  ◦ Mastery of writing conventions

6. Encourage students to reflect on the feedback and revise their first draft.

FIGURE 17.4 Student's Sample Four Thought Organizer

Topic: Hurricane Katrina

Pre-reading Associations

hurricane	Gulf of Mexico	wind	death
New Orleans	Red Cross	flood	disease
Mississippi	Superdome	levees	evacuation

Four Thought

Describe It	React to It
Hurricane Katrina hit the United States from the Gulf of Mexico. Most of New Orleans was covered with water and parts of other states were flooded too. After the storm, most people did not have clean water, power, food, or medicine and diseases started to spread.	I can't believe that a hurricane could destroy an entire city so quickly! So many people were hurt or killed. And the people that survived dont have jobs, schools, or homes to go back to. It is still a sad situation.
Analyze It	**Solve It**
Nothing can be done to prevent powerful and dangerous storms like Hurricane Katrina. There was too much water for the levees to handle so New Orleans quickly flooded. Evacuation before a storm is the best thing to do but not everyone can leave.	We have very good weather forecasts. Officials should know early enough to evacuate people. Supplies should be stored in shelters before a storm hits so they can be used right away. The levees need to be fixed in New Orleans so they are stronger and never fail again. Everyone should be prepared in case of a storm or an emergency. Family, friends, and pets are so important. Anything else can be fixed or replaced.

How does the strategy fit into unit design?
(Blueprint for Learning)

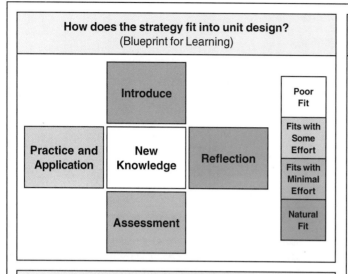

Introduce	Poor Fit
Practice and Application — New Knowledge — Reflection	Fits with Some Effort
	Fits with Minimal Effort
Assessment	Natural Fit

What learning styles does the strategy engage?
(Motivation/Differentiation)

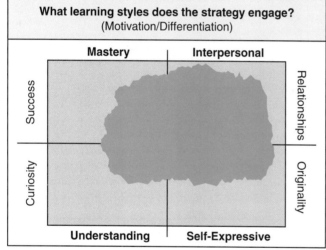

Mastery | Interpersonal
Success — Curiosity (left axis)
Relationships — Originality (right axis)
Understanding | Self-Expressive

What facets of understanding does the strategy develop?
(Understanding by Design)

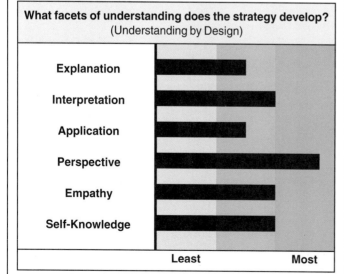

- Explanation
- Interpretation
- Application
- Perspective
- Empathy
- Self-Knowledge

Least — Most

What skills does the strategy build?
(The Hidden Skills of Academic Literacy)

Read and Study
- ● Collect/organize ideas through note making
- ○ Make sense of abstract academic vocabulary
- ○ Read/interpret visuals

Reason and Analyze
- ● Draw conclusions; make/test inferences, hypotheses, conjectures
- ○ Conduct comparisons using criteria
- ● Analyze demands of a variety of questions

Create and Communicate
- ● Write clear, coherent explanations
- ○ Write comfortably in major nonfiction genres
- ● Read and write about two or more documents*

Reflect and Relate
- ○ Construct plans to address questions and tasks
- ○ Use criteria and guidelines to evaluate work
- ● Control/alter mood and impulsivity

How does the strategy incorporate the research on instructional effectiveness?
(Classroom Instruction That Works)

- ○ Identifying similarities and differences
- ● Summarizing and note taking
- ● Reinforcing effort and providing recognition
- ○ Homework and practice
- ○ Nonlinguistic representation
- ● Cooperative learning
- ○ Setting objectives and feedback
- ○ Generating and testing hypotheses
- ● Cues, questions, and advance organizers

What types of knowledge does the strategy teach?

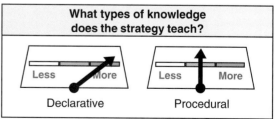

Declarative (Less — More) | Procedural (Less — More)

*Text-driven discussions are even more central to the strategy known as Socratic Seminar (pp. 225–227).

18

Circle of Knowledge

Strategy Overview

Discussion is central to all our lives. In school, discussion is the foundation for intellectual and personal growth. One of the most useful skills students can learn is how to listen, integrate information, and respond to a range of ideas that they then use to formulate their own ideas and beliefs. By engaging in informed dialogue and by exchanging ideas with others, students learn an invaluable social, academic, and vocational skill.

Despite its enormous potential as a teaching and learning strategy, discussion can also be very fragile. No strategy is more involving, yet none suffers as much from students who choose not to participate. No strategy is more likely to lead students to new insights, yet none can so easily be sidetracked by trivial details. Clearly, learning how to conduct an effective discussion is an essential skill in any teacher's repertoire. Circle of Knowledge (and its more text-based cousin, Socratic Seminar) provides teachers with a strategic framework for planning and conducting discussions in any classroom—discussions marked by high levels of participation, a clear and content-driven focus, and active, in-depth thinking on the part of students.

The Strategy in Action

High school math teacher Eileen Cho thinks too many math classrooms run through critical concepts too quickly.

With so many concepts coming one on top of the next, students never get an opportunity to explore the core ideas of the discipline or get the "big picture." In my experience, this isolation of ideas—this failure to let students enter into the rich and provocative issues and questions that drive the discipline of mathematics—is one of the main reasons that so many students "turn off" math and end up leaving high school with negative impressions of our subject.

In response, Eileen has structured her classroom not only around learning key algorithms and procedures, but also around focused discussions on big ideas in math.

Currently, it is the second week of school. Students have already learned about the foundations of geometry and developed a set of visual and linguistic notes outlining the key concepts of the discipline: *point*, *plane*, *line*, *line segment*, *ray*, *angle*, and so on. A typical entry in a student's notebook looks like the entry shown in Figure 18.1.

Armed with this background information, Eileen feels her students are ready to engage in one of these "big idea" discussions. She introduces Circle of Knowledge by saying, "I'd like to spark our discussion by posing a simple but very deep question: How do you know when something is real? Take a few minutes and jot down some ideas in your Learning Logs." After students have written their initial thoughts, Eileen breaks the class up into groups of four. Each group of four students exchanges and compares ideas, and then Eileen has students share their ideas with the class. During the excerpt that follows (and the entire discussion), Eileen ensures a high level of participation by using a variety of recognition techniques. She calls on students randomly, asks for volunteers, redirects questions to other students, surveys the class, and lets students direct questions to one another.

Eileen: OK, so who has an idea? Stephan?

Stephan: Well, I think you know something is real if you can see it.

Eileen: OK, I see a lot of hands that just went up when you said that, so I'm going to check in with someone else. Casey, why did what Stephan said make you so adamant?

Casey: Because there are lots of things you can see that aren't real. Like in the movies. With special effects, you can "see" dinosaurs and dragons and spaceships and. . . . Do you see what I'm saying, Stephan?

Stephan: Well, I mean, I guess. . . . Yeah, you're right. What I mean is if you can sense it, if you can see it and touch it and smell it, then it's real.

Eileen: OK, so then can we agree that one way we know something's real is through our senses? Good. Who has another idea? Tonia?

Tonia: Well, I agree that senses are one way to find out if something's real, but not the only way. I don't know, but to me, something's only really real if you can . . . how do I say this? If you can feel it. Like happiness or sadness . . . or love. If you can feel it in your heart, then it's real.

FIGURE 18.1   Student's Sample Notebook Entry

	Definition	Physical Model	Visual Representation
○	A line segment is a line that has two endpoints and does not continue on forever.	A physical model for a line segment would be the red and blue lines on a hockey rink, or the white lines on a football or soccer field.	*(diagram: line segment from C to D)* Line segment $\overline{CD}$ is named for its two endpoints.

Eileen: That's very interesting, Tonia. Let's summarize where we are. We have two ideas: One is that "real" is confirmed by the senses. The other is that we know things are real when we can feel them. What does the class think? Which idea do you agree with more? Raise your hand if you agree with Stephan. . . .

The discussion continues for a few more minutes before Eileen decides to sharpen the focus of the lesson. "Believe it or not," she tells students, "some of the world's great thinkers have been wrestling with the question of what's real for thousands of years. Especially in geometry, where the question has been taken up by the Greek philosopher Plato and Albert Einstein, among others."

Eileen distributes to her students three brief readings on the question of whether geometry is real: one taken from Plato's *Republic* arguing that geometric figures are ideal forms that exist only in our minds; one taken from a speech by Albert Einstein claiming that geometry happened by human discovery; and one laying out the "mirror" argument, which claims that geometry simply reflects what we see in nature (e.g., the line of the horizon becomes the geometric line). Eileen poses the focusing question—"How do each of these three positions contribute to (or conflict with) your understanding of geometry?"—and then gives students a few minutes to read, make notes, and prepare for the next round of discussion.

During this phase of the discussion, Eileen again encourages student participation by using a variety of recognition techniques. The feedback Eileen provides to students is similarly varied: Sometimes she is silent; sometimes she corrects responses; sometimes she requests clarification or asks students to expand on their initial ideas. Throughout the discussion, Eileen records responses and asks students to summarize what has been said thus far.

A few minutes before the discussion ends, Eileen asks students what they have discovered. As she surveys students, she records their ideas on the board:

- There is no simple agreement about whether geometry is real.
- One theory argues that geometry reflects nature.
- Plato claims geometric figures are ideal forms in our minds.
- Einstein believes geometry happened by discovery, and could have been very different if the shortest space between two places were a curved line.
- Most of us had no idea that this topic was up for debate.

For homework, Eileen assigns a closing task: Students have to select the position that is closest to their own position and defend it against the other two.

Why the Strategy Works

Discussion is an essential component in any thoughtful classroom. Dialogue and conversations are foundations for serious thought, and learners in discussion-rich classrooms enjoy irrefutable benefits: deeper comprehension, increased ability to handle complex and rigorous content, improved conflict resolution skills, and a greater passion for learning in general (Polite & Adams, 1996; Tredway, 1995). This research also tells us that effective discussions are characterized by three essential criteria:

- High levels of participation
- A high degree of focus
- High levels of thinking

Circle of Knowledge provides teachers with a framework for designing and conducting discussions that consistently meet these criteria. The framework rests on a set of techniques, or "moves" teachers can make during any discussion to raise the level of participation, focus, and thought.

Moves for Increasing Participation

- **Allow students to test and share ideas in small groups.** Practice may not make perfect performance, but it nearly always makes for better performance. If we are going to ask students to participate in class, it seems only fair to let them practice first. After posing an open-ended question, encourage students to share and compare their answers with a neighbor or a small group. Keep small-group work focused by giving groups a specific task to accomplish: "Talk with the people at your table, and make a list of how your responses are similar and different."

• **Use a variety of recognition techniques.** Orchestrating the discussion to maximize participation and keep the discussion on track requires a wide variety of recognition techniques. You can significantly increase the level and quality of participation by applying these six techniques:

  ◦ *Volunteering* (raised hands) should be used when the question is difficult and you don't want to put a particular student on the spot.

  ◦ *Random calling* (teacher selects a student to respond) should be used when you want all students to know that they are expected to have an answer; when you know through observation that a particular student has something to offer; when you want to keep a record to make sure that everyone has a chance to say something.

  ◦ *Student calling* (one student addresses a question to another) should be used when you want to increase interaction among students; when you want students to stop talking to you and start speaking to each other.

  ◦ *Round robin* (every student has a turn to talk) should be used when you want students to know that they will have an opportunity and a responsibility to speak; it is especially useful when your students may feel tense about sharing.

  ◦ *Surveying* (everyone shares a response at once through raised hands or other signs) and sampling (you ask the same question of a number of students in turn to get a sample of students' responses) should be used when you want your students to see where their classmates stand on a particular issue.

  ◦ *Redirection* (you redirect a student's question to another student or to the group as a whole) should be used when you want your students to explore a student-raised proposition that moves the discussion forward and keeps it on track.

The important thing about this list is its variety. Restricting a discussion to volunteers or to students you have selected is like restricting a painter to a single color. By using a variety of recognition techniques in a discussion, you can move from mere question-and-answer drills to genuine conversations.

Moves for Keeping Focus

• **Use a variety of techniques to help students pull their ideas together.** Frequently students flounder in discussion because they have not pulled their many thoughts together into a cohesive answer or position. Giving them paper and asking them to jot down some notes to themselves, to draw a sketch that illustrates their answer, or, for the very young, to scribble what comes to mind when they hear the question are ways to get students to focus their thinking in response to the question.

• **Record responses and summarize frequently.** Because a discussion is made up of the contributions of many, its structure is often hard to see. To establish and maintain focus, you need to record, clarify, and summarize what has been said.

To record a discussion, jot down students' key ideas on the board, an easel, or an overhead projector. Draw lines between statements to suggest relationships based on agreement or disagreement. Recording slows the pace of discussion. This is sometimes a plus because it gives students more time to think. On the other hand, if recording seems to be hindering the excitement of a discussion, wait a while before recording, and then use the process of recording to review the ground covered.

To clarify a discussion, frequently ask students to restate what previous speakers have said. To summarize a discussion, stop every five minutes or so and ask students to paraphrase the ideas that are on the table. If students have trouble summarizing, help them by asking a question such as "Do I hear you saying . . . ?" After soliciting several summaries, help your students combine these into a group summary.

Moves for Encouraging High Levels of Thinking

• **Encourage your students to stop and think about the question.** Perhaps the most common cause of thoughtless responses in a discussion is student impulsiveness. When students grab at a ready-made answer, their responses will likely be routine, shallow, or unrelated to the question. Thoughtful discussion requires students to stop and think about the question. Teachers can help students slow down and internalize the question by writing the question on the board, asking students to repeat the question quietly to themselves, and encouraging students to visualize information related to the question or possible answers.

• **Use Q-SPACE to shape discussions.** Q-SPACE (Strong, Hanson, & Silver, 1998) stands for

- **Q**uestion
- **S**ilence and wait time
- **P**robing
- **A**ccepting
- **C**larifying and correcting
- **E**laborating

Once a **q**uestion has been posed, your behaviors will give shape to the lesson. Remember that "**s**ilence is golden": Students require three to five seconds of wait time to process a question adequately (Rowe, 1978; Stahl, 1994). Use **p**robing questions that ask students to support their answers further to increase the sense of challenge in a discussion, to keep your students on their toes, and to provide practice and guidance in the always difficult skill of looking for proof. Use **acceptance** to increase the quantity and diversity of students' answers, to help students feel more comfortable about sharing, and to build a pool of responses you can use for later reflection. Use **clarification** and **correction** judiciously to increase the precision of students' responses. When you clarify and correct, student answers will tend to be briefer and the discussion will take on more of a question-and-answer or drill session feeling. Finally, use **elaboration** to encourage students to expand on their ideas and make generalizations that unite the various ideas that have emerged during the discussion.

How to Use the Strategy

1. Spark the discussion by posing an open-ended question that hooks students into the material.

2. Allow students time to stop and think about the question. You may also want students to jot down and share responses with a partner or small group before opening the discussion.

3. Sharpen the focus of the discussion by posing a focusing question that highlights the central topic or theme of the discussion.

4. Have students "kindle" their responses by jotting down their initial responses and then sharing and comparing their responses in small groups.

5. Engage the whole class in the discussion. Encourage students to share their ideas, respond to prompts and questions from the teacher or other students, refine their ideas, and evaluate the depth of their understanding.

6. During the discussion, use a variety of recognition techniques to maximize participation and Q-SPACE to shape the discussion.

7. Record students' responses and summarize key content with students.

8. Allow students to reflect on the discussion and their own participation.

9. Synthesize student learning with a task that asks them to apply what they learned during the discussion.

Planning a Circle of Knowledge Lesson

Good discussions rarely happen by accident; good discussions are planned. To plan a Circle of Knowledge for your classroom, follow these six steps:

1. **Establish the topic and purpose for the discussion.** In selecting the content for your lesson, look for topics that are magnets for controversy,

are rich with implications, and will stimulate a high degree of student interest. Once you've selected your topic, determine the purpose of the discussion. Do you want students to obtain new knowledge, develop a new perspective, explore connections between contents, tease out hidden information, or empathize with characters or content?

2. **Develop a focus question.** Focus questions set the tone for the lesson and provide students with the initial entryway into the topic. From the focus question, the structure of the discussion will unfold. Effective focus questions are clear and tend to be highly divergent. They ask students to marshal evidence in support of a position. Here are some examples of effective focus questions:

- A U.S. history teacher who wanted his students to explore the concept of checks and balances asked, "Is there really a balance of power between the three branches of federal government?"
- A calculus teacher wanted her students to explore the foundations of calculus. After providing a short reading about Isaac Newton, she posed the question, "What does it mean when we say someone invented calculus?"
- A primary school teacher whose students had just read Susan Meddaugh's *Tree of Birds* (in which the main character wants to keep a bird he finds in the wild) asked students, "Can people and animals be friends?"

3. **Develop a sparking question.** In terms of the lesson sequence, sparking questions or activities are asked before focus questions; they are designed to build bridges between the students' prior knowledge and the content to be discussed. Sparking questions also generate interest in the content. You may use a single sparking question or a set to help students make the appropriate connections. In creating sparking questions, you need to think about your students. What do they already know from their own experiences or from what they have already studied? How can you activate that prior experience and bring it to bear on the lesson? Here are the sparking questions developed by the three teachers mentioned in Step 2.

- Checks and balances lesson—What First Amendment rights are especially important to you? How are all three branches involved in protecting those rights?
- Origins of calculus lesson—What inventions can you think of that completely changed the world?
- *Tree of Birds* lesson—Have you ever had a pet or animal that you were very close to? What kinds of feelings do people have for pets and animals?

4. **Decide how students will acquire the information they need to participate in the discussion.** What sources of knowledge will your students need to draw upon for this information? Some possibilities include:

- A reading selection
- The student's own notes

- A teacher demonstration
- A lab experiment
- An audio or video presentation (CD, DVD, cassette)
- A mini-lecture

5. **Develop a kindling activity.** The teaching process known as *kindling* helps get the "fire" of discussion burning. Kindling consists of three steps. In the first step, students internalize the focus question and generate their initial response. For the planning phase, you need to consider how students will record their responses. Will they write responses, sketch ideas, or make notes? The second step of kindling involves breaking students into pairs or small groups to complete a brief task and discuss ideas. Small-group discussion gives students an opportunity to test their thinking and evaluate the cohesiveness of their ideas. Planning for this step means creating a simple task that will help students prepare for the discussion. Possibilities include sharing ideas and answering questions, formulating positions, creating visual organizers, and comparing and contrasting group members' ideas. The third step entails returning to the large-group discussion. For this step you need to plan how you will record what students say. Recording responses, drawing lines to show agreement or disagreement, and highlighting by circling or underlining key points are some of the ways you can help students keep track of what has been said so that their energy is not spent trying to remember the points they should be discussing or challenging.

6. **Create a synthesis activity for the discussion.** You now need to consider how students will apply what they have learned from the discussion. What will students do to pull together all of the ideas and information to which they have been exposed? Some possible product formats include:

- a written summary of all the opinions
- a defense of one's own opinion against the others
- a group project
- a visual organizer
- a persuasive or rhetorical essay
- an oral presentation
- a survey

Variations and Extensions

An important variation on Circle of Knowledge is the Socratic Seminar (Adler, 1982). The strategy is based on the teaching techniques of the Greek philosopher Socrates, who posed provocative questions to his students but did not answer them. Instead, Socrates allowed rich, student-based discussions to unfold. The underlying idea of the Socratic Seminar is that students are responsible for their own learning.

In a typical Socratic Seminar, discussion is focused around a text or set of texts that the entire class has already read. Before the seminar, students think carefully about the reading(s) and form preliminary ideas based on a set of questions provided by the teacher. During the seminar, the classroom is arranged in a circle so that all participants can see and address one another as equals. Although the teacher poses thought-provoking questions that call for discussion and divergent thinking, it is important to emphasize that students are talking to each other and not to the teacher. Usually, the seminar culminates in an essay.

The steps for conducting a Socratic Seminar follow, along with a running example from the classroom of high school English teacher Jolene Baccay:

1. **Assign a reading or thematically linked group of readings. Ask students to take notes that will help them understand and talk about the central issues in their reading(s).** Jolene is conducting an interdisciplinary lesson about the struggle for literacy on the part of enslaved African Americans. For the seminar, she chooses three readings: a selection from Booker T. Washington's autobiography, an autobiographical selection by Frederick Douglass, and Frances Ellen Watkins Harper's poem "Learning to Read." To help students organize their notes and prepare for the seminar, Jolene asks them to focus their attention on why literacy was so important to the authors and what obstacles faced enslaved persons who wanted to learn how to read.

2. **Share the criteria for the seminar with students before they begin.** Jolene and her students discuss the four criteria for thoughtful seminars: preparation, comprehension of content, participation, and use of evidence.

3. **Arrange the classroom in a circle, and begin the seminar by posing a sparking question.** Jolene begins the seminar by asking, "Why was learning to read so important to enslaved persons?"

4. **Allow students to exchange their ideas about the question.** Students do not need to raise their hands to respond; the only rules are that they must allow each other to speak, must show respect to all speakers' ideas, and must use evidence from the text whenever they make claims.

   Jolene sits in the circle and becomes a participant. She reminds students that they are conducting the discussion and steps in as a teacher only once to help two students resolve a dispute by reminding them of the rules of the seminar. At key points during the seminar, when Jolene would normally intervene, she lets the students work it out themselves. At first, this is as awkward for Jolene as it is for students, but after a few minutes the message is clearly received by students: They are responsible for what happens during the seminar.

5. **Use a few focusing questions throughout the seminar to keep the discussion close to the central issues. Pose a closing question to synthesize the discussion.** As she participates, Jolene periodically poses a

new focusing question. For today's seminar, she asks three focusing questions: the opening question plus two more (*What were the attitudes of slave owners toward their slaves' literacy? What were the obstacles facing enslaved persons who wanted to learn to read?*). Just before the end of the discussion, Jolene poses the closing question: *How did the enslaved persons overcome the obstacles they encountered in learning to read?*

6. **Present the final task and discuss the criteria for success.** Jolene wants students to reflect on the seminar and then to develop an essay discussing the struggle for literacy among enslaved African Americans, noting similarities and differences among the three readings. Before students begin, Jolene reviews the criteria for success with her students.

- The essay demonstrates a thorough understanding of all three selections.
- The essay is based on evidence from the selections.
- The essay is specific, detailed, and comprehensive.
- The organization of the essay is logical, coherent, and easily discernible.
- The language of the essay is interpretive and communicates information and ideas effectively.
- The essay demonstrates a command of the conventions of standard written English.

How does the strategy fit into unit design?
(Blueprint for Learning)

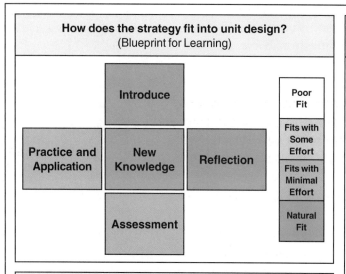

Introduce	Poor Fit
Practice and Application / New Knowledge / Reflection	Fits with Some Effort
	Fits with Minimal Effort
Assessment	Natural Fit

What learning styles does the strategy engage?
(Motivation/Differentiation)

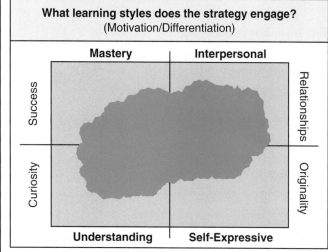

Mastery | Interpersonal
Success — Relationships
Curiosity — Originality
Understanding | Self-Expressive

What facets of understanding does the strategy develop?
(Understanding by Design)

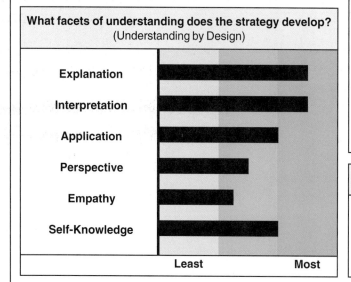

- Explanation
- Interpretation
- Application
- Perspective
- Empathy
- Self-Knowledge

Least   Most

What skills does the strategy build?
(The Hidden Skills of Academic Literacy)

Read and Study
- ● Collect/organize ideas through notemaking
- ● Make sense of abstract academic vocabulary
- ○ Read/interpret visuals

Reason and Analyze
- ○ Draw conclusions; make/test inferences, hypotheses, conjectures
- ○ Conduct comparisons using criteria
- ● Analyze demands of a variety of questions

Create and Communicate
- ● Write clear, coherent explanations
- ● Write comfortably in major nonfiction genres
- ● Read and write about two or more documents

Reflect and Relate
- ○ Construct plans to address questions and tasks
- ● Use criteria and guidelines to evaluate work
- ○ Control/alter mood and impulsivity

How does the strategy incorporate the research on instructional effectiveness?
(Classroom Instruction That Works)

- ● Identifying similarities and differences
- ● Summarizing and note taking
- ○ Reinforcing effort and providing recognition
- ● Homework and practice
- ○ Nonlinguistic representation
- ● Cooperative learning
- ● Setting objectives and feedback
- ○ Generating and testing hypotheses
- ○ Cues, questions, and advance organizers

What types of knowledge does the strategy teach?

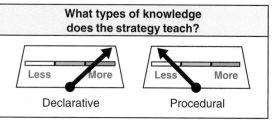

Less   More   Less   More

Declarative   Procedural

19

Do You Hear What I Hear?

Strategy Overview

Scan a set of state or national standards at any grade level and in any discipline and you'll find an unmistakable emphasis on literacy skills. Much more than basic reading and writing, literacy now implies a whole host of critical academic skills central to all the content areas, from separating essential from nonessential information, to monitoring comprehension, to finding evidence, to producing high-quality written products in various genres and styles. If teachers are to develop these standards-based skills, they need strategies that

- Are easy to implement;
- Allow them to work effectively with all students, not just high achievers;
- Engage various forms of thinking and all forms of communication—listening, speaking, reading, and writing;
- Scaffold key literacy skills and support the development of these skills over time; and
- Provide them with time to diagnose literacy problems and provide coaching to students.

Do You Hear What I Hear? (Strong, Silver, Perini, & Tuculescu, 2002) is one such strategy. The strategy is so named because of the initial emphasis it places on the important but often neglected skill of listening. The teacher reads a brief but rigorous text aloud to students two separate times. Students are afforded the opportunity to simply listen the first time and then create a set of notes during the second reading. Student partners then coach each other to a complete retelling of the text, checking to see if their retellings capture the same big ideas and important details (in effect asking each other, "Do you hear what I hear?"). After the retelling, the strategy engages students in a set of increasingly sophisticated literary skills. Students respond to higher-order comprehension questions, support claims with textual evidence, craft a written product, and refine the written product through peer feedback and teacher coaching—precisely the skills needed to raise literacy standards in every classroom and to help every student learn how to manage and respond to challenging texts and content.

The Strategy in Action

More than any other course, Penny Watts loves teaching the half-year elective she developed two years ago, called "Writing the Real: The Importance of Nonfiction in the 21st Century." What excites her most is not the syllabus of first-rate nonfiction texts that she and her students explore together; what excites her most is the way she can actually see the drastic improvement that students make in only a few months. Penny credits this turnaround in her students' reading, writing, speaking, and listening skills to the regular use of Do You Hear What I Hear? (DYHWIH?). Penny uses the strategy once each week, and this week is no exception. The topic for today's DYHWIH? lesson is the famous speech delivered by Sojourner Truth known as "Ain't I a Woman?"

Penny reads the speech aloud—twice. During the first reading, students just listen, trying to pick up the gist of the reading. During the second reading, students create a set of notes that will allow them to retell the main ideas and key details in their own words.

After Penny completes the second reading, students partner up. Each student in the pair retells the passage to the other student, who acts as a retelling coach. As student pairs work, Penny moves around the room, listening in on student pairs and providing assistance and coaching to struggling students. As Penny listens in on one pair, she is pleased to hear Ryan (the coach) help Allison (the reteller) through a difficult section of the reading:

Allison: This is the part that gave me trouble, the part where Sojourner Truth talks about the quarts and pints.

Ryan: Well, that's not what she's really talking about. Remember? She's really comparing how much different people have of something.

Allison: Right, I remember. She's talking about people's intellect.

Ryan: That's right, and why would she use units of measurement, like quarts and pints to make her point?

Allison: Oh . . . um . . . OK, now I get it. She's saying that it doesn't matter how much intellect someone has, whether someone has a quart or a pint. It's a comparison.

Ryan: Good. So now finish your retelling.

After each student in each pair has completed a retelling, each pair meets up with another pair. Penny provides groups with four questions, which she asks them to preview and formulate their initial responses to.

- Vocabulary Question: What does Sojourner Truth mean by the word *intellect*?
- Quotation Question: What does she mean when she keeps saying, "Ain't I a Woman?"
- Technique Question: What can you learn from the speech about responding to counterarguments when trying to persuade others?
- Motivation Question: What does Sojourner Truth hope to accomplish through this speech?

At this point, Penny distributes a written copy of Sojourner Truth's speech to students. Students read the text and must use specific evidence from it in responding to the questions with their groups. Meanwhile, Penny moves around the room again, observing student groups as they formulate and discuss their responses, and providing assistance and coaching as needed. After student groups have come to agreement on their responses, Penny assigns them a task:

> Now that you've shared some of your ideas about how to persuade people through language, we're going to put some of these ideas into action. Imagine that a publishing company is preparing a new compilation of the great short persuasive speeches of all time and is looking for suggestions on which speeches to include. Write a letter to the editors persuading them that "Ain't I a Woman?" should be included in their compilation. Remember to be like Sojourner Truth, and anticipate and respond to possible counterarguments.

Penny uses Do You Hear What I Hear? in this way for the first three Mondays of every month. On the final Monday of the month, students choose their best work from the three previous lessons and meet in Writer's Clubs to read their pieces and collect notes on how to improve them. As always, Penny sits in on these Writer's Club sessions to help group members fine-tune their communication skills, generate constructive feedback, and produce their best work. In addition, while this process is helpful to students, it is more helpful to Penny: With only one product to grade, Penny is able to commit much more time to helping students identify and overcome their liabilities as writers.

Why the Strategy Works

As state and national standards are emphasizing literacy skills, teachers are faced with the task of developing a skill-based curriculum without cutting into content. Do You Hear What I Hear? is a strategy that helps teachers and students meet the challenge posed by these new and demanding literacy standards. More specifically, the strategy leads to significant improvements in students' reading, writing, speaking, and listening skills for the following reasons:

• **It is built on the research-based practice known as retelling.** Students' initial efforts during a DYHWIH? lesson go into the development of a high-quality retelling of the text. Unlike traditional summarizing, which requires deleting some information, substituting some information, and keeping some information, retelling asks students to develop their own personal way of representing their emerging understanding for another reader.

While a significant body of research (Brown & Cambourne, 1987; Gambrell, Koskinen, & Kapinus, 1991; Moss, 2002) confirms the benefits of retelling as a way to both build and assess students' comprehension skills, what is especially eye-opening about retelling are its overall effects on students' literacy skills when used regularly. Brown and Cambourne (1987) have demonstrated that repeated use of retelling strategies leads to

  ◦ a greater variety of sentence forms and structures in student writing;
  ◦ an increased confidence in reading, discussing, and writing about new texts; and
  ◦ improvements in grammar, spelling, and other semantic and syntactical conventions.

• **It front-loads comprehension.** Before students ever see a written text in a DYHWIH? lesson, they have already listened to it twice, made notes about it, retold it to a partner, and coached their partner through another retelling. By the time the text arrives, students already understand it. For this reason, DYHWIH? is an ideal way to assist less-proficient readers and bolster the confidence of all students in preparing them to read and respond to the text.

• **It increases the level of rigor in the classroom.** "The decision to withhold rigor from some students is one of the most important reasons why schools fail" (Strong, Silver, & Perini, 2001, p. 7). The argument behind this claim is simple: "Dumbing down" content yields few, if any, educational benefits while regular exposure to challenging texts and content compels attention, teaches students how to manage uncertainty, develops flexibility in thinking, and leads to increased self-confidence among students. Thus, each and every Do You Hear What I Hear? lesson is designed around a brief but rigorous text—one that will challenge students to think without overwhelming them with too much content.

• **It scaffolds and supports the evolution of students' thinking.** Do You Hear What I Hear? begins with listening and then moves through a series of increasingly sophisticated thinking processes, from developing notes to retelling and peer coaching, to responding to higher-order questions about themes and passages, all the way to the creation and revision of a written product. In this way, DYHWIH? does more than employ the research showing that generative post-reading tasks improve students' retention and comprehension (Morrow, 1985; Taylor & Beach, 1984); it also provides teachers with a clear method for preparing students to succeed at these higher-order tasks.

 • **It reduces grading time and increases coaching time.** DYHWIH? recognizes that diagnosis and coaching from the teacher are the true building blocks of students' skill development. That's why the strategy yields only one graded product each month. Students choose their best product for the month and work in Writer's Clubs (see p. 202 for more on Writer's Clubs) to refine their product before submitting it. This leaves the teacher free to work with students in diagnosing and helping them overcome the challenges they face as readers, retellers, and writers.

How to Use the Strategy

1. Leave time to read a short, rigorous text to your students, preferably once each week. Read each text twice: once for students to get the gist through listening and once for them to take notes for retelling.

2. Instruct students to find a partner and review their notes together. One student puts the notes aside, while the other coaches him to a complete retelling. Students then switch roles.

3. Pose two to four guiding questions. Guiding questions often focus on vocabulary (e.g., *What does "prime" mean in math?*), the meaning of quotations (e.g., *What does Robert Frost mean when he says, "And that has made all the difference"?*), characters' or authors' motivations (e.g., *Why do Frog and Toad decide to eat all the cookies? Why does the author paint the Romans in such an unflattering way?*), and themes (e.g., *How are birds and dinosaurs related, according to this article?*). Shift from listening to reading by having students read the text.

4. Have student pairs team up. In groups of four, students discuss answers and resolve differences. Observe and coach groups.

5. Establish a writing product based on the reading. The product should be short (one to one-and-a-half pages) and can be in any of these formats: a retelling, a review, an essay, a creative response (story, poem, play, etc.), or a personal response.

6. To maximize the benefits of DYHWIH? use the strategy regularly. Once per week is ideal.

7. Have students review their written products, select their best one, and work in Writer's Clubs (see p. 202) to collect feedback and revision ideas from their peers. Sit in on Writer's Clubs and provide coaching.

8. Give students time to revise their products according to the feedback. Inform students that only their selected, revised product will be graded.

Planning a Do You Hear What I Hear? Lesson

Designed to keep planning to a minimum (thereby leaving more time for diagnosis and coaching), Do You Hear What I Hear? requires only three planning steps.

1. **Select your text.** The text you choose should take no more than 10 minutes to read aloud, and most texts chosen tend to be considerably shorter than that. One teacher we know constructed a series of wonderful lessons around the three-line poems known as haiku. However, whatever text you select should be rigorous. That is, it should be more challenging than reading that is regularly assigned.

   ◦ A high school science teacher uses Do You Hear What I Hear? to explore "Science on the Edge"—science being worked on by real scientists in today's world. Each Friday, the class uses Do You Hear What I Hear? to develop a deep understanding of an article taken from the science section of the local paper.

   ◦ A middle school English teacher who is reading *The Miracle Worker* (a play about Helen Keller) with his 7th graders selects three scenes for in-depth exploration. Each Friday over the course of the month-long unit, students focus on one of the three selected scenes.

   ◦ An elementary teacher creates her Do You Hear What I Hear? lessons using the *Touchpebbles* program (Zeiderman, 2003). *Touchpebbles* is a collection of short, rigorous readings from various disciplines for students in grades 2–5.

2. **Prepare your guiding questions.** Questions for Do You Hear What I Hear? lessons work best when they are fairly predictable, when they can be repeated in slightly different forms from week to week. This repetition leads to a growing sense of confidence as students learn how to recognize, think about, and wrestle with questions that call for particular kinds of thinking. Students should answer no more than four questions. In a literature setting, questions typically require students to think about vocabulary, a quotation from the text, a character's motivation, and theme. Of course, many other types of questions are possible, depending on your text, instructional goals, content area, and students. For example, learning styles provide a great frame of reference for creating different kinds of questions as well as for engaging different kinds of thinking. Figure 19.1 outlines the four styles of questions and provides question stems for creating 13 different kinds of style-based questions.

3. **Choose a writing prompt or assignment you can repeat from week to week with slight variations.** Do You Hear What I Hear? capitalizes on repetition, using it as a key to student growth. Assigning a similar task (e.g., a comparative essay) three or four weeks in a row keeps students' energies focused on the same skill or genre for an extended period

FIGURE 19.1 Questions in Style

Mastery questions ask students to	**Interpersonal questions ask students to**
Focus on recalling facts: • Who was involved? • Where did it take place? • When did it occur? • What happened? • How did it occur? Supply information based on observations: • What did you observe? • What is wrong with this? How would you correct it? • Can you describe the data? Establish procedures or sequences: • What are the steps? • How would you go about doing this? • What comes first? Next? • What is the correct order for this?	Empathize and describe feelings: • How would you feel if _____ happened to you? • How do you think _____ felt? • Can you describe your feelings? Value and appreciate: • Why is _____ important to you? • What is the value of _____? • What decision would you make? Explore human interest problems: • How would you advise or console _____? • What is the issue facing _____? What would you do about it? • How would you help each side come to an agreement?
Understanding questions ask students to	**Self-Expressive questions ask students to**
Focus on making connections: • What are the important similarities and differences? • What is the cause? • What are the effects? • How are the parts connected? Make inferences and interpret: • Yes, but why? • How would you explain _____? • Can you prove it? • What can you conclude? • What evidence do you have to support your position? Focus on underlying meanings: • What are the hidden assumptions? • What does this prove? • What have you discovered?	Rethink their ideas: • What comes to mind when you think of _____? • How is _____ like _____? Develop images, hypotheses, and predictions: • What would happen if _____? • Can you imagine _____? What would it look like? What would it be like? Focus on alternatives and original solutions: • How many possible ways can you _____? • What is another way to do this? • Is there a better way to design a _____? Think metaphorically and creatively: • How is _____ like _____? • Can you create a poem, icon, or skit that represents this?

Source: Adapted from Silver, H. F., Strong, R. W., & Perini, M. J. (2001). Tools for promoting active, in-depth learning, 128. Thoughtful Education Press: Ho-Ho-Kus, NJ.

of time—an important condition for improvement. Here's how each of the three teachers introduced in Step 1 designed their repeating tasks:

- The high school teacher who had students read an article from the science section of the newspaper each week asked students to write a lab-style report on each article, describing the methodology, conclusions, hypotheses, and potential future of the research.

- The middle school teacher who read *The Miracle Worker* with his 7th graders asked students to assume the role of a theater critic and review the selected scenes by focusing on the strengths and weaknesses of each scene.

- The elementary teacher who used the short, rigorous selections from *Touchpebbles* wanted to concentrate on persuasive writing. For each text that students read, they had to write a letter telling a friend why the text is important and convincing the friend to read it.

Variations and Extensions

Retelling and summarizing are more complex skills than they seem at first sight. Both retelling and summarizing require students to make decisions about what content is essential and nonessential, sort information into meaningful sets, and communicate their ideas as a cohesive whole. Following you will find two techniques designed to help students—especially struggling students—develop these crucial skills. We have also included in this section a strategy known as Do You See What I See? The strategy puts the structure of DYHWIH? to work in mathematics classrooms.

Retelling Rubrics

One of the main causes of difficulty for students when they write retellings is that they're not sure what a good retelling looks or sounds like. You can help students conduct focused analyses of their own and others' retellings by providing them with a double-input rubric (see Figure 19.2). With a double-input rubric, both the student and teacher assess the retelling and make suggestions for how to improve it.

Collaborative Summarizing

Picking out only the most essential information from the text is another problem facing students when they develop retellings and summaries. Collaborative Summarizing (Strong, Silver, & Perini, 2001) uses a cooperative learning structure and peer negotiation to scaffold the skill of separating the important from the trivial. Collaborative Summarizing moves through five basic steps, as listed on page 238.

FIGURE 19.2   Double-Input Retelling Rubric

Organization

Your retelling shows that you are able to organize information so that it is clear and easy to understand for the reader.

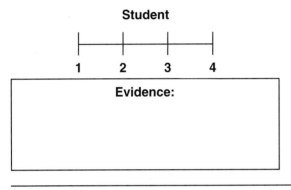

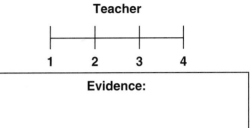

Accuracy

Your retelling shows that you carefully check your notes and summaries against the original text to make sure your information is accurate.

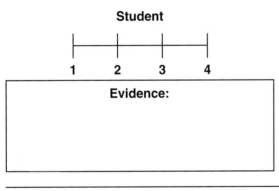

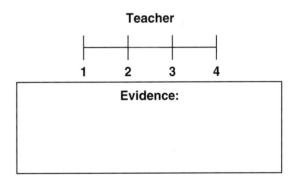

Balance

Your retelling shows that you know how to strike the right balance between main ideas and supporting details. It includes all the important information and leaves out everything that is trivial or redundant.

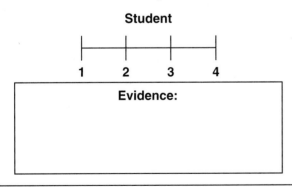

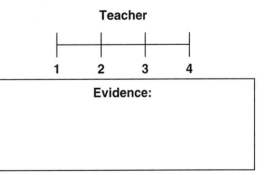

Source: From *Reading for Academic Success, Grades 2–6: Differentiated Strategies for Struggling, Average, and Advanced Readers* (p. 43), by H. F. Silver, R. W. Strong, & M. J. Perini (2007), Thousand Oaks, CA: Corwin. Figure copyright © Thoughtul Education Press. Adapted with permission.

1. After reading, ask students to list three to six ideas they believe are the most important.

2. In pairs, have students review the rules for peer negotiation.
   - Use evidence from the text to show why an idea is important.
   - Avoid quick and simple solutions. Negotiate through your ideas.
   - This is not a vote or a contest of wills, so avoid win-lose thinking in your negotiations.

   Have students use these three rules to come to an agreement on the three to six most important ideas in the text.

3. Allow each student pair to meet with another pair to exchange negotiated lists. In groups of four, students should negotiate their lists to create a final consensus on the most important ideas. Remind students that this final list will serve as the foundation for the summary or retelling, so they should organize the ideas so that they can be written out easily. For example, here is the final negotiated list that a group of high school art students created for an assigned reading on the movement known as Impressionism:
   - By breaking many established rules of painting, the Impressionists created a new movement in art.
   - Unlike painters before them, who were interested in topics of historical significance, the Impressionists attempted to catch the simple and natural beauty of their surroundings at a given moment.
   - Impressionist painters were more concerned with capturing the essence of their subjects than they were in getting all of the details exactly right.
   - Among the Impressionists' technical innovations were a new and vibrant way of using color and short, thick brushstrokes that the viewer of the painting could actually see.
   - In the late 1800s, Impressionism looked strange to most people, who sometimes thought the paintings were unfinished.
   - Today, Impressionist paintings by artists such as Monet, Renoir, and Degas are among the most famous and beloved of all time.

4. Ask students to convert their lists into summaries or retellings individually.

5. Have each original team of four join another group of four. In groups of eight, students read and discuss their summaries and then use their discussion to generate a set of criteria for creating high-quality summaries. Discuss and refine criteria through a whole-class discussion. Then, over the course of the year, remind students to refer to these criteria to help them create powerful summaries.

Do You See What I See? A Technique for Improving Students' Mathematical Problem-Solving Skills

One of the most common blocks to student performance on state math tests is that students tend to be impulsive. Students decide too quickly what a problem is asking for and how to solve it. The same features that make DYHWIH? an effective strategy for improving thinking and communication skills also make it ideal for helping students become more careful, more strategic problem solvers in math. This math-based variation of DYHWIH? known as Do You See What I See? (because of its emphasis on visual representation), leads students through seven steps:

1. Devote one class period a week to exploring complex and nonroutine problems connected to current math topics from your curriculum. A wealth of these Problem-of-the-Week-type problems is available online. Some of our favorite sites for juicy problems include the National Council of Teachers of Mathematics (NCTM) weekly problems (www.nctm.org), the Franklin Institute's library of open-ended math problems (www.fi.edu/school), and the Education Development Center's "Problems with a Point" (www2.edc.org/mathproblems).

2. Read the problem aloud twice to your students. During the first reading, ask students to make notes that capture the most important information from the problem. During the second reading, ask students to create a sketch representing the problem. Students may use numbers and letters in their sketches, but no words.

3. Provide students with a written copy of the problem and ask them to revise their notes and sketches. Make sure students do not solve the problem yet.

4. Create small collaborative groups of three to four students and ask groups to
   ◦ Share their notes and sketches.
   ◦ Define what the problem is asking.
   ◦ Develop a plan to solve the problem. (Groups should still not solve the problem.)

5. As students work, circulate around the room to listen to and observe student groups. Invite two or three groups with different problem-solving approaches to describe their plans. Allow class members to ask questions and provide feedback.

6. Assign the problem for homework. Ask students to submit a written justification for their approach along with their solution.

7. Have students engage in this process once a week for three weeks. On the fourth week of the month, ask students to select their best effort from the three previous sessions. Allow students to meet in small groups to revise and publish their work. Grade only the one published piece each month.

How does the strategy fit into unit design?
(Blueprint for Learning)

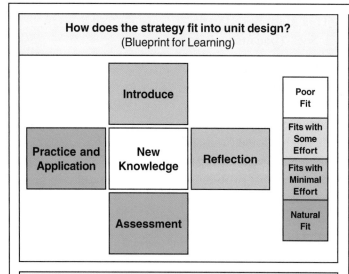

	Poor Fit
	Fits with Some Effort
	Fits with Minimal Effort
	Natural Fit

Introduce

Practice and Application | New Knowledge | Reflection

Assessment

What learning styles does the strategy engage?
(Motivation/Differentiation)

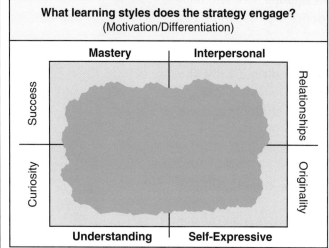

Mastery | Interpersonal

Success

Curiosity

Relationships

Originality

Understanding | Self-Expressive

What facets of understanding does the strategy develop?
(Understanding by Design)

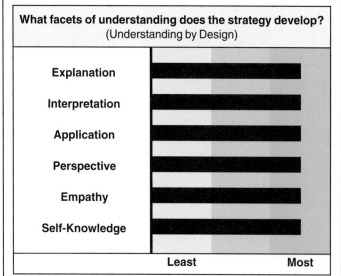

Explanation

Interpretation

Application

Perspective

Empathy

Self-Knowledge

Least | Most

What skills does the strategy build?
(The Hidden Skills of Academic Literacy)

Read and Study
- ○ Collect/organize ideas through note making
- ○ Make sense of abstract academic vocabulary
- ○ Read/interpret visuals

Reason and Analyze
- ○ Draw conclusions; make/test inferences, hypotheses, conjectures
- ○ Conduct comparisons using criteria
- ● Analyze demands of a variety of questions

Create and Communicate
- ● Write clear, coherent explanations
- ○ Write comfortably in major nonfiction genres
- ○ Read and write about two or more documents

Reflect and Relate
- ● Construct plans to address questions and tasks
- ● Use criteria and guidelines to evaluate work
- ● Control/alter mood and impulsivity

How does the strategy incorporate the research on instructional effectiveness?
(Classroom Instruction That Works)

- ○ Identifying similarities and differences
- ○ Summarizing and note taking
- ● Reinforcing effort and providing recognition
- ● Homework and practice
- ○ Nonlinguistic representation
- ● Cooperative learning
- ● Setting objectives and feedback
- ○ Generating and testing hypotheses
- ● Cues, questions, and advance organizers

What types of knowledge does the strategy teach?

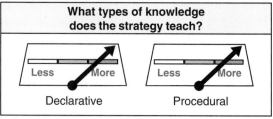

Less More | Less More

Declarative | Procedural

20

Task Rotation

Strategy Overview

Imagine you have just signed up for a new course in college. On the first day of class, your professor informs you that 50 percent of your grade will be based on your choice of two of the following four tasks:

1. A 150-question, timed multiple-choice final exam
2. An essay in which you identify a central thesis of the course and assemble evidence for and against the thesis
3. A project in which you use four major concepts from the course to create an application to your work as a classroom teacher
4. An extended letter in which you explore the personal meaning of the course to you

Which two tasks would you choose? Which one would you do your best to avoid?

Task Rotation provides teachers with a classroom-friendly framework for differentiating teaching and learning. In using Task Rotation, teachers present students with four different styles of tasks.

1. **Mastery tasks** ask students to remember and describe.
   ◦ Sample task: Select an irritating or dangerous animal from our unit. Develop a profile sheet that highlights at least eight important features of your animal.
2. **Understanding tasks** ask students to reason and explain.
   ◦ Sample task: Why is your animal important? Develop a plan that will help others understand the role your animal plays in the world.

3. **Self-Expressive tasks** ask students to imagine and create.
   ◦ Sample task: Create a myth that tells how your animal developed an important trait or behavior.
4. **Interpersonal tasks** ask students to explore feelings and relate personally.
   ◦ Sample task: Write a friendly letter explaining why you love your animal.

By designing and assigning tasks that represent the four learning styles, teachers can create differentiated assessment systems that are manageable, that provide powerful insights into how each student learns, and that are meaningful and motivating for all the learners in their classrooms.

The Strategy in Action

Fifth grade math teacher Kathy Padilla knows how important learning styles are to motivating all her students. Over the course of the year, Kathy differentiates teaching and learning through learning styles by

- Developing learning style profiles for each student and using the profiles to help struggling readers and writers capitalize on their natural strengths and minimize weaknesses.
- Rotating teaching strategies across all four learning styles so that all students are accommodated (by strategies that speak to their dominant style) and challenged (by strategies that call for them to use less-developed styles).
- Using the *Learning Style Inventory for Students* (Silver & Strong, 2004) to help students discover their learning style profile and engaging students in a yearlong conversation about how they learn best and how they can improve as learners.

Kathy's commitment to differentiated learning is also apparent in her assessment system, which is anchored by Task Rotation. Currently, Kathy is using Task Rotation to synthesize a unit on area and perimeter. Using her state standards as her guide, Kathy designs tasks in all four styles. Figure 20.1 shows the state standards Kathy chose to address as well as the Task Rotation she developed for her unit.

Students begin by reviewing the four tasks with Kathy. She explains that students must complete all four tasks, but may work in any order they like. Students may refer back to their notes to monitor their understanding and to make sure they have the information they need to complete each task. Kathy ensures that students understand what exemplary work looks and sounds like for each task by providing criteria for all four in the Task Rotation. She makes sure that the criteria are clear and written in student-friendly language. Kathy's criteria are on page 243.

• Do you know how to compute area and perimeter accurately?
• Can you explain the mathematical reasoning behind the computation process?
• Can you use your understanding to create and solve sophisticated perimeter and area problems?
• Can you use area and perimeter to describe and explain concepts from your own life?

FIGURE 20.1   Kathy's State Standards and Task Rotation

Kathy used these standards:

Academic Expectations
• **Students use mathematical ideas and procedures to communicate, reason, and solve problems.**

• **Students understand space and dimensionality concepts and use them appropriately and accurately.**
  Core Content Standards:
    • Students will use measurements to describe and compare attributes of objects to include length, width, height, perimeter, area, and volume, and compare attributes.
    • Students will identify, describe, and give examples of basic two-dimensional shapes, and will use these shapes to solve real-world and/or mathematical problems.

Kathy developed this Task Rotation:

Mastery Task	Interpersonal Task
If a rectangle that is 4 in. × 10 in. is placed next to a rectangle that is 5 in. × 12 in., what is the perimeter of the combined figure? What is the area of the combined figure? 	Draw a picture of the floor plan of your home showing the dimensions of each room. Then, compute the perimeter and area for each room and order the rooms from largest to smallest according to their perimeter. How much time do you spend in each room? Can you find a correlation between area, perimeter, and time spent in each room?
In the figure below, what are the fewest number of sides whose measures you must know to accurately calculate perimeter and area? Explain your answer. 	Create a problem in which you must find the perimeter and area of two rectangles, a square, and an equilateral triangle. The problem must be solved using four measurements. Can you create another problem only using three measurements? How about two?
Understanding Task	**Self-Expressive Task**

What Kathy likes best about Task Rotation is how it enables students to explore mathematical concepts and problem-solving procedures from multiple angles using a variety of reading strategies. As students work through the tasks and add new layers to their comprehension of area and perimeter, they are also learning how to apply a set of general skills and strategies that all mathematics learning demands:

- Computing accurately (Mastery)
- Discovering and explaining mathematical principles (Understanding)
- Solving nonroutine problems (Self-Expressive)
- Connecting mathematical ideas to personal experiences (Interpersonal)

To maximize the value of this style-based approach to reading and assessment, Kathy does two things. First, she observes students as they work and asks them questions about how they go about completing various tasks. Second, she holds a follow-up discussion during which students talk about which tasks they liked least, which tasks they liked best, and how they can grow as learners. Through these observation and discussion sessions, Kathy gathers a wealth of assessment data, allowing her to pinpoint those mathematical skills that students need to develop further.

A Potpourri of Task Rotations

Now that you've seen how a teacher designs and implements a Task Rotation in mathematics, take a look at the Task Rotations shown in Figure 20.2. These Task Rotations span a variety of grade levels and subjects. Which ones do you like best? Why?

Why the Strategy Works

Encouraging a full range of student diversity while, at the same time, helping all students meet rigorous state and national standards is a challenge facing nearly every educator. Task Rotation is a differentiated teaching and learning strategy that helps teachers meet this challenge by giving students the opportunity to process content and demonstrate what they know in a variety of learning styles.

Learning styles come out of the work of famed psychologist Carl Jung (1923). A core theme in Jung's work is that much apparently random variety in human behavior is due to the preferences individuals

FIGURE 20.2   A Potpourri of Task Rotations

Primary—Plants	
Mastery Task Draw a flowering plant and label its parts.	**Interpersonal Task** How would you feel on a sunny (or rainy) day if you were a plant?
Understanding Task Why are plants important to our world? Think of three reasons.	**Self-Expressive Task** What would our world look like if there were no plants?

Elementary—Nouns	
Mastery Task Nouns are words that name a person, place, or thing. Underline the nouns in the sentences below. Next, write each noun in the correct column of this chart: Person | Place | Thing	**Interpersonal Task** Ask your mother or father to help you make a list of the first words you ever spoke when you were an infant. Look over your list. What do you notice about the first words?

Understanding Task
Before you can use better nouns, you must be able to find the nouns. If you are a good noun detective, you can find the nouns hidden in these three sentences. Explain how you discover them.
  1. Lethargy is difficult to combat.
  2. Those fallacies are often believed.
  3. Did you write those six formulae?
	Self-Expressive Task
	Now try this: Write sentences that are full of nonsense words like "My beautiful snagrid won the porfgret." Write your sentences so that a friend can easily spot the nouns no matter how many nonsense words are in the sentences.

Middle School—"Casey at the Bat"	
Mastery Task "Casey at the Bat" is a poem written in 13 stanzas. Can you retell the poem in seven sentences: six sentences for the first 12 stanzas and one sentence for the last stanza?	**Interpersonal Task** Everyone is a little like Casey. What attitudes do you have that help you perform well in school? What attitudes do you have that might make school more difficult for you? Explain how these attitudes are beneficial to you.
Understanding Task Prove or disprove this statement with evidence from the poem: Casey's attitude is responsible for his failure.	**Self-Expressive Task** Let's write a little poetry ourselves. We'll add just one stanza. Imagine Casey is being interviewed after the game. Based on your discussion about his attitude, what would Casey say in the interview? Be sure to follow the style and rhyme scheme of the poem.

High School—Constitutional Complexities	
Mastery Task Read through the selection of legal briefs in our Citizenship Library. Then, using these briefs as a model, develop a legal brief for this case.	**Interpersonal Task** Put together a portfolio of cases that reflect similar ambiguities in our right to free speech and two other basic rights. Accompany your portfolio with a journal that explores your personal feelings about these cases.
Understanding Task Put together a debate team to discuss this issue: Resolved, it is possible to rewrite our Constitution to eliminate problems in freedom of speech relating to obscenity, political correctness, and the denigration of ethnic identity.	**Self-Expressive Task** Create a folk song about this case. Your song should take a position on the case and its resolution.

develop for certain styles of thinking and learning. Years later, Isabel Myers and Kathleen Briggs (1962/1998) expanded on Jung's work to create a comprehensive model of human differences, culminating in the well-known Myers-Briggs Type Indicator. Since then, new generations of educational researchers—including Bernice McCarthy (1982), Kathleen Butler (1984), Carolyn Mamchur (1996), Harvey Silver and J. Robert Hanson (1998), Edward Pajak (2003), and Gayle Gregory (2005)—have explored the implications of these ideas and applied them specifically to education.

Our own model of learning styles synthesizes this research in light of our 30 years of helping schools engage, motivate, and raise the achievement of all learners, and it identifies four main learning styles. These styles are outlined in the introduction to this book. (See Figure C: The Four Learning Styles, p. 7.)

All styles are equally important and all styles are used by every learner; however, it is also true that people usually develop style preferences. If, in the classroom, some students' style preferences are ignored, then those learners will likely disengage from, or even feel threatened by, new learning. By failing to reach out to different learning styles, teachers produce unmotivated, uncomfortable students. On the other hand, students become willing to stretch and grow as learners when their styles are validated in the classroom. The evidence for this fact can be found in a number of studies showing significant improvement in student motivation and achievement when teachers take their students' styles into account (Carbo, 1992; Dunn, Griggs, & Beasley, 1995; Hanson, Dewing, Silver, & Strong, 1991).

By putting the power of learning styles to work through Task Rotation, teachers can more easily meet several key educational goals, including these:

- **Increasing the depth of student learning**—Students' comprehension of new material becomes deeper because they regularly examine new content from different perspectives.
- **Improving the quality of student thinking**—Students become more proficient in four distinct styles of thinking: remembering (Mastery), reasoning (Understanding), creating (Self-Expressive), and relating (Interpersonal).
- **Motivating all learners**—Students become more engaged in the learning process because Task Rotation lessons balance work in their own personal style with explorations of new and different approaches to learning.
- **Increasing students' mental flexibility**—Students' thinking becomes more open and flexible as they work on tasks requiring different ways of thinking and learning.

How to Use the Strategy

1. If your students are unfamiliar with learning styles, introduce them to the four styles and allow time for reflection and discussion.

2. Introduce the four tasks. Explain students' roles: Will they be completing all of the tasks, some of the tasks, or one of the tasks? Do they get to choose which tasks to complete? Do they have to complete the tasks in a prescribed order?

3. Allow students to complete the tasks either alone or with a cooperative learning group. Provide criteria for success if needed.

4. Move around the room while students work. Observation of students while they select and complete tasks is an ideal way to learn more about each student's preferences and personal approach to learning.

5. Conduct a discussion session in which students talk about:
   ◦ The kind of thinking required by each task
   ◦ Which tasks they liked best and which they liked least
   ◦ What they learned about themselves as learners during the lesson
   ◦ How they can improve themselves as learners by capitalizing on their strongest styles and growing their underdeveloped capacities

Planning a Task Rotation

To plan a Task Rotation, follow these six steps:

1. **Collect your standards.** Begin by reviewing your standards. What content and skill standards do you want students to be able to meet?

2. **Identify your purpose.** While standards are critical to planning your Task Rotation, they also tend to be abstract and, to be honest, a little mind-numbing with their language of compulsion (*Students will . . .*) and their tendency to separate too many distinct ideas with nothing more than a series of flimsy commas (*Students will use measurements to describe objects according to length, width, height, temperature, weight, and monetary value; sort objects; and compare attributes*). That's why we recommend converting your standards into something more useful—a clear purpose. Defining your purpose(s) means taking your standards and asking yourself:
   ◦ What do I want students to *know*? (Core content knowledge)
   ◦ What do I want students to *understand*? (Themes, questions, big ideas)
   ◦ What *skills* do I want students to develop?
   ◦ What *attitudes* do I want to foster in students?

Unlike a typical standard from a state standards document, your answer to each question should be easy to read and digest. For example, a 1st grade teacher who decided to use Task Rotation to synthesize a unit on plants (see top of Figure 20.2, p. 245) answered the four purpose questions this way:

- *Know*—The main parts of flowering plants
- *Understand*—Why plants are important to us and our world
- *Skills*—Visual representation and explanation
- *Attitudes*—Empathy (students get to "be" plants); appreciation (for the "gifts" plants give us)

3. **Design tasks in all four learning styles.** In designing your four tasks, remember these basic guidelines:

- *Mastery tasks* ask students to remember, describe, summarize, or sequence.
- *Understanding tasks* ask students to compare, reason, prove, or explain.
- *Self-Expressive tasks* ask students to imagine, create, think metaphorically, or ask "What if?"
- *Interpersonal tasks* ask students to empathize, connect to real life, relate personally, or explore feelings and values.

Consult Figure 20.2 for a potpourri of Task Rotations across grade levels and content areas. These Task Rotations will help you get a better sense of how to design your own style-based tasks.

4. **Create a "hook" to pique students' interest and activate prior knowledge.** Before presenting your Task Rotation, it is always a good idea to begin with a hook. A hook is a question or activity designed to capture student interest, help students access their background knowledge related to the content, and set up the Task Rotation to follow. For example, in designing a Task Rotation focused on building students' argument skills, a 5th grade teacher framed a Task Rotation around a crucial argument scene between a British loyalist and an American patriot from the novel *My Brother Sam Is Dead*. He decided to "hook" students into the lesson by posing two questions:

- What's the difference between a good argument and a bad one?
- Think of someone you know who argues well. What does this person do that makes him or her so persuasive?

5. **Develop criteria for success.** You can develop criteria for each task or look for criteria that unite all four tasks. Whichever you choose, remember to keep things simple: There is no need to overwhelm yourself with long lists of highly specific criteria. For example, the 1st grade teacher who developed a Task Rotation on flowering plants (see Figure 20.2), developed these four criteria for her Task Rotation—one criterion for each task.

- Can students identify the main parts of a flowering plant and draw them accurately?

- Can students provide three central reasons for the importance of plants?
- Can students imagine and describe a world without plants?
- Can students personalize the life of a plant?

Before the lesson, share the criteria with students so that they know what to strive for when completing their tasks.

6. **Establish a work plan.** Task Rotation is a highly flexible strategy; it can be used in a variety of ways to meet a host of instructional and assessment purposes. In creating a work plan for your Task Rotation you can:

- Ask students to complete all four tasks in a specified sequence.
- Ask students to complete all four tasks in any sequence they like.
- Assign one or two tasks, and allow students to choose another one.
- Permit students to choose only the task(s) they wish to complete.

One of the great benefits of Task Rotation is that it provides you with valuable information about how each student learns. However you design your work plan, pay close attention to the tasks that students are drawn to and those that they avoid or seem to like least. Regular use of Task Rotation coupled with observation of student work and discussion after the lesson will give you a wealth of data about students' preferences as learners—a kind of window into each student's mind. You can then use this information to help students target and overcome their weaknesses as learners.

Variations and Extensions

Task Rotations help teachers create a culture of comfort (by providing work in every student's style) and challenge (by asking students to work in less preferred styles). The following spin-offs of the strategy show teachers how to adopt this model in order to get a quick reading on students' comprehension levels (Comprehension Menus), differentiate assessment by ability level as well as by learning style (Assessment Menus), and design tasks that incorporate a wide range of multiple intelligences (style-intelligence Task Rotations).

Comprehension Menus

A Comprehension Menu is a pared-down Task Rotation: It asks students questions in all four styles, but the work required to answer each question usually takes only one to five minutes to complete. Unlike Task Rotations, which may or may not ask students to complete all four tasks, Comprehension Menus always require that students respond to all four questions. Comprehension Menus are especially useful when teachers want to make sure students have completed and understand the work they have been assigned. Figure 20.3 shows a comprehension menu designed by a 4th grade teacher to assess her students' understanding of the initial chapters of Betsy Byars's *The Pinballs*, a novel about three foster children who learn to depend on one another.

Assessment Menus

When it comes to assessment, providing an equal opportunity for all four styles of learners can be a challenge, especially because different students perform at different levels of ability and readiness. Assessment Menus solve this problem by fusing the four learning styles with an ability-level approach to differentiation (a là Graduated Difficulty, see pp. 45–55). Assessment Menus allow students to develop their own portfolio of activities and performances over the course of a learning unit—one from each level of difficulty, and one from each style. A sample Assessment Menu can be found in the Variations and Extensions section of the Graduated Difficulty strategy (Figure 3.4, p. 54).

Style-Intelligence Task Rotations

Task Rotation provides students with activities in each of the four learning styles. Often, Task Rotation calls for students to produce written products. However, the strategy readily accommodates many other kinds of products. As such, Task Rotation is tailor-made for integrating learning styles and multiple intelligences.

Multiple intelligence theory is the work of Harvard psychologist Howard Gardner (1999). He proposed that traditional notions of intelligence such as IQ testing were inadequate in explaining the great diversity of human accomplishment. Instead of a single form of intelligence, Gardner found evidence for eight different forms of human intelligence:

• *Verbal-linguistic intelligence* is the intelligence involving language. It is used to comprehend the spoken and written word and to communicate orally and on paper.

• *Logical-mathematical intelligence* involves numbers and logic. We rely on logical-mathematical intelligence when we reason, sequence, and identify conceptual and numerical patterns.

• *Spatial intelligence* focuses on pictures and images. Sketching, visualizing, and the graphic arts all require spatial intelligence.

FIGURE 20.3   Comprehension Menu—The Pinballs

Comprehension Menu	
Mastery Comprehension Who are the three main children in the book? How did each end up in the Mason's foster home?	**Interpersonal Comprehension** Think about the different characters you have read about. Which character do you identify with the most?
Understanding Comprehension What do you think Mrs. Mason means when she says "I guess 'homesickness' is a very real kind of illness, like measles or mumps"?	**Self-Expressive Comprehension** The character Thomas J. is very quiet. What do you imagine he is thinking when he meets the other children for the first time?

• *Musical intelligence* involves our sensitivity to sound and rhythms and our ability to express ourselves through music.

• *Bodily-kinesthetic intelligence* involves the movement of the body. Athletics, dance, and physical work are expressions of this intelligence.

• *Interpersonal intelligence* is at the heart of human relationships, including our ability to understand, empathize with, and respond to other people.

• *Intrapersonal intelligence* deals with self-knowledge. Whenever we seek to access and understand our own feelings and emotional states, we are employing intrapersonal intelligence.

• *Naturalist intelligence* is used to make sense of the natural world. It includes our ability to recognize, discriminate among, and classify living things and natural objects.

What multiple intelligence theory lets teachers do is shift assessment away from primarily written work and toward many different kinds of assessment products. In addition, the incorporation of multiple intelligences into Task Rotation enables teachers to connect the disciplines and engage students by appealing to their natural talents and interests. Notice how the Task Rotation created by a 7th grade science teacher (Figure 20.4, p. 252) allows students to obtain a deep understanding of the scientific concept of work through the visual arts, mathematics, language arts, and physical education in addition to the linguistic and logical-mathematical intelligences all the tasks require.

FIGURE 20.4   Style-Intelligence Task Rotation

Showing What You Know About Your Work	
Mastery Style **Spatial Intelligence** **ATE Wants You!** The Army of Temporary Employees wants you to design a recruitment poster. Your poster must include a slogan, four illustrations of physical work, a written section describing the kind of people ATE wants to hire, and a good description of physical work.	**Interpersonal Style** **Bodily–Kinesthetic Intelligence** **That's not work!** Two students are arguing about whether isometric exercise is more or less beneficial than weight training. With a classmate, complete two exercises, one using weights, the other using isometrics. Discuss which workout was more strenuous, which was more beneficial, and which would be considered work according to scientific principles. (You may argue that both or neither are work provided you use evidence.) Then, take the side of one of the arguing students, or argue against both students.
Understanding Style **Logical–Mathematical Intelligence** **Chimney construction analysis:** You have been asked to replace four chimney tops on an old mansion. The estate is 4 m above ground, and each chimney top will be 1 m high. Each requires 100 bricks and 100 kg of mortar. Each brick is 10 cm square and weighs 1 kg. 1. Identify all aspects that require physical work. 2. Calculate the total mass of all materials. 3. Calculate how much force will be needed to lift the materials. 4. Suggest a method for the workers to lift the materials. 5. Calculate the total distance materials will be moved. 6. Calculate how much work (in Joules) is needed to position the materials on the roof.	**Self-Expressive Style** **Linguistic Intelligence** **The New Fables of Aesop.** Sierra Publishing Co. is interested in fables written by new authors. Read two fables and analyze their characteristics. Next, look over some maxims about work (e.g., "Many hands make light work"). Write a fable based on one of these expressions. Your fable should teach the idea contained in the expression and demonstrate your understanding of physical work.

Postscript
To Be Fair . . .

This country will not be a good place for any of us to live in unless
we make it a good place for all of us to live in.
—Theodore Roosevelt

So much of today's discussions on instruction are driven by a kind of ideological fixation on effectiveness for good and pressing reasons: the stakes are high, the tests are difficult, and the worlds of work and citizenship that await students beyond school demand highly skilled thinkers and learners. With so much riding on the decisions teachers make in their classrooms, effectiveness is bound to play a central role, to become the name of the game. *What skills are being modeled and taught? Is there research that supports this practice? Will it lead to measurable gains in student performance?*

However, effectiveness is not the only game in town. There is, as Teddy Roosevelt reminds us, another impulse—perhaps the noblest one of all—residing in all of our cherished democratic institutions. Our Bill of Rights, our attempt to create a "blind" legal system, our belief in public education—all of these are potent reminders of the commitment we have made as a society to the ideal of fairness. While a wide range of social and economic factors slant the playing field to the advantage of some students and to the disadvantage of others, in our schools and in our classrooms, we seek to give every student an equal opportunity to succeed.

Fortunately, the drive toward effectiveness and the drive toward fairness need not impose themselves on us as a battle for supremacy. Teaching strategies put an end to the possibility of a drawn-out war of either-or thinking by speaking loudly to both of these drives. On the one hand, teaching strategies are the ultimate engine for creating highly effective schools and classrooms. A simple glance at one of the Strategic

Dashboards and its array of indicators pointing to academic skills, research bases, and facets of understanding makes this point rather clearly. On the other hand, a repertoire of teaching strategies is as good a way as there is to address the diverse needs, motivational patterns, and learning styles found in any classroom. Taking a nonstrategic approach to instruction is unfair because it guarantees boredom, frustration, and needless difficulty in achieving success for an arbitrary majority of your students whose style happens to be different from yours. However, take the time to put a variety of strategies across all four styles into classroom action and you give all your students what they want and what they need. What could be fairer, or more effective, than that?

References

Introduction

Brown, R., Pressley, M., Van Meter, P., & Schuder, T. (1996). A quasi-experimental validation of transactional instruction with low-achieving second-grade readers. *Journal of Educational Psychology, 88,* 18–37.

Connecticut State Department of Education [State Department of Education Web site]. (2001). *Connecticut Academic Performance Test: Second Generation Science Handbook,* 38. Retrieved January 10, 2007, from http://www.sde.ct.gov/sde/lib/sde/PDF/Curriculum/captsci/scicapt_36-39.pdf

Cotton, K. (2000). *The schooling practices that matter most.* Alexandria, VA: Association for Supervision and Curriculum Development.

Ellis, A. K., & Fouts, J. (1997). *Research on educational innovations.* Larchmont, NY: Eye on Education.

Gregory, G. (2005). *Differentiating instruction with style.* Thousand Oaks, CA: Corwin Press.

Hunter, M. (1984). Knowing, teaching, and supervising. In P. Hosford (Ed.), *Using what we know about teaching* (pp. 169–192). Alexandria, VA: Association for Supervision and Curriculum Development.

Jung, C. G. (1923). *Psychological types.* (H. G. Baynes, Trans.) New York: Harcourt, Brace.

Mamchur, C. (1996). *A teacher's guide to cognitive type theory and learning style.* Alexandria, VA: Association for Supervision and Curriculum Development.

Marzano, R. J. (2003). *What works in schools: Translating research into action.* Alexandria, VA: Association for Supervision and Curriculum Development.

Marzano, R. J., Pickering, D., & Pollock, J. (2001). *Classroom instruction that works: Research-based strategies for increasing student achievement.* Alexandria, VA: Association for Supervision and Curriculum Development.

McCarthy, B. (1982). *The 4mat system.* Arlington Heights, IL: Excel Publishing.

Myers, I. B. (1962/1998). *The Myers-Briggs Type Indicator.* Palo Alto, CA: Consulting Psychologists Press.

Pajak, E. (2003). *Honoring diverse teaching styles: A guide for supervisors.* Alexandria, VA: Association for Supervision and Curriculum Development.

Silver, H. F., & Hanson, J. R. (1998). *Learning styles and strategies* (3rd ed.). Woodbridge, NJ: Thoughtful Education Press.

Wiggins, G., & McTighe, J. (2005). *Understanding by design.* Alexandria, VA: Association for Supervision and Curriculum Development.

1. New American Lecture

Anderson, J. R. (1995). *Learning and memory: An integrated approach.* New York: John Wiley & Sons.

Ausubel, D. (1963). *The psychology of meaningful verbal learning.* New York: Grune & Stratton.

Ausubel, D. (1968). *Educational psychology, a cognitive view.* New York: Holt, Rinehart, & Winston, Inc.

Jensen, E. (2005). *Teaching with the brain in mind* (2nd ed.). Alexandria, VA: Association for Supervision and Curriculum Development.

Marzano, R. J. (2004). *Building background knowledge for academic achievement: Research on what works in schools.* Alexandria, VA: Association for Supervision and Curriculum Development.

Paivio, A. (1990). *Mental representations: A dual coding approach.* New York: Oxford University Press.

Sprenger, M. (2005). *How to teach so students remember.* Alexandria, VA: Association for Supervision and Curriculum Development.

2. Direct Instruction

Hastings, F. L., Raymond, G., & McLaughlin, T. F. (1989). Speed counting money: The use of direct instruction to train learning disabled and mentally retarded adolescents to count money efficiently. *B.C. Journal of Special Education, 13*(2), 137–146.

Hunter, R. (2004). *Madeline Hunter's mastery teaching: Increasing instructional effectiveness in elementary and secondary schools.* (Updated edition.) Thousand Oaks, CA: Corwin Press.

Marzano, R. J., Norford, J. S., Paynter, D. E., Pickering, D. J., & Gaddy, B. B. (2001). *A handbook for classroom instruction that works.* Alexandria, VA: Association for Supervision and Curriculum Development.

Marzano, R. J., Pickering, D., & Pollock, J. (2001). *Classroom instruction that works: Research-based strategies for increasing student achievement.* Alexandria, VA: Association for Supervision and Curriculum Development.

Rosenshine, B. (1985). Direct instruction. In Torsten Husen & T. Neville Postlethwaite, (Eds.), *International encyclopedia of education, 3,* pp. 1395–1400. Oxford: Pergamon Press.

Tarver, S. C., & Jung, J. S. (1995). A comparison of mathematics achievement and mathematics attitudes of first and second graders instructed with either a discovery-learning mathematics curriculum or a direct instruction curriculum. *Effective School Practices, 14,* 49–57.

Wilson, C. L., & Sindelar, P. T. (1991). Direct instruction in math word problems: students with learning disabilities. *Exceptional Children, 57*(6), 512–519.

Woodward, J. (1991). Procedural knowledge in mathematics: The role of the curriculum. *Journal of Learning Disabilities, 24*(4), 242–251.

3. Graduated Difficulty

Erwin, J. C. (2004). *The classroom of choice: Giving students what they need and getting what you want.* Alexandria, VA: Association for Supervision and Curriculum Development.

Glasser, W. (1998). *Choice theory: A new psychology of personal freedom.* New York: Harper Collins Publishers.

Jensen, E. (1998). *Teaching with the brain in mind.* Alexandria, VA: Association for Supervision and Curriculum Development.

Marzano, R. J., Pickering, D., & Pollock, J. (2001). *Classroom instruction that works: Research-based strategies for increasing student achievement.* Alexandria, VA: Association for Supervision and Curriculum Development.

Mosston, M. (1972). *Teaching: From command to discovery.* Belmont, CA: Wadsworth Publishing.

Tomlinson, C. A., & McTighe, J. (2006). *Integrating differentiated instruction and understanding by design.* Alexandria, VA: Association for Supervision and Curriculum Development.

4. Teams-Games-Tournaments

DeVries, D. L., Edwards, K. J., & Slavin, R. E. (1978). Biracial learning teams and race relations in the classroom: Four field experiments using teams-games-tournaments. *Journal of Educational Psychology, 70*(3), 356–362.

Jensen, E. (2005). *Teaching with the brain in mind* (2nd ed.). Alexandria, VA: Association for Supervision and Curriculum Development.

Johnson, D. W., & Johnson, R. T. (1999). *Learning together and alone: Cooperative, competitive, and individualistic learning* (5th ed.). Boston: Allyn & Bacon.

Sylwester, R. (2003). *A biological brain in a cultural classroom* (2nd ed.). Thousand Oaks, CA: Corwin Press.

5. Compare and Contrast

Marzano, R. J., Pickering, D., & Pollock, J. (2001). *Classroom instruction that works: Research-based strategies for increasing student achievement.* Alexandria, VA: Association for Supervision and Curriculum Development.

Thomas, E. (2003). *Styles and strategies for teaching high school mathematics.* Ho-Ho-Kus, NJ: Thoughtful Education Press.

6. Reading for Meaning

Herber, H. (1970). *Teaching reading in the content areas.* Englewood Cliffs, NJ: Prentice Hall.

Ogle, D. (1986). K-W-L: A teaching model that develops active reading of expository text. *Reading Teacher, 39*(6), 564–570.

Strong, R. W., Silver, H. F., Perini, M .J., & Tuculescu, G. M. (2002). *Reading for academic success: Powerful strategies for struggling, average, and advanced readers, grades 7–12.* Thousand Oaks, CA: Corwin Press.

Tierney, R. J., & Cunningham, P. M. (1984). Research on teaching reading comprehension. In P. D. Pearson (Ed.), *Handbook of reading research.* New York: Longman.

Young, E., Righeimer, J., & Montbriand, C. (2002). *Strategic teaching and reading project: Comprehension resource handbook.* Naperville, IL: North Central Regional Educational Laboratory.

7. Concept Attainment

Bruner, J. (1973). *Beyond the information given: Studies in the psychology of knowing.* Oxford: W.W. Norton.

Marzano, R. J., Pickering, D., & Pollock, J. (2001). *Classroom instruction that works: Research-based strategies for increasing student achievement.* Alexandria, VA: Association for Supervision and Curriculum Development.

8. Mystery

Hansell, T. S. (1986). One student's learning cycle in an interpretive reading discussion. *Reading Psychology, 7*(4), 297–304.

Koedinger, K. R., & Anderson, J. R. (1993). Reifying implicit planning in geometry: Guidelines for model-based intelligent tutoring systems. In S. Lajoie & S. Derry (Eds.), *Computers as cognitive tools.* Hillsdale, NJ: Lawrence Erlbaum.

Koedinger, K. R., & Tabachneck, H. J. M. (1994, April). *Two strategies are better than one: Multiple strategies used in word problem solving.* Paper presented at the annual meeting of the American Educational Research Association, New Orleans.

Marzano, R. J., Pickering, D., & Pollock, J. (2001). *Classroom instruction that works: Research-based strategies for increasing student achievement.* Alexandria, VA: Association for Supervision and Curriculum Development.

Suchman, J. R. (1966). *Developing inquiry.* Chicago: Science Research Associates.

9. Inductive Learning

Jensen, E. (1998). *Teaching with the brain in mind.* Alexandria, VA: Association for Supervision and Curriculum Development.

Marzano, R. J., Pickering, D., & Pollock, J. (2001). *Classroom instruction that works: Research-based strategies for increasing student achievement.* Alexandria, VA: Association for Supervision and Curriculum Development.

Taba, H. (1971). *Hilda Taba teaching strategies program.* Miami, FL: Institute for Staff Development.

Thomas, E. (2003). *Styles and strategies for teaching high school mathematics.* Ho-Ho-Kus, NJ: Thoughtful Education Press.

10. Metaphorical Expression

Chen, Z. (1999). Schema induction in children's analogical problem solving. *Journal of Educational Psychology, 91*(4), 703–715.

Cole, J. C., & McLeod, J. S. (1999). Children's writing ability: The impact of the pictorial stimulus. *Psychology in the Schools, 36*(4), 359–370.

Gordon, W. J. J. (1961). *Synectics, the development of creative capacity.* New York: Harper.

Gottfried, G. M. (1998). Using metaphors as modifiers: Children's production of metaphoric compounds. *Journal of Child Language, 24*(3), 567–601.

Marzano, R. J., Pickering, D., & Pollock, J. (2001). *Classroom instruction that works: Research-based strategies for increasing student achievement.* Alexandria, VA: Association for Supervision and Curriculum Development.

11. Pattern Maker

Gick, M. L., & Holyoak, K. J. (1980). Analogical problem solving. *Cognitive Psychology, 12,* 306–355.

Jensen, E. (2005). *Teaching with the brain in mind* (2nd ed.). Alexandria, VA: Association for Supervision and Curriculum Development.

Perkins, D. N. (1986). *Knowledge as design.* Hillsdale, NJ: Lawrence Erlbaum.

Strong, R., Silver, H., & Perini, M. (2001). *Teaching what matters most: Standards and strategies for raising student achievement.* Alexandria, VA: Association for Supervision and Curriculum Development.

12. Mind's Eye

Brownlie, F., Close, S., & Wingren, L. (1990). *Tomorrow's classrooms today: Strategies for creating active readers, writers, and thinkers.* Markham, Ontario: Pembroke Publishers, Ltd.

Gambrell, L. B., & Bales, R. J. (1986). Mental imagery and the comprehension-monitoring performance of fourth-and fifth-grade poor readers. *Reading Research Quarterly, 21*(4), 454–464.

Keene, E. O., & Zimmerman, S. (1997). *Mosaic of thought: Teaching comprehension in a reader's workshop.* Portsmouth, NH: Heinemann.

Lindamood, P., Bell, N., & Lindamood, P. (1997). Sensory-cognitive factors in the controversy over reading instruction. *Journal of Developmental and Learning Disorders, 1*(1), 143–182.

Paivio, A. (1990). *Mental representations: A dual coding approach.* New York: Oxford University Press.

Pressley, M. (1976). Mental imagery helps eight-year-olds remember what they read. *Journal of Educational Psychology, 68*(3), 355–359.

Pressley, M. (2002). *Reading instruction that works: The case for balanced teaching. Solving problems in the teaching of literacy.* New York: Guilford Publications.

Sadoski, M., & Paivio, A. (2001). *Imagery and text: A dual coding theory of reading and writing.* Mahwah, NJ: Lawrence Erlbaum.

Sadoski, M., & Paivio, A. (2004). A dual coding theoretical method of reading. In R. B. Ruddell & N. J. Unrau (Eds.), *Theoretical models and processes of reading.* Newark, DE: International Reading Association.

Sadoski, M., & Willson, V. L. (2006). Effects of a theoretically based large-scale reading intervention in a multicultural urban school district. *American Educational Research Journal, 43*, 135–152.

Silver, H. F., Strong, R. W., & Perini, M. J. (2000). *Discovering nonfiction: 25 powerful teaching strategies, grades 2–6.* Santa Monica, CA: Canter & Associates.

13. Reciprocal Learning

Butler, F. M. (1999). Reading partners: Students can help each other learn to read! *Education and Treatment of Children, 22*(4), 415–426.

Fuchs, D., Fuchs, L. S., Mathes, P. G., & Simmons, D. C. (1997). Peer-assisted learning strategies: Making classrooms more responsive to academic diversity. *American Education Research Journal, 34*(1), 174–206.

Hashey, J. M., & Connors, D. J. (2003). Learn from our journey: Reciprocal teaching and action research. *The Reading Teacher, 57*(3), 224–232.

King-Sears, M. E., & Bradley, D. F. (1995). Classwide peer tutoring: Heterogeneous instruction in general education classrooms. *Preventing School Failure, 40*(1), 29–35.

Whimbey, A., & Lochhead, J. (1999). *Problem solving and comprehension* (6th ed.). Mahwah, NJ: Lawrence Erlbaum Associates.

14. Decision Making

Hart, M. (1992). *The 100: A ranking of the most influential persons in history* (revised edition). Secaucus, NJ: Carol Publishing Group.

Jimenez-Aleixandre, M., & Pereiro-Munoz, C. (2002). Knowledge producers or knowledge consumers? Argumentation and decision making about environmental management. *International Journal of Science Education, 24*(11), 1171–1190.

Naftel, M. I. (1993). Problem solving and decision making in an eighth grade class. *Clearinghouse, 66*(3), 177–180.

Rowland, P., & Adkins, C. (1992). *Developing environmental decision-making in middle school classes.* Paper presented at meeting of the World Congress for Education on Communication on Environment and Development.

15. Jigsaw

Aronson, E., Blaney, N., Stephan, C., Sikes, J., & Snapp, M. (1978). *The jigsaw classroom.* Beverly Hills, CA: Sage Publications.

Ellis, A. K., & Fouts, J. (1997). *Research on educational innovations.* Larchmont, NY: Eye on Education.

Gardner, H. (1999). *Intelligence reframed: Multiple intelligences for the 21st century.* New York: Basic Books.

Johnson, D. W., & Johnson, R. T. (1999). *Learning together and alone: Cooperative, competitive, and individualistic learning* (5th ed.). Boston: Allyn & Bacon.

Johnson, D. W., Johnson, R. T., & Holubec, E. J. (1994). *New circles of learning: Cooperation in the classroom and school.* Alexandria, VA: Association for Supervision and Curriculum Development.

Marzano, R. J., Pickering, D., & Pollock, J. (2001). *Classroom instruction that works: Research-based strategies for increasing student achievement.* Alexandria, VA: Association for Supervision and Curriculum Development.

Slavin, R. E. (1986). *Using student-led team learning* (3rd ed.). Baltimore, MD: Johns Hopkins University, Center for Research on Elementary and Middle Schools.

Slavin, R. E. (1995). *Cooperative learning: Theory, research, and practice* (2nd ed.). Boston: Allyn & Bacon.

Slavin, R. E., & Cooper, R. (1999). Improving intergroup relations: Lessons learned from cooperative learning programs. *Journal of Social Issues, 55*(4), 647–663.

Silver, H. F., Strong, R. W., & Perini, M. J. (1999). *The teaching and learning strategies library: Cooperative learning.* Woodbridge, NJ: Silver, Strong, and Associates.

16. Community Circle

Ashby, F. G., Isen, A. M., & Turken, A. V. (1999, July). A neuropsychological theory of positive affect and its influence on cognition. *Psychological Review, 106*, 529–550.

Cahill, L., Prins, B., Weber, M., & McGaugh, J. (1994, October). Adrenergic activation and memory for emotional events. *Nature, 371*(6499), 702–704.

Damasio, A. (1994). *Descartes' error.* New York: Grosset/Putnam.

Given, B. (2002). *Teaching to the brain's natural learning systems.* Alexandria, VA: Association for Supervision and Curriculum Development.

Jensen, E. (2005). *Teaching with the brain in mind* (2nd ed.). Alexandria, VA: Association for Supervision and Curriculum Development.

Kolb, B., & Taylor, L. (2000). Facial expression, emotion, and hemispheric organization. In R. Lane & L. Nadel (Eds.), *The cognitive neuroscience of emotion* (pp. 62–83). New York: Oxford University Press.

LeDoux, J. (1994). Emotion, memory, and the brain. *Scientific American, 270*(6), 50–57.

Peterson, R., & Eeds, M. (1990). *Grand conversations: Literature groups in action.* Richmond Hill, Ontario: Scholastic-TAB.

Sousa, D. (2001). *How the brain learns* (2nd ed.). Thousand Oaks, CA: Corwin Press.

17. Window Notes

Beecher, J. (1988). *Note-taking: What do we know about the benefits. ERIC Digest #37.* Bloomington, IN: ERIC Clearinghouse on Reading, English, and Communications. (ERIC Document Reproduction Service No. EDO CS 88 12)

Kierwa, K. A. (1985). Students' note-taking behaviors and the efficacy of providing the instructor's notes for review. *Contemporary Educational Psychology, 10*, 378–386.

Kobayashi, K. (2006). Combined effects of note-taking/reviewing on learning and the enhancement through interventions: A meta-analytical review. *Educational Psychology, 26*(3), 459–477.

Marzano, R. J., Pickering, D., & Pollock, J. (2001). *Classroom instruction that works: Research-based strategies for increasing student achievement.* Alexandria, VA: Association for Supervision and Curriculum Development.

Silver, H. F., Strong, R. W., & Perini, M. J. (2001). *Tools for promoting active, in-depth learning* (2nd ed.). Ho-Ho-Kus, NJ: Thoughtful Education Press.

Strong, R. W., Silver, H. F., Perini, M. J., & Tuculescu, G. M. (2003, September). Boredom and its opposite. *Educational Leadership, 61*(1).

Strong, R. W. (2005, January). From blasé to hooray. *Education Update, 47*(1), 2.

18. Circle of Knowledge

Adler, M. (1982). The paideia proposal: Rediscovering the essence of education. *American School Board Journal, 169*(7), 17–20.

Polite, V. C., & Adams, A. H. (1996). *Improving critical thinking through Socratic seminars. Spotlight on student success, no. 110.* Philadelphia: Mid-Atlantic Laboratory for Student Success.

Rowe, M. B. (1978). Wait . . . wait . . . wait . . . *School Science and Mathematics, 78*(3), 207–216.

Stahl, R. J. (1994). *Using "think-time" and "wait-time" skillfully in the classroom.* Bloomington, IN: ERIC Clearinghouse for Social Studies/Social Science Education.

Strong, R. W., Hanson, J. R., & Silver, H. F. (1995). *Questioning styles and strategies* (3rd ed.). Woodbridge, NJ: Thoughtful Education Press.

Tredway, L. (1995). Socratic seminars: Engaging students in intellectual discourse. *Educational Leadership, 53*(1), 26–29.

19. Do You Hear What I Hear?

Brown, H., & Cambourne, D. (1987). *Read and retell.* Portsmouth, NH: Heinemann.

Gambrell, L., Koskinen, P. S., & Kapinus, B. (1991). Studies for retelling as an instructional strategy. *Journal of Educational Research, 84,* 358–362.

Morrow, L. M. (1985). Reading and retelling stories: Strategies for emergent readers. *The Reading Teacher, 38*(9), 870–875.

Moss, J. F. (2002). *Literary discussion in the elementary school.* Urbana, IL: National Council of Teachers of English.

Silver, H. F., Strong, R. W., & Perini, M. J. (2001). *Tools for promoting active, in-depth learning.* Ho-Ho-Kus, NJ: Thoughtful Education Press.

Silver, H. F., Strong, R. W., & Perini, M. J. (2007). *Reading for academic success, grades 2–6: Differentiated strategies for struggling, average, and advanced readers.* Thousand Oaks, CA: Corwin.

Strong, R. W., Silver, H. F., & Perini, M. J. (2001). *Teaching what matters most: Standards and strategies for raising student achievement.* Alexandria, VA: Association for Supervision and Curriculum Development.

Strong, R. W., Silver, H. F., Perini, M. J., & Tuculescu, G. M. (2002). *Reading for academic success: Powerful strategies for struggling, average, and advanced readers grades 7–12.* Thousand Oaks, CA: Corwin Press.

Taylor, B. M., & Beach, R. W. (1984). The effects of text structure instruction on middle-grade students' comprehension and production of expository text. *Reading Research Quarterly, 19*(2), 134–146.

Zeiderman, H. (2003). *Touchpebbles, Vol. A—Teacher's guide.* Annapolis, MD: Touchstones Discussion Project.

20. Task Rotation

Butler, K. (1984). *Learning and teaching style in theory and practice.* Columbia, CT: Learner's Dimension.

Carbo, M. (1992). Giving unequal learners an equal chance: A reply to a biased critique of learning styles. *Remedial & Special Education, 13*(1), 19–29.

Dunn, R., Griggs, S. A., & Beasley, M. (1995, July). A meta-analytic validation of the Dunn & Dunn model of learning style preferences. *Journal of Educational Research, 88*(6), 353–362.

Gardner, H. (1999). *Intelligence reframed: Multiple intelligences for the 21st century.* New York: Basic Books.

Gregory, G. (2005). *Differentiating instruction with style.* Thousand Oaks, CA: Corwin Press.

Hanson, J. R., Dewing, T., Silver, H. F., & Strong, R. W. (1991). Within our reach: Identifying and working more effectively with at-risk learners. In *Students at-risk* (Produced for the 1991 ASCD Conference, San Francisco, CA). Alexandria, VA: Association for Supervision and Curriculum Development.

Jung, C. G. (1923). *Psychological types.* (H.G. Baynes, Trans.) New York: Harcourt, Brace & Co.

Mamchur, C. (1996). *A teacher's guide to cognitive type theory and learning style.* Alexandria, VA: Association for Supervision and Curriculum Development.

McCarthy, B. (1982). *The 4mat system.* Arlington Heights, IL: Excel Publishing.

Myers, I. B. (1962/1998). *The Myers-Briggs Type Indicator.* Palo Alto, CA: Consulting Psychologists Press.

Pajak, E. (2003). *Honoring diverse teaching styles: A guide for supervisors.* Alexandria, VA: Association for Supervision and Curriculum Development.

Silver, H. F., & Hanson, J. R. (1998). *Learning styles and strategies* (3rd ed.). Woodbridge, NJ: Thoughtful Education Press.

Silver, H. F., & Strong, R. W. (2004). *Learning Style Inventory for Students.* Ho-Ho-Kus, NJ: Thoughtful Education Press.

Index

Note: Page numbers followed by *f* refer to figures.

About the Authors

Harvey F. Silver

Harvey Silver, president of Silver Strong & Associates and Thoughtful Education Press, was named one of the 100 most influential teachers in the country. He has conducted numerous workshops for school districts and state education departments throughout the United States. He was the principal consultant for the Georgia Critical Thinking Skills Program and the Kentucky Thoughtful Education Teacher Leadership Program.

Richard W. Strong

Richard Strong, vice president of Silver Strong & Associates and Thoughtful Education Press, is an author, a program developer, and a trainer/consultant to school districts around the world. As cofounder of the Institute for Community and Difference, Richard has been studying democratic teaching and leadership practices in public and private schools for more than 25 years.

Matthew J. Perini

Matthew Perini serves as director of publishing for Silver Strong & Associates and Thoughtful Education Press. Over the last 10 years, Matthew has authored more than 20 books, curriculum guides, articles, and research studies covering a wide range of educational topics including learning styles, multiple intelligences, reading instruction, and effective teaching practices.

Harvey Silver, Richard Strong, and Matthew Perini have collaborated on a number of recent best sellers in education including *So Each May Learn: Integrating Learning Styles and Multiple Intelligences* and *Teaching*

What Matters Most: Standards and Strategies for Raising Student Achievement, both published by ASCD; *Reading for Academic Success: Powerful Strategies for Struggling, Average, and Advanced Readers, Grades 7–12* for Corwin Press; and Thoughtful Education Press's *Tools for Promoting Active, In-Depth Learning*, which won a Teachers' Choice Award in 2004.

Related ASCD Resources: The Strategic Teacher

Audiotapes

Instructional Approaches of Superior Teachers by Lloyd Campbell (#299202)

Putting Best Practices to Work on Behalf of Improving Student Learning by Kathleen Fitzpatrick (#298132)

Teaching for the 21st Century by Linda Darling-Hammond (#297247)

Print Products

Classroom Instruction That Works: Research Based Strategies for Increasing Student Achievement by Robert J. Marzano, Debra J. Pickering, Jane E. Pollock (#101010)

Classroom Management That Works: Research Based Strategies for Every Teacher by Robert J. Marzano, Jana S. Marzano, Debra J. Pickering (#103027)

Enhancing Professional Practice: A Framework for Professional Practice 2nd edition by Charlotte Danielson (#106034)

Grading and Reporting Student Learning by Robert J. Marzano and Tom Guskey (Professional Inquiry Kit; # 901061)

A Handbook for Classroom Instruction That Works by Robert J. Marzano, Jennifer S. Norford, Diane E. Paynter, Debra J. Pickering, Barbara B. Gaddy (#101041)

Improving Student Learning One Teacher at a Time by Jane Pollock (#107005)

Research-Based Strategies to Ignite Student Learning: Insights from a Neurologist and Classroom Teacher by Judy Willis (#107006)

Schooling by Design: Mission, Action, and Achievement by Grant Wiggins and Jay McTighe (#107018)

So Each May Learn: Integrating Learning Styles and Multiple Intelligences by Harvey F. Silver, Richard W. Strong, and Matthew J. Perini (#100058)

Tests That Teach: Using Standardized Test to Improve Instruction by Karen Tankersley (#107022)

Understanding by Design (expanded 2nd edition) by Grant Wiggins and Jay McTighe (#103055)

Videotapes

"Helping Students Acquire and Integrate Knowledge" Series with Robert J. Marzano (5 videos; #496065)

How to Use Graphic Organizers to Improve Student Thinking (Tape 6 of the "How To" Series; #499048)

Library of Teaching Strategies Parts I & II (#614178)

What Works in Schools: School Factors with Robert J. Marzano (Tape 1; # 403048)

What Works in Schools: Teacher Factors with Robert J. Marzano (Tape 2; #403049)

For more information: send e-mail to member@ascd.org; call 1-800-933-2723 or 703-578-9600, press 2; send a fax to 703-575-5400; or write to Information Services, ASCD, 1703 N. Beauregard St., Alexandria, VA 22311-1714 USA.